CASE STUDIES IN

CULTURAL ANTHROPOLOGY

GENERAL EDITORS

George and Louise Spindler

STANFORD UNIVERSITY

THE AZTECS OF CENTRAL MEXICO

An Imperial Society

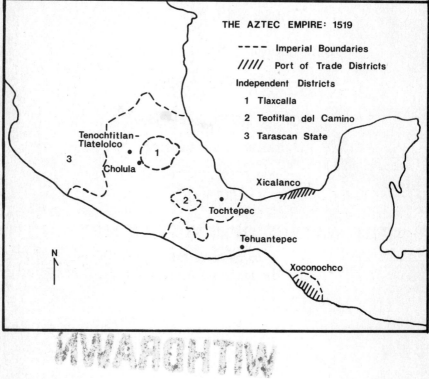

THE AZTEC EMPIRE: 1519

- - - - Imperial Boundaries
///// Port of Trade Districts
Independent Districts
1 Tlaxcalla
2 Teotitlan del Camino
3 Tarascan State

Tenochtitlan-
Tlatelolco

3

Cholula

1

Xicalanco

2

Tochtepec

Tehuantepec

N

Xoconochco

THE AZTECS OF
CENTRAL MEXICO

An Imperial Society

By

FRANCES F. BERDAN

California State College, San Bernardino

HOLT, RINEHART AND WINSTON

NEW YORK   CHICAGO   SAN FRANCISCO   PHILADELPHIA

MONTREAL   TORONTO   LONDON   SYDNEY   TOKYO

MEXICO CITY   RIO DE JANEIRO   MADRID

Credits

León-Portilla, Miguel. *Pre-Columbian Literatures of Mexico.* Norman: University of Oklahoma Press, 1969. Copyright © 1969 by the University of Oklahoma Press, publishing division of the University.

León-Portilla, Miguel. *Aztec Thought and Culture.* Norman: University of Oklahoma Press, 1963. Copyright © 1963 by the University of Oklahoma Press, publishing division of the University.

Durán, Fray Diego. *Book of the Gods and Rites* and *The Ancient Calendar* (transl. and ed. by Fernando Horcasitas and Doris Heyden). Norman: University of Oklahoma Press, 1971. Copyright © 1971 by the University of Oklahoma Press, publishing division of the University.

Zorita, Alonso de. *Life and Labor in Ancient Mexico: The Brief and Summary Relation of the Lords of New Spain* (transl. and with introduction by Benjamin Keen). New Brunswick, New Jersey: Rutgers University Press, 1963. Copyright © 1963 by Rutgers, the State University. Reprinted by permission of Rutgers University Press.

Sahagún, Fray Bernardino de. *The Florentine Codex: A General History of the Things of New Spain, Book 2, The Ceremonies* (transl. by Charles E. Dibble and Arthur J. O. Anderson). Santa Fe and Salt Lake City: School of American Research and the University of Utah, 1951.

Sahagún, Fray Bernardino de. *The Florentine Codex: A General History of the Things of New Spain, Book 4, The Soothsayers* (transl. by Charles E. Dibble and Arthur J. O. Anderson). Santa Fe and Salt Lake City: School of American Research and the University of Utah, 1957.

Sahagún, Fray Bernardino de. *The Florentine Codex: A General History of the Things of New Spain, Book 6, Rhetoric and Moral Philosophy* (transl. by Charles E. Dibble and Arthur J. O. Anderson). Santa Fe and Salt Lake City: School of American Research and the University of Utah, 1969.

Sahagún, Fray Bernardino de. *The Florentine Codex: A General History of the Things of New Spain, Book 8, Kings and Lords* (transl. by Arthur J. O. Anderson and Charles E. Dibble). Santa Fe and Salt Lake City: School of American Research and the University of Utah, 1969.

Sahagún, Fray Bernardino de. *The Florentine Codex: A General History of the Things of New Spain, Book 10, The People* (transl. by Charles E. Dibble and Arthur J. O. Anderson). Santa Fe, New Mexico, and Salt Lake City: School of American Research and the University of Utah, 1961.

Figs. 1–3, 1–4: Reproduced by permission of the Society for American Archaeology from *American Antiquity* 37(1):108, 109, 1972.

Library of Congress Cataloging in Publication Data
Berdan, Frances F.
    The Aztecs of Central Mexico.
    (Case studies in cultural anthropology)
    Bibliography: p. 189
    1. Aztecs. I. Title. II. Series.
F1219.73.B47   972'.01   81–7055
ISBN 0–03–055736–4   AACR2

CBS COLLEGE PUBLISHING
Holt, Rinehart and Winston
The Dryden Press
Saunders College Publishing

Foreword

ABOUT THE SERIES

These case studies in cultural anthropology are designed to bring to students, in beginning and intermediate courses in the social sciences, insights into the richness and complexity of human life as it is lived in different ways and in different places. They are written by men and women who have lived in the societies they write about and who are professionally trained as observers and interpreters of human behavior. The authors are teachers, and in writing their books they have kept the students who will read them foremost in their minds. It is our belief that when an understanding of ways of life very different from one's own is gained, abstractions and generalizations about social structure, cultural values, subsistence techniques, and the other universal categories of human social behavior become meaningful.

ABOUT THE AUTHOR

Frances F. Berdan was born in Wellsville, New York, in 1944. She received her B.A. degree in geography at Michigan State University (1965) and her Ph.D. degree in anthropology at the University of Texas at Austin (1975). Dr. Berdan has engaged in archaeological field research in the American Southwest, participated in ethnographic research in a Mexican peasant community, and conducted archival research in Mexico City and Seville, Spain. She has published numerous articles on Aztec culture and society and co-authored a book on colonial period Nahuatl documents (*Beyond the Codices*, 1976). She is presently involved in completing a monograph on the Aztec imperial economic system, co-authoring a second book on colonial Nahuatl documentation, and researching the linguistic and cultural bases of the Aztec hieroglyphic writing system. Dr. Berdan is currently associate professor and chair of the Department of Anthropology at California State College, San Bernardino, is married, and has two children.

ABOUT THE BOOK

This case study is about the Aztecs of Central Mexico, a people who dominated a vast area of what is now Mexico by the time the Spanish conquistadors arrived in A.D. 1519, but who had humble beginnings as despised nomads. The story of the confrontation and the defeat of the Aztecs by the small force of Spaniards led by Hernán Cortés is told in the last chapter.

The larger part of this book is devoted to an ethnographic reconstruction of Aztec culture as it flourished in the period immediately preceding the Conquest. It is based upon a variety of documents, in Nahuatl and in Spanish, most of which were written immediately or soon after the Conquest. Although this case study is based on documents produced by others, the reconstruction of Aztec life is as vivid and detailed as though it were the product of direct participation–observation, as most ethnographies are.

The richness and complexity of Aztec life in its aesthetic, ideological, and material dimensions is beautifully developed in this case study. For many potential readers the fact that the Aztecs sacrificed thousands of lives in religious ceremonies has loomed so large that the other dimensions of Aztec life have been overshadowed or even obliterated. This study provides detailed information on occupational special-ization, the role of merchants and artisans, modes of production, the marketplace, social class, kinship, education, etiquette, morals, marriage, social control and law, warfare, religion, the calendric system, medicine, literature and music, and many other aspects of the Aztec way of life. Human sacrifice and cannibalism are discussed in the perspective of opposing interpretations of both their magnitude and their significance.

This study is essential reading for anyone interested in native life in the New World. Aztec culture was complex and sophisticated, rivaling the high cultures of the Old World. This culture and the other centers of cultural development in Mesoamerica and South America, such as the Mayas and Incas, had far ranging influences on cultural development elsewhere in the New World. In fact, some interpreters argue that the indigenous North American cultures represented, in varying degrees, diminished cultural complexes; human sacrifice among the Pawnee, the "priest–temple–idol cult" among the Natchez, and the Feast of the Dead among the Iroquois are believed to have originated from the Aztec or other high Central American cultures. Although these diffusionist interpretations have been challenged, and by many interpreters discarded, the profound influence of Aztec and other complex state societies on the cultural development of the rest of the Americas cannot be denied. An understanding of Aztec culture, therefore, is essential to understanding other cultural developments in the Americas.

Aztec culture, however, is so interesting in itself that no extraneous justification is needed for its study. Never again will any human culture replicate even the outlines of this unusual way of life.

We are fortunate to have this reconstruction of pre-conquest Aztec life readily available. Other available literature tends to be either too massive or technical for anyone but a specialist or highly motivated aficionado to assimilate, or too super-ficial to be adequate for class use. This study by Professor Berdan achieves a fine balance between complexity and simplicity. She does not avoid the complexities and contradictions of Aztec culture but writes about them in understandable language. The result is both a contribution to the serious literature on pre-conquest Mexico and an excellent text for both undergraduate and graduate courses in ethnology, cultural anthropology, world ethnography, ethnohistory, New World history, and other courses in the social sciences and in history, religion, and philosophy. It is also a fine and informative book for the general reader interested in human cultures.

GEORGE AND LOUISE SPINDLER
General Editors

Calistoga, California

Preface

Seeking an ever broader understanding of mankind, anthropologists have trekked to remote corners of the globe, excavated deep into the earth, and penetrated the complexities of urban life. More recently anthropologists have also begun to probe historical documents for ethnographic data, and with considerable success. In fact, for some societies, the investigator is almost entirely restricted to written documents for information. This is the case with the Aztecs of pre-Spanish, sixteenth-century Mexico.

Although supported by some archaeological evidence, knowledge of the culture portrayed in *The Aztecs of Central Mexico: An Imperial Society* leans heavily on documents composed for the most part during and immediately following the Spanish conquest in 1521. These documents include a tremendous amount and variety of written material: pictorial manuscripts painted in pre-conquest style, eye-witness reports of the Spanish conquest, detailed ethnographic data collected by Spanish friars from Indian nobles, and much "local-level" documentation, such as wills, tax records, correspondence, and other documents generated by various kinds of disputes between persons or communities.

This is, therefore, an historical ethnography. It is drawn not from the direct experience of the author but is based on accounts written by others, others who were not, and did not intend to be, anthropologists. Thus, it is also interpretive history. This implies certain problems. One is the selective nature of the documentation: It tends to emphasize certain aspects of life, while barely touching on many other areas of interest to the ethnographer. Beyond selectivity, even documents which abundantly record particular areas of life sometimes leave considerable gaps in specific information; or several documents recording the same category of information may leave behind a trail of confusing contradictions. And since the vast bulk of the documentation regarding the Aztecs was created after the arrival of the Spaniards, some of the documents reflect Indian adaptations to new conditions, rather than pre-Spanish Indian life.

To minimize these problems, an attempt has been made here to draw on as wide an array of documentation as possible: formal and informal, Nahuatl and Spanish, state level and local level, pictorial and textual. Quotations from original sources are used extensively to provide cultural insights and to maintain the special flavor of the original documentation.

The goal is to provide an overall understanding of Aztec culture. This poses a particular challenge in a society as heterogeneous and complex as the Aztec empire. Despite its limitations, the documentation allows a detailed analysis of the major themes underlying Aztec culture, reflected in highly diverse phenomena such as settlement patterns, warfare, legal codes, ceremonies, human sacrifice, formal education, and the creative arts. The cultural themes were given unique content by the people themselves, each bringing a special flavor to traditional roles and activities. An appreciation of the broad variety and diversity of life encompassed under the rubric "Aztec" is a particular concern in this book. Whether noble or commoner, male or female, young or old, merchant or artisan, urbanite or rural dweller, each person had different roles in, and orientations to, the shared culture.

ACKNOWLEDGMENTS

It is a pleasure to acknowledge the kind support and assistance I have received from many quarters in developing this book. Over the years my understanding of Aztec culture has been continually refined and enriched by Dr. H. B. Nicholson of UCLA, who has always given generously of his time and knowledge and has helped instill in me a strong appreciation of the potential of primary ethnohistorical sources. Likewise, Dr. James Lockhart of UCLA has consistently been a stimulating and insightful colleague, especially enhancing my understanding of life in early colonial Mexico. Dr. Patricia Anawalt has been an extremely supportive and wise colleague and critic and has generously shared her extensive knowledge and resources. I would also like to express my gratitude to Drs. George and Louise Spindler. Their encouragement and constructive suggestions have contributed greatly to the final form of this book.

Bruce Compton provided many hours of invaluable assistance in the details of manuscript production and in rendering the maps. My grateful thanks also go to Chris Rasmussen for her perseverance, dedication, and skill in typing the manuscript. Earl Jamgochian and Peter Bradford photographed and produced the illustrations—their accommodating and talented services are gratefully acknowledged. I would also like to express my gratitude to California State College, San Bernardino, for providing assistance in the production of the manuscript.

My very special thanks go to my linguist husband, Bob, who spent endless hours discussing, reading, and editing drafts of this book, and who provided strong intellectual and moral support in bringing this book into final form.

Contents

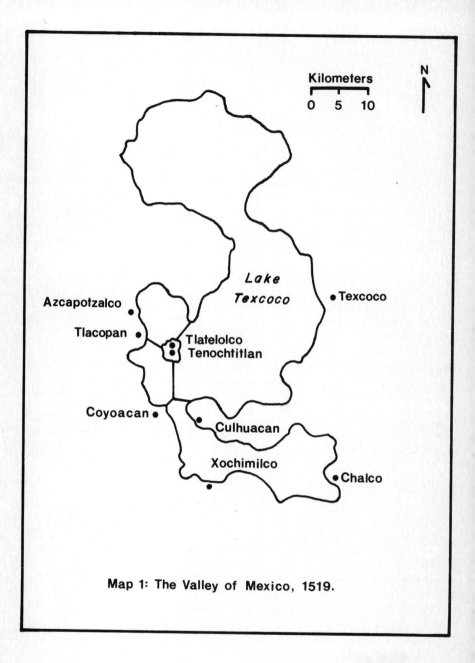

Map 1: The Valley of Mexico, 1519.

1/Mexico and the Mexica

The people of this province are well proportioned, tending to be tall rather than short; they are swarthy or brownish, of good features and mien. For the most part they are very skillful, stalwart and tireless, yet they sustain themselves with less food than any other people. They are very warlike and fearless of death (Anonymous Conqueror, 1520s; in de Fuentes 1963:168).

Their understanding is keen, modest, and quiet, not proud or showy as in other nations (Motolinía, 1536–1543; 1950:238).

Many of [the warriors] carried standards and gold shields, and other insignia which they wore strapped to their backs, giving them an appearance of great ferocity, since they also had their faces stained, and grimaced horribly, giving great leaps and shouts and cries. These put such fear into us that many of the Spaniards asked for confession (Francisco de Aguilar, 1560; in de Fuentes 1963:139).

. . . the men or women who were to be sacrificed to their gods were thrown on their backs and of their own accord remained perfectly still. A priest then came out with a stone knife . . . and with this knife he opened the part where the heart is and took out the heart, without the person who was being sacrificed uttering a word. . . . [The priests] went about very dirty and blackened, and wasted and haggard of face. They wore their hair hanging down very long and matted, so that it covered them, and went about infested with lice. . . . At night they walked like a procession of phantoms to the hills where they had their temples and idols and houses of worship (Francisco de Aguilar, 1560; in de Fuentes 1963:163–164).

. . . when we saw so many cities and villages built on the water and other great towns on dry land and that straight and level Causeway going towards Mexico [Tenochtitlan], we were amazed and said that it was like the enchantments they tell of in the legend of Amadis, on account of the great towers and cues [temples] and buildings rising from the water, and all built of masonry. And some of our soldiers even asked whether the things that we saw were not a dream (Bernal Díaz del Castillo, 1560s; 1956:190–191).

Like fine burnished turquoise thou givest thy heart.
It cometh to the sun.
Thou wilt yet germinate—
Wilt once again blossom
On earth.
Thou wilt live among Uexotzinco's drums—
Wilt gladden the nobles.
Thy friends will behold thee (Aztec song; in Sahagún 1950–1969, book 6:115).

1

Skillful and tireless, keen and modest. Ferocious in battle and stoic in sacrifice. Builders of magnificent cities and composers of sensitive songs and poems. Who were these people—so clever in both war and poetry?

They called themselves Mexica, although it has become popular today to refer to them as Aztecs. They arrived in central Mexico in the thirteenth century as a despised nomadic tribe. Through clever alliances and relentless warfare, they rapidly emerged as the leading military and political power in central Mexico. By the time of the Spanish arrival in 1519, the Mexica, with their capital at Tenochtitlan, had formed a strong alliance with their neighbors to the east and west: the Acolhuacans of Texcoco and the Tepanecas of Tlacopan (see Map 1). Together, these three groups forged a vast empire in Mesoamerica[1] which may be called the Triple Alliance empire, or the Aztec empire.

The Valley of Mexico was the center of Aztec activity. Here they built their grandest marketplaces and greatest temples. Here they celebrated the most extravagant rituals, with gala processions and solemn priestly rites. Here was the empire's greatest concentration of wealth—nobles living in exquisite palaces and wearing fancy clothes; wealthy merchants fond of giving lavish feasts. Here elderly sages examined the wisdom of the ages, while inspired poets reflected on the virtues of beauty, honor, and death. And from this valley marched the great armies of conquest, often returning in glory with riches and slaves.

Covering some 2500 square miles, the Valley of Mexico lies at an elevation of over 7000 feet. It is circumscribed by low-lying hills to the north, and impressive mountains to the west, south, and east, with some perpetually snow-capped peaks reaching elevations of more than 17,000 feet. Rimming the valley, this mountainous and hilly terrain presented a variety of micro-ecological zones, each offering slightly different potentials for human use.

Also adding to variety in ecological potential was a series of connected lakes. Water from mountainside runoff and numerous springs collected in them, yet they had no natural outlet. As a result, flooding and water quality were persistent problems for human habitation. Major feats of hydraulic engineering would be undertaken in the fifteenth century to control this powerful resource. Some of these massive hydraulic projects, which included dikes, aqueducts, canals, and causeways, were also designed to alleviate a second problem: the highly saline nature of the central lake, Lake Texcoco. Lying at a slightly lower elevation than the lakes to the north and south, it tended to collect salts deposited from those lakes and from the eastern drainage area. Securing access to freshwater supplies became an important motivation for some instances of early Aztec imperial expansion.

Although they sometimes posed a severe threat to life, property, and urban expansion, these lakes also favored the human populations residing along their shores and on their islands. The lakes provided an effective means of transportation.

---

[1] The culture area designated by anthropologists as Mesoamerica encompasses a large area extending from central Mexico, south through Belize and Guatemala, and into Honduras. It is particularly set apart from the rest of Mexico and Central America by the presence of a settled agricultural life leading to the growth of a succession of great civilizations in pre-Spanish times. In addition, this culture area embraced a great variety of ethnic groups living in an atmosphere of shifting alliances and open conflicts.

At least by the time of the Spanish arrival, they were laden with canoe traffic, inviting commerce and other forms of interaction throughout the valley. The lakes also supplied varied and abundant aquatic resources: fish and fowl, reptile and amphibian. *Chinampa* cultivation, a highly productive form of agriculture, was practiced in several lacustrine districts by claiming lands from the lakes (see Chapter 2).

ORIGIN OF THE MEXICA AND ARRIVAL IN CENTRAL MEXICO

Like many earlier groups, the Mexica migrated into the Valley of Mexico. As related in myths and histories collected by indigenous and Spanish chroniclers of the sixteenth century, this migration extended over some 200 years (A.D. 1111–1325). Although numerous pictographic manuscripts and texts recorded the migration, it is now difficult to separate fact from myth, and to establish clearly many details.

The migration began from a place called Aztlan ("Place of the Herons"). The exact location of Aztlan is in hot dispute: Some claim it was as distant as the southwestern United States; others, as close as 60 miles northwest of the final destination of the Mexica. There is general agreement, however, that Aztlan was probably located in a northwesterly direction from the Valley of Mexico.

From the elusive lake site of Aztlan the Mexica traveled to Chicomoztoc ("Seven Caves"), another unidentified locale. Chicomoztoc reputedly served as a jumping-off spot for a large number of nomadic groups. From here had departed the Tlaxcalans, settling to the east of the Valley of Mexico and later becoming bitter enemies of the Mexica. The Xochimilca, Chalca, Tepaneca, Culhua, Tlahuica, and others apparently congregated at Chicomoztoc; and each in turn subsequently traveled southeast, settling in the Valley of Mexico. The Mexica were reputedly the last to leave. By the time the Mexica arrived in central Mexico, the area was densely populated by sedentary populations of great antiquity and by recently arrived nomads from the north.

The Mexica, like other migrants before them, called themselves and were called by others Chichimeca. The Chichimeca included a large number of ethnic groups (such as the Mexica), and may be broadly defined as nomadic hunting and gathering tribes of the northern desert regions. The sixteenth-century ethnohistorical accounts actually identify more than one type of Chichimeca. The classic type was called the Teochichimeca, or "true Chichimecs." Groups so labeled were nomadic hunters and gatherers; they relied heavily on the bow and arrow, wore clothing made from animal skins, produced fine objects of stone and feathers, and used peyote (Sahagún 1950–1969, book 10:171–175).

The Mexica, both during their long journey and at the time of their arrival in the Valley of Mexico, more closely resembled a second type of Chichimeca, the Tamime: peoples who were neither truly nomadic and "barbaric," nor truly settled and "civilized."

A sixteenth-century Franciscan friar, Bernardino de Sahagún, provides the following description of the Tamime as they were known in his time:

This name Tamin means "shooter of arrows." And these Tamime were only an offshoot, a branch, of the Teochichimeca, although they were somewhat settled. They made their homes in caves, in gorges; in some places they established small grass huts and small corn fields. And they went mingling with the Mexica, or the Nahua, or the Otomí. There they heard the Nahuatl language, they spoke a little Nahuatl or Otomí, and in a measure they there learned a civilized way of life from them. Also they put on a few rags—tattered capes. Also in places they laid out small maize plots; they sowed them, they harvested them (Sahagún 1950–1969, book 10:171).

In this statement, Sahagún mentions Tamime of the early sixteenth century coming into contact with settled groups such as the Mexica; in the twelfth century, the Mexica themselves would have been much like these Tamime, associating with earlier settled peoples.

This picture of the early Mexica as Tamime is supported by pictographic and textual accounts produced in the sixteenth century. During their extended journey into the Valley of Mexico, the Mexica are reported to have cultivated maize, chile, and other crops. They constructed "great and curious buildings," including temples. They were aware of luxury goods such as jade, cacao, and rich capes (Durán 1964:9, 15, 17).

They appear to have been a heterogeneous lot; they had a social hierarchy with priests as well as followers, and they developed internal factions. One sixteenth-century pictorial manuscript, the Codex Boturini, illustrates three priests and a priestess leading various nomadic groups; one of the priests carried the god Huitzilopochtli, patron deity of the Mexica, and was responsible for transmitting the will of that deity to the followers (see Figure 1–1). The priests apparently

Figure 1–1: The long journey of the Mexica. The priests and priestess are illustrated on the left, the leading priest carrying the god Huitzilopochtli. On the right are three sacrifices in honor of Huitzilopochtli (Codex Boturini 1964:plate IV).

were in a position of significant authority, as attested by the sixteenth-century chronicler Durán:

> The people held this idol [Huitzilopochtli] in such reverence and awe that no one but his keepers [priests] dared approach or touch him. . . . The priests made the people adore the idol as a god, preaching to them the law they were to follow, and the ceremonies and rites to be observed in honor of their divinity (1964:13).

Whenever they stopped, even for short periods, the people were commanded to build a temple for their patron deity, Huitzilopochtli, and even occasionally to construct a ball court for the already widespread Mesoamerican ritual ball game (Tezozomoc 1949:32). Ceremonies at times included human sacrifice. These sacrifices were used to honor Huitzilopochtli, but they may also have served a social control function. Durán (1964:18–21) speaks of certain Mexica who opposed the will of Huitzilopochtli. These people were content to stay in an inviting place near Tula, even though their god, through the priests, commanded them to continue on their journey. Under cover of night, the hearts of the upstarts were torn out: The wrath of Huitzilopochtli was expressed, and the rebellious faction was eliminated.

The journey from Aztlan to nearby Chicomoztoc and eventually to the Valley of Mexico was long and arduous. The wandering tribe not only encountered unfriendly peoples along the route but also was plagued with rivalries and tensions within its own group. The example cited above suggests that consensus was not necessarily the rule; disagreements were present, and some dissenters were simply eliminated through sacrifice. Apparently, parts of the nomadic population also were intentionally left behind along the route. The events at Malinalco offer an example:

> The god of the Aztecs had a sister who was called Malinalxochitl, Wild Grass Flower, who came with the tribe. She was very beautiful and was possessed of such intelligence that she became skillful in the magic arts. Her cunning was so great that she caused much harm in the tribe and made herself feared in order to be adored later as a goddess. The people had endured her because she was the sister of Huitzilopochtli, but finally they asked the latter to try to get rid of her for the sake of the tribe. The god advised the priests through dreams, as was his custom, to abandon her in the place that he would indicate, together with her attendants and certain elders (Durán 1964:16).

Whether or not true in detail, accounts such as this suggest that dissension and factions were present in this wandering population.

Other aspects of Mexica culture at this time suggest ties with the settled Mesoamerican way of life. During their more than 200 years' journey the Mexica celebrated, at 52-year intervals, the "new fire" ceremony. This ritual commemorated the passage of a calendrical cycle, and indicates knowledge of the sophisticated Mesoamerican calendrical systems. Even their patron deity, Huitzilopochtli, was born of a goddess (Coatlicue) with deep Mesoamerican roots.

Although the Mexica, like earlier nomadic migrants, had many traditional Mesoamerican cultural traits, they were Chichimeca. They were nomadic and skilled in hunting. Their specialists were apparently limited to the religious realm. They wore clothing made from maguey fiber. They were viewed by the sedentary peoples they encountered as vile and barbaric in their customs. However, by the time they arrived in the Valley of Mexico in the thirteenth century, their culture had become an intricate blend of nomadic and sedentary, "barbaric" and "civilized."

Also by this time, the classic features of civilizational states were already well entrenched in the Valley of Mexico. Cities, characterized by monumental public constructions and conscious urban planning, surrounded Lake Texcoco. Sophisticated irrigation agriculture, based on knowledge of a complex and specialized technology, produced abundant harvests of a variety of crops. Occupational specialization was common, complemented by a variety of exchange mechanisms including markets, foreign trade, and state-administered tax and tribute systems. A number of political states, composed of bureaucratic machineries and built on complex social stratification, exercised some control over the production and allocation of critical resources. Polytheistic religions reflected both cultural heterogeneity (through numerous specialized and patron deities) and hierarchical principles of organization (through the ranking of both deities and their public servants, the priests).

Primarily through warfare and conquest, these principles of heterogeneity and hierarchy were woven into concrete social realities. The structure of social classes and means for attaining rewards and social mobility were closely tied to military activities; imperial territorial structures were established on a foundation of domination through conquest. A companion of warfare is alliance, and alliances were established through marriage and through purely political arrangements between rulers. As the Mexica became integrated into these patterns, they would enlarge upon these already existing themes, creating in some cases new and unique content.

The entrance of the Mexica into this complex urban situation was neither spectacular nor welcomed. Traveling through the valley and guided by their patron deity, they searched for some unoccupied place to settle. By the end of the thirteenth century, they had occupied Chapultepec, a strategic hilltop site beside Lake Texcoco. Twice forcefully expelled from Chapultepec, feared and despised by more powerful groups, the Mexica retreated to Culhuacan for asylum. The rulers there sent the Mexica to Tizapan, a dismal, volcanic, snake-infested place a few miles east of Culhuacan. Surprised at the ability of the Mexica to thrive in such an environment, the Culhua finally accepted the new arrivals. Conforming to an apparently traditional pattern, the Mexica then served the Culhua as mercenaries, exhibiting exceptional abilities in the martial arts.

These capabilities, as well as certain of their customs, generated some fear and a great deal of hatred for the Mexica. The most notable example of the latter involves the deterioration of the previously amiable relations with the Culhua. Durán describes the following series of events:

> The Aztecs . . . went to the ruler of Colhuacan and asked for his daughter to be mistress of the Aztecs and bride of their god. . . . When the Aztecs had carried her to their camp and placed her upon the altar, Huitzilopochtli spoke to his priests . . . "Now you must kill her and sacrifice her in my name. . . . After she is dead, flay her and with her skin dress one of the principal youths . . ." (1964:26).

The Culhua ruler was then asked by the Mexica to attend a ceremony dedicating his daughter as a goddess:

> The king, with great confidence, arose and went to the temple. He entered the chamber of the idol and began to perform many ceremonies. He cut off the heads of the quail and the other birds and offered sacrifice by scattering the birds' blood and placing the food before the idols. Then he offered incense and flowers which he had brought for that purpose. . . . Taking with his hand a brazier with fire, he threw incense into it fervently. This began to burn and the room lighted up with the fire. Thus the king suddenly perceived the priest who was seated next to the idol, dressed in his daughter's skin. This was such a frightful sight that the king was filled with a wild terror (*ibid.*:27).

The wrath of the Culhua ruler forced the Mexica to retreat. Fleeing into the marshes of Lake Texcoco, they were informed by their patron god that nearby they would soon see an eagle perched upon a prickly pear cactus. This sign was to indicate the location of their final destination, the goal of an extended and difficult journey. Seeing this sight on a nearby island, they immediately occupied the island and set to erecting a small temple to Huitzilopochtli. They named their settlement Tenochtitlan ("Place of the Fruit of the Prickly Pear Cactus"), commemorating perhaps the symbolism of the founding event or perhaps the priest-ruler named Tenoch who had led them there or both. In the European calendar, the year was probably A.D. 1325.[2]

Both symbolism and practicality played a part in the choice of this site. Present-day historian Nigel Davies (1973:37) has noted that for the Mexica the eagle symbolized the sun, as did their patron deity. Also, the fruit of the prickly pear cactus (*nochtli*) represented the human hearts which were the sustenance of Huitzilopochtli. Symbolically, then, this was truly a place destined for occupation by the Mexica, Huitzilopochtli's servants.

On a practical level, the island site presented both advantages and problems. Fish and aquatic birds and animals were abundant. The surrounding lake was amenable to intensive chinampa cultivation. The little island location was also advantageous in terms of transportation and communication: In Mesoamerica transport was by foot or canoe, with the canoe having obvious advantages of ease of effort and size of load.

But this struggling settlement was also beset by problems: the total lack of certain essential raw materials (particularly wood and stone for construction), the periodic threat of flooding, and (later on) limited access to potable water.

HISTORICAL BACKGROUND OF THE AZTEC EMPIRE

From the founding of Tenochtitlan in 1325 to the time of the Spanish arrival in 1519, the Mexica strove to carve a niche for themselves in this physical and socio-political environment. Their history may be viewed as a dynamic process of adapta-

---

[2] A.D. 1325 is the date traditionally assigned to the founding of Tenochtitlan. However, some modern writers, using a different year count, place the event in A.D. 1345.

tion to an environment in some respects hospitable, in others, hostile. In the first phase of this history, 1325–1428, the Mexica were subject to forces already at play in the Valley of Mexico, and they primarily adapted to existing patterns. From 1428–1519, they took an aggressive, imperial position, actively shaping and directing the course of history of much of Mesoamerica.

For the first century after the founding of Tenochtitlan, the Mexica successfully tackled numerous problems. They had settled on land which formed the boundary among three powerful political entities. Unsure of their political status in this situation (although assuredly it was a weak position), they faced the problem of becoming tributaries of one of these states or of striving to maintain political independence. Although the latter alternative was most desirable to them, and in fact attempted, they quickly became subjects of the Tepanec city of Azcapotzalco. By the mid-fourteenth century, Azcapotzalco had taken aggressive military action in central Mexico, conquering one by one the numerous cities dotting the valley. In some cases, conquest involved actual military engagements; in others, agreements were made recognizing Azcapotzalco as the dominant power. The Mexica took the latter course. In a subordinate position to the growing Tepanec empire, they rendered tribute in lake products and in military service.

To strengthen their political position, the Mexica sought allies. Marriage provided an effective means of establishing alliances, and the Mexica rulers made a series of clever marriages into long-established dynasties (see Figure 1–2). Their first ruler, Acamapichtli, was reputedly the son of a Mexica nobleman and a Culhua princess. He married a woman from the royal line of Culhuacan, thus cementing a close alliance with the Culhua. This choice of ruler and his strategic marriage also provided future generations of Mexica rulers with a claim to Toltec heritage. In the

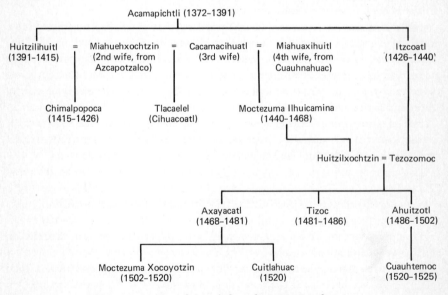

Figure 1–2: Genealogy of the ruling Mexica dynasty.

Valley of Mexico, descent from the ancient Toltec nobility was translated into legitimacy to rule.

Acamapichtli's son and successor, Huitzilihuitl, used the same means to create firm ties with the famed Tepanec ruler of Azcapotzalco, Tezozomoc. Huitzilihuitl's second wife was a granddaughter of the old Tepanec ruler himself. Following this marriage, and particularly after the birth of a son, relations between Tenochtitlan and Azcapotzalco became quite amiable. The Tepanec ruler seemed to favor the Mexica, lightening their tribute burdens and involving them in numerous conquests from which they gained some territory for themselves. This favored position was also reflected in a gradual shift in power relations:

> In proportion to the rate at which the [Tepanec] conquests grew, the importance of the Aztecs also increased. They were treated less and less as ordinary vassals and mercenaries and more and more as allies. A number of regions which they had conquered for Atzcapotzalco were made over to them and from there they obtained the timber which they lacked and a constantly increasing supply of food. As their strength increased their influence in the making of political decisions seems also to have risen (Katz 1972:138).

Although not well documented until 1428, when the Mexica defied Azcapotzalco, a definite system of social differentiation characterized Mexica society in this earlier time. A growing nobility class, headed by rulers descended from Acamapichtli, claimed special rights and privileges. Such privileges included private ownership of land and rights to serve in major public offices. The bulk of the Mexica population were commoners (*macehualtin*), who served as tillers of the soil and wielders of arms on the battlefield. Between these two distinct classes developed groups of occupational specialists: professional merchants and artisans of luxury wares, many of whom may have been later immigrants into the new city.

Military strategies and political machinations must have occupied much of the energy of the nobility, but the slow, everyday drudgery of building a city fell primarily to the commoner population. A major problem was the lack of building materials on the little island. Initially, the Mexica took advantage of a well-established market system to obtain stone and wood, trading available lacustrine products such as fish and frogs, mosquitos and worms, ducks and other waterfowl. Later the Mexica supplemented the market system with a tribute system, obtaining many necessary goods from conquered peoples. Although little detailed information remains, the construction of dwellings, temples, palaces, and administrative buildings must have occupied a considerable portion of the time of the early settlers.

Another tremendously time-consuming task was the construction of chinampas. The claiming of lands from the lake for cultivation was a complicated yet vital activity. If the Mexica were to retain some degree of political autonomy, they would have to provide for the bulk of their own needs. With very little land available for cultivation, chinampas not only provided this land but also afforded a means for urban expansion.

The Mexica population seems to have quickly outgrown the tiny island. This rapid growth stemmed from both natural increases and a substantial amount of immigration. The expanding population was divided, territorially, into four large quarters. Each quarter was then divided into smaller territorial units usually called *calpulli* (see Chapter 3). Some elders and their followers were apparently displeased with their position in this new arrangement. They left to settle at Tlatelolco, a small island to the north and nearly adjacent to Tenochtitlan. Tlatelolco rapidly assumed considerable status as a commercial center, developing the largest and most active marketplace in the Valley of Mexico.[3]

The Mexica accomplished much in their first century at Tenochtitlan. They established alliances with the major Valley of Mexico cities. Strategic marriages cemented these alliances, and also allowed the Mexica rulers to claim Toltec ancestry, the key to political legitimacy. The city of Tenochtitlan grew in size and splendor, its population augmented by a variety of immigrant groups. Chinampa production provided the population with a reliable and intensive resource base. This resource base broadened as the Mexica succeeded in conquering others, from whom they demanded tribute.

The time spent under Tepanec domination allowed the Mexica to develop a strong and effective military force. This force, allied with neighboring and embittered Texcoco, turned against Azcapotzalco in 1428. The success of these allied forces in crushing the Tepanec empire of Azcapotzalco in 1430 ushered in another chapter in Mesoamerican history, a chapter dominated by the Mexica and their two allies: the Acolhuacans of Texcoco and the Tepanecs of Tlacopan. For the next 90 years this Triple Alliance embarked on a course of military expansion unparalleled in the history of Mesoamerica.

URBAN SETTLEMENT AND ORGANIZATION

By 1519, the dual city of Tenochtitlan-Tlatelolco was connected to the mainland by three large manmade causeways—one stretching south, another north, and another west (see Figure 1–3). From the southern causeway the Spanish conquistadors gained their first awed impressions of the Mexica capital and surrounding cities (see Chapter 8).

The causeways extended from the shores of the lake to the central ceremonial district of Tenochtitlan. There, in an area enclosed by a wall, rose the major ceremonial buildings of the capital. Beyond this were the palaces of rulers, the houses of nobility, and the numerous buildings necessary for the administration of the empire. The vast remainder of the city was composed of urban dwelling sites, many with accompanying chinampas.

Although few writers agree on the dimensions of the central ceremonial area of Tenochtitlan, it probably measured as much as 500 meters square. Its immensity greatly impressed Cortés, who remarked that it could have contained "a town of fifteen thousand inhabitants" (1928:90). Friar Diego Durán, speaking of a preconquest festival, states that the ceremonial area "must have been immense, for it accommodated eight thousand six hundred men, dancing in a circle" (1971:78). The district was the scene of the major public ceremonies of the Mexica. Most of

---

[3] Tlatelolco was conquered by the Mexica in 1473.

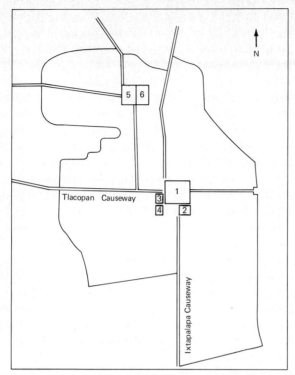

Figure 1–3: Tenochtitlan–Tlatelolco in 1519. The central district of Tenochtitlan (1) was connected to the mainland by causeways. Adjacent to the ceremonial district were the palaces of Moctezuma Xocoyotzin (2), Axayacatl (3), and the cihuacoatl (4). Causeways and canals linked Tenochtitlan with the Tlatelolco ceremonial center (5) and marketplace (6). Urban boundaries on the north and west are approximations (adapted from a map in Calnek 1972:108).

these Aztec ceremonies involved human sacrifice, which was a particularly common activity here.

Sahagún enumerates 78 different structures within this district; Cortés mentions that there must have been at least 40 "towers" within the confines of the wall. Durán, drawing on the memory of another conquistador, adds elaborate detail:

> . . . the eight or nine temples in the city were all close to one another within a large enclosure. Within this compound they all stood together, though each had its own staircase, its special courtyard, its chambers, and its sleeping quarters for the priests of the temples. . . . How marvelous it was to gaze upon them. . . . All stuccoed, carved, and crowned with different types of merlons, painted with animals, (covered) with stone figures . . . (1971:75–76).

The central district was restricted to religious edifices and activities. Just beyond its wall were found the palaces of rulers and nobles, and the various buildings necessary for the administration of a great empire. It was apparently customary for each new ruler to construct a new palace for himself on his accession to the throne. When the Spaniards first arrived, they were housed in the palace of Axayacatl; they also found the palace of Ahuitzotl still standing nearby.

Moctezuma Xocoyotzin's palace was apparently not only a residence but also comprised several buildings and courtyards, all important in the administration of an empire. These included a "courthouse," where the most important judges presided; a council chamber for the leading warriors; rooms for storing the extensive imperial tributes, along with a dwelling for the caretakers of these stores; housing for other rulers, both allies and enemies; rooms for dancers and singers of the palace; and even a room where those in charge of the activities of young men received their daily instructions. In addition, Díaz (1956:211–214) observed that Moctezuma had two armories filled with lances, bows and arrows, slings, *macquauitl* (wooden clubs inset with numerous sharp obsidian blades), shields, and quilted cotton armor. He also described an extensive aviary, as well as a zoo, the inhabitants of which gave off an "infernal noise." Díaz also mentioned a library, gardens, and ponds.

Moctezuma's palace housed artisans and servants, nobles and government officials. Cortés speaks of 300 men to look after the royal aviary and zoo, and over 600 nobles present at Moctezuma's palace every day (the servants of these nobles overflowed two or three palace courtyards). Díaz (1956:211) estimates that over 1000 dishes of food and 2000 containers of cacao were served to the ruler's palace guard. Add to these people the vast numbers of artisans, laborers (such as masons and carpenters), dancers, and royal wives and children, and the palace must have been an awe-inspiring, animated, and colorful scene.

The dwellings of the nobility were concentrated in the central part of the city, although many were also found in the outer quarters. In contrast to the humbler dwellings of the macehualtin, the residences of nobles were frequently stuccoed and had two stories.

Outside this central ceremonial and administrative area, the city was divided into four large quarters: Cuepopan, Teopan, Moyotlan, and Aztacalco. These quarters were further divided into numerous other territorial divisions, or calpulli. There is little agreement as to the exact number of calpulli in Tenochtitlan at the time of the Spanish conquest; a good estimate is 80.

As each quarter possessed a ceremonial district, so also did each calpulli. The public areas of the calpulli contained a temple for the calpulli god, a school for the young men (*telpochcalli*), and an administrative building (see Chapter 3). Life at the local level was carried on primarily within the confines of an inward-looking house site with an all-important patio and, in some cases, an adjacent chinampa. Based on extensive archival research, Edward Calnek concludes that

> The basic residential unit in each [documented] case was a walled or fenced compound. . . . This enclosed a number of separately entered dwelling units which faced inward on an open patio space. Access to the compound . . . was frequently indirect, so that the living area was visually isolated from the outside world (1972:111).

These residential units were occupied primarily by joint families; Calnek reports populations ranging from 2–3 to 25–30 per unit, the average being around 10–15 persons per unit (see Chapter 3).

Traffic was regulated by numerous waterways, footpaths, and combinations of the two:

> The principal streets are very broad and straight, the majority of them being of beaten earth, but a few and at least half the smaller thoroughfares are waterways along which they pass in their canoes (Cortés 1928:86).

Most canals and streets were apparently arranged in alternation with one another; house sites faced the streets, while adjacent chinampas faced the canals. Where chinampas (ranging in size from 100–805 square meters) had been built, this pattern resulted in a "mirror image" effect (see Figure 1–4 and Calnek 1972).

The adjacent city of Tlatelolco was similarly organized, with a central ceremonial square and several calpulli, but apparently without the four larger divisions. In addition, Tlatelolco boasted the largest marketplace in central Mexico, located beside its ceremonial center. The total urban area of Tenochtitlan-Tlatelolco encompassed at least 12 square kilometers.

The dual city of Tenochtitlan-Tlatelolco contained a diversified population. It would be a mistake to assume that this city was exclusively Mexica. Urban areas

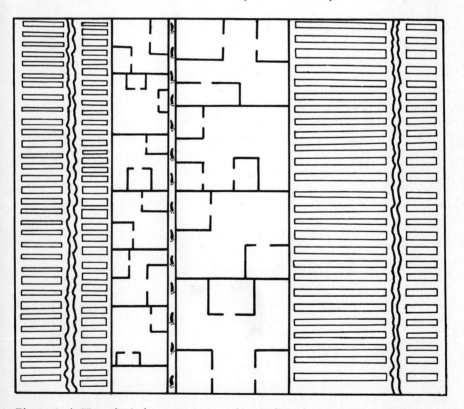

Figure 1–4: Hypothetical reconstruction of a residential area in Tenochtitlan. Note that the chinampas (narrow rectangles) face canals (wavy lines), while the house sites face streets or footpaths. Each house site was composed of a number of separate rooms facing an open patio (based on data in Calnek 1972, 1976).

characteristically have the ability to incorporate a wide array of groups. And not only did Tenochtitlan grow through immigration, for Mexica peoples were found inhabiting sections of neighboring cities. Groups specializing in particular crafts (e.g., lapidaries and manuscript painters) may have originated elsewhere and migrated to Tenochtitlan, becoming concentrated in special calpulli. Nezahualcoyotl, ruler of Texcoco from 1418–1472, encouraged such immigration of specialists into that lakeshore city. In addition, Calnek (1976:289) suggests that some immigrants were war refugees seeking asylum after military defeats they had suffered elsewhere. Through immigration and natural growth, the island city of Tenochtitlan had reached a population of approximately 150,000–200,000 persons by 1519.[4]

---

[4] At the same time, Paris had an approximate population of 300,000, and London 50,000 (Robert A. Smith, personal communication). Seville, jumping-off point for the Spanish empire, had approximately 60,000–70,000 inhabitants in 1500; by 1519, their numbers had been seriously reduced by epidemics and emigration (Elliott 1964:177). Estimates of the population of the entire Valley of Mexico in 1519 range from 1,000,000–2,560,000 (Sanders, Parsons, and Santley 1979; Cook and Borah 1963).

2/Economic organization

Large cities and complex civilizations require extensive and reliable material bases if they are to continue as viable, ongoing systems generation after gene ation. The environmental and cultural milieus of central Mexico at the time (f the Spanish arrival were conducive to civilizational achievements. The environment provided a wealth and variety of natural resources, the cultures stressed human industriousness, and the society was built upon complex social arrangements. All these elements stimulated extensive surplus production of material necessities and luxuries.

The distinguishing physical feature of central and southern Mexico may be said to be its diversity and, hence, its great potential for variable human adaptations. Capitalizing on this environmental diversity, the indigenous inhabitants of this region developed a varied diet and an increasing desire for luxury goods. Considerable surpluses resulted from the intensive production of certain key resources and a high degree of economic specialization. Linked to this complex production system were intricate exchange networks, differential controls over the means of production, and varied standards of living.

At the Aztec empire's core was the Valley of Mexico. (The environmental potential of this valley is discussed in Chapter 1.) Significant micro-environmental variations, the presence of large lakes, and the availability of a wide range of essential resources made this valley a likely location for the heartland of an empire. Surrounding this valley were other, similar valleys, although few had lake systems comparable to that of the Valley of Mexico. To the east, west, and south, and along the coasts, more temperate highlands and tropical lowlands predominated, offering still different resources for food and clothing, tools and housing.

MODES OF FOOD PRODUCTION

Agriculture served as the material foundation for the Aztec empire, as it had for earlier Mesoamerican civilizations. Some agricultural products were uniformly produced throughout the area encompassed by the empire: maize, beans, chia, amaranth, chiles, and squashes. These differed only in specific variety from area to area. Other food and nonfood crops were adapted to special environments. In particular, some

15

could be grown only in the more tropical areas of the empire: fruits, cacao, and cotton.

At the heart of Aztec agriculture was maize (corn).[1] It was the dietary mainstay, prepared in a multitude of ways. Most commonly, maize was formed into tortillas, but the Mexica were also extremely fond of tamales, which they prepared with great imagination:

> White tamales with beans forming a sea shell on top;
> white tamales with maize grains thrown in . . .
> red tamales with beans forming a sea shell on top;
> tamales made of a dough of maize softened in lime . . .
> tamales of maize softened in wood ashes . . .
> tamales of meat cooked with maize and yellow chili . . .
> tamales made of maize flowers with ground amaranth seed
>   and cherries added . . .
> tamales made with honey (Sahagún 1950–1969, book 8:37–38).

A maize gruel, called *atolli,* was also a frequent dish served with many variations:

> maize gruel with honey, with chili and honey, with yellow
>   chili;
> white, thick gruel with a scattering of maize grains;
> sour, white maize gruel;
> sour, red maize gruel with fruit and chili . . .
> maize gruel with fish-amaranth seeds and honey . . .
> maize gruel with wrinkled chia, covered with green
>   chilis or small, hot chilis . . .
> maize gruel with chia, covered with squash seeds and
>   with chili (*ibid.*:39).

Maize was grown successfully from the tropical lowlands to the high plateaus. Throughout Mesoamerica, the rains were concentrated in the summer (May–September), and this provided optimal conditions for the maturation of maize. In the lower elevations, two crops a year were often possible; but in the higher elevations, such as the Valley of Mexico, only one crop per year was normal—and even that could fail because of droughts or early frosts. In the maize cycle, timing was all important. It was critical that the summer rains begin in May or June so that the maize could be planted early and mature before the onset of the frosts, which often appeared as early as November; late rains often spelled disaster for the Valley of Mexico.

In the more temperate and tropical zones outside the valley, threats of drought or frosts were minimal. Aztec conquest of these areas may have initially been motivated by a need to control a reliable supply of maize. In the years 1450–1454, a great famine had spread throughout central Mexico. The famine was so severe it forced some Mexica to sell their own family members into servitude in exchange for the life-sustaining maize successfully produced in the fertile areas outside the

---

[1] The maize grown in sixteenth-century Mexico was similar in size and overall characteristics to some varieties grown in parts of rural Mexico today.

Valley of Mexico: ". . . they sold their sons and daughters to merchants and to rulers of towns who could maintain them. They would trade a child for a small basket of maize and the new owner was obliged to maintain the infant while the famine lasted" (Durán 1964:147). Later, some of these areas fell to Aztec conquest. By 1519, the Triple Alliance had gained political control of vast areas of maize production in different environmental zones. This minimized the effect of local agricultural disaster for the Mexica and their allies. Furthermore, maize was harvested in different seasons throughout these regions. This allowed stores of maize to be replenished at intervals during the year, lessening the impact of the mid-summer "lean months." Nonetheless, lean times still befell the Mexica, particularly just before harvest during the summer month of Uey tecuilhuitl ("Great Feast of the Lords"). At this time "there was much hunger; when dried maize was costly, then there was much want, (and) it was hard to gain a livelihood" (Sahagún 1950–1969, book 2:93). The rituals and feasts of this month were dedicated to the goddess of the young maize plant, Xilonen. In her honor, the ruler provided the populace with an abundance of tamales for seven days, and later offered the people green corn tortillas, indicating that the maize had just begun to ripen (*ibid.*: 92–99, Durán 1971:436–437). This feasting helped offset the effects of a particularly difficult time of year.

Many deities were dedicated to fertility, and some looked specifically after the maize.[2] During May, in the Mexica month Uey toçoztli, the Mexica venerated the maize goddess Chicomecoatl ("Seven Serpent") and carried out rituals to ensure the imminent arrival of sufficient rain and a bountiful crop. In one event of that month,

> The people tore out stalks of corn, calling them centeotlana, which means "to tear out the god of the ears of corn." When these plants had been ripped out, they were offered as first fruits of the fields. And the women cried out in loud voices, "O my lady, come quickly!" They said this to the cornfields so that they would ripen soon, before the frost could fall upon them. Then the men took up their flutes and went about playing in the fields (Durán 1971:425).

During this same annual ceremony, maize was dedicated as seed that would be used for the coming planting. After dedicating the seed, the people honored the maize goddess by saying,

> "Yea, verily, this one is our sustenance"; that is to say, she is truly our flesh, our livelihood; through her we live and are strong. If she (were) not, we should die of hunger.

> For he who eateth no tortillas, he then fainteth; he falleth down; he droppeth quickly; there is a twittering as of birds in his ears; darkness descendeth upon him.

> And it is said, it is this Chicome coatl who maketh all our food (Sahagún 1950–1969, book 2:62).

[2] It is probably more correct to talk about one or two deities, each with a number of different guises. For example, the maize goddess was referred to as Chicomecoatl ("Seven Serpent") when there was frost and famine, as Chalchiuhcihuatl ("Jade Woman"; Durán probably means Chalchiuhtlicue, "Jade-Her Skirt") when the harvests were abundant, and as Xilonen when the young maize began to ripen (Durán 1971:222).

Maize was awarded an exalted position in virtually all aspects of Mexica culture. This was undoubtedly due to the critical role maize played in subsistence, combined with the hazards of its production in the Valley of Mexico. The Mexica, in keeping with this overwhelming concern with maize, elaborated numerous terms for maize varieties, maize characteristics, maize life cycle. For example, the Nahuatl language distinguished among *centli*, "ear of maize"; *xiuhtoctli*, "tender maize stalk"; *tlatlauhcacintli*, "reddish maize ear"; *tzatzapalli*, "double maize ear"; *cuitlacochi*, "ears of maize which appear malformed"; *cinuechtli*, "maize which appears anywhere"; *cimpala*, "rotten ear of maize"; and so on (*ibid.*: book 11:279–282).

Maize was more than an impersonal food. It was highly personalized, deified, and an intimate part of the everyday life of the Mexica and their neighbors. The individual felt very close to maize, and with ritual precision would address the seed before planting it in the ground; this relationship has continued in central Mexico in communities such as Tepoztlán to the present time: "My beloved body and strength, go and bear the cold and the storm of the seasons; all is for us" (Oscar Lewis 1951:137). Many sayings or adages linked people to maize: A person who had gained honor and esteem was one who had "reached the season of the green maize ear"; one who revealed a secret wrong of another was likened to an "ear of green maize whose entrails open" (Sahagún 1950–1969, book 6:235, 228).

Interest in maize penetrated the poetry and hymns of the Mexica. Frequent allusions to maize are made, as in this segment of a hymn to Xipe Totec, a deity associated with agricultural fertility:

> Mayhap I shall die and perish—I, the tender maize. Like a precious green stone is my heart, (yet) I shall see gold in it. I shall be content if first I mature. The war chief is born.

> My god, (give me) in part plenteous tender maize. Thy worshipper looketh toward thy mountain. I shall be content if first I ripen. The warrior chief is born (*ibid.*: book 2:213).

Of lesser importance ideologically, but excellent complements to maize in the diet, were cultigens such as beans, chia, amaranth, chiles, squashes, prickly pear cactus, maguey, and a multitude of other fruits and vegetables. Varieties of all these were widely cultivated throughout the Aztec empire.

Beans were frequently served with tortillas and as an ingredient in the ever-present tamales. Chia and amaranth were used much like maize; the seeds of each could be made into a nourishing gruel (*pinole*), and the amaranth seeds were often mixed with ground maize for tamales. Additionally, cakes of amaranth seed dough (*tzoalli*) were used to form and adorn idols of the deities and other religious symbols (*ibid.*, book 2:69, 121). The greens of some varieties of amaranth were eaten, but those of chia were considered inedible. Chiles accompanied virtually every meal, and—along with salt and some flowers—seasoned a variety of dishes. In fact, religious fasting sometimes meant serving full meals, but without chile (*ibid.*, book 1:13). The many varieties of squashes provided seeds and fruit, which could be eaten raw or cooked, and flowers, which were used widely for flavoring.

Two cacti, nopal and maguey, were also cultivated. These cultigens were especially important in areas of low or marginal rainfall, and they invariably survived and produced well, even when the maize failed (see Figure 2–1). The nopal, or prickly pear cactus, yielded a popular fruit (nochtli) and succulent green joints which were almost always available. From the versatile maguey plant were produced extensive quantities of an alcoholic drink (octli, or pulque), medicinal cures, fibers for clothing, and thorns for sewing needles and sacrificial barbs. Like maize, maguey was important in Mexica religion. It was personified as Mayahuel, a fertility goddess with 400 (i.e., innumerable) breasts. She and her offspring, the Four Hundred Rabbits, formed the religious world of drink and drunkenness. Although pulque was formally forbidden to all but the aged, it apparently found its way into general consumption. It was widely used as an additive to medicines. Pulque, one yellow chile, and some shelled gourd seeds were combined with a sweatbath to cure the patient who had suffered a relapse from a recent illness. The ground, cooked pulp of the maguey leaves was blended with salt and applied directly to open wounds. Combined with pine resin, this same pulp was used as a compress; applied to afflicted parts of the body, it provided relief from gout (ibid., book 11:179). According to the sources, those who did overindulge in pulque were viewed with great

Figure 2–1: A colonial period rendering of maguey cultivation (Historia General de las Cosas de Nueva España 1926:lámina CXXII, illus. 750).

disdain: They were portrayed as physically and mentally disheveled, as bringing poverty and ruin upon their families, and as ultimately committing a serious crime or suffering a fatal accident. This behavior, however, was not directly attributed to the person, but to fate, the pulque, and the pulque deities. A person unfortunate enough to be born under the day-sign Two Rabbit was destined to succumb to drink. When the inevitable happened, people simply said, "He is like his rabbit." In addition to its uses as a beverage and a remedy, the maguey plant also provided coarse fibers which were woven into cloth. Capes and other articles of clothing were made from this cloth; this constituted the upper-torso attire of the commoners, but was normally shunned by the nobility, who preferred cotton.

In the more distant reaches of the empire, in the tropical lowlands, cotton and cacao (chocolate) were cultivated along with most of the food crops already mentioned. Cotton fibers were woven into the "prestige clothing" of Mesoamerica, much as cacao constituted the "prestige drink." Cacao beans also apparently provided the indigenous money system with its "small change." As will be shown, these items moved readily from the lowlands to the highlands through tribute and trade systems.

Techniques for cultivating these many crops fall into two broad categories: fallowing, or *tlacolol*, and irrigation. In some cases, these techniques may have been supplemented by the use of terracing, crop rotation, or fertilizers.

In large areas of the highlands, particularly on sloping land or land not conducive to irrigation, the fallowing system was the basic agricultural adaptation. A field was cultivated for two to three years, allowed to rest for an equal length of time, recultivated, rested, and so on. All of the major crops could be cultivated in this manner. Terracing may have been an adjunct to fallowing in some areas; it allowed the cultivator to increase the soil depth, at the same time inhibiting runoff and erosion. Crop rotation has also been suggested for the Mesoamerican tlacolol cultivator. Most likely he alternated maize, chia, and amaranth (Sanders 1971:8).

The cultivator also had at his disposal many different kinds of natural fertilizers. Some of these are emphasized in the classification of soil types: *tlazollalli* (soil fertilized by turning under weeds or other vegetation), *quauhtlalli* (land with humus formed from rotten wood or oak leaves), *tlalauiyac* (land that is fertilized). It is also probable that human excrement was used, but whether it was applied to tlacolol fields is not clear. Bernal Díaz del Castillo, startled by many of the Mexica customs, made special note of its use:

> . . . I must also mention, with all apologies, that they sold many canoe-loads of human excrement, which they kept in the creeks near the market. This was for the manufacture of salt and the curing of skins, which they say cannot be done without it. I know that many gentlemen will laugh at this, but I assure them it is true. I may add that on all the roads they have shelters made of reeds or straw or grass so that they can retire when they wish to do so, and purge their bowels unseen by passers-by, and also in order that their excrement shall not be lost (1963:233).

In addition, this collection of excrement would have also served as an efficient sanitation system, especially in crowded urban areas. William Sanders (1971:7) points out that the supplies of human excrement must have far surpassed the demands of the specialists observed by Díaz; its additional use as a fertilizer is highly likely.

On relatively flat lands and in some shallow lakebeds, irrigation agriculture was the rule. Floodwater irrigation systems were constructed over large areas. The soils were fortified and replenished by nutrients and soil particles carried in the water; thus, the need for fallowing was eliminated. Irrigation was far more intensive than the tlacolol technique, providing greater surpluses and supporting larger populations. Crop rotation and fertilizers may have been used to further increase yields. Lands with easy access to natural springs could be irrigated permanently with springwater. Springs were numerous in the southern part of the Valley of Mexico, and vast systems of irrigation agriculture were concentrated there. These permanent systems, along with floodwater networks favorably situated near springs, could draw on water supplies prior to the onset of the rainy season. Crops could be planted early and mature with certainty before the frost season began. Reliability of production, therefore, was high.

The most intensive form of irrigation agriculture was the *chinampas*. Chinampas were highly productive plots of land claimed from the shallow beds of freshwater lakes. Misnamed "floating gardens," chinampas are still cultivated in and around Xochimilco and are a popular tourist attraction. A chinampa was constructed by piling alternating layers of vegetation and mud in shallow areas of the lakes. The parcel was held secure at first by posts, and later, when the plot was established, by the roots of willow trees planted at the corners and along the sides. The entire plot thus served as a deep, humus-filled foundation for continuous cultivation. It was bordered by canals and walkways, and irrigation was provided by dipping into an adjacent canal. Although nutrients constantly replenished the soil in this manner, other fertilizers and crop rotation may have been used to increase production.[3] A variety of crops were grown on chinampas, including maize, beans, chiles, amaranth, tomatoes, and flowers. There are good indications that, like today, the *chinampero* planted his seeds in small seedbeds, allowed them to germinate there, and then transplanted them throughout the chinampa. Maize, apparently, was the only crop which could bypass this stage (Coe 1964:94–95). The seedbed technique assured greater returns, since only germinated plants were transplanted. Furthermore, it allowed the cultivator some overlap in cropping: While one crop was about to be harvested, another could be germinating in the seedbeds. This would have reduced the intervals between croppings. Today, and probably in the sixteenth century, seven different crops are possible on any chinampa annually. While the intensiveness, reliability, and versatility of this system cannot be overemphasized, it must be placed in the context of the population it supported. After extensive investigations of sixteenth-century documents, Edward Calnek has concluded that, on the average, approximately 500 square meters of chinampa land would be necessary to support a single individual. In the city of Tenochtitlan, chinampas ranged in

---

[3] In the early twentieth century, many cultivators rotated maize, chiles, and tomatoes on their chinampa plots (Parsons 1976:244).

size from 100–850 square meters (see Chapter 1) and were occupied by 2–3 to 25–30 persons (with an average of 10–15 persons per chinampa). These figures have led Calnek to state that:

> The larger chinampa holdings would normally have provided no more than 15% of family subsistence income; in a large number of cases, the actual contribution must be estimated at a fraction of 1% of family needs. With respect to the smaller sites, it is difficult to imagine why chinampas were maintained at all (1972:112).

Calnek provides an answer by suggesting that the value of the plots lay less in their overall productive yields than in their specialization in the production of fresh vegetables (*ibid.*). Flowers also were an important perishable which could be produced on the urban chinampas; hardly a religious festival or political feast took place without an abundance of aromatic flowers. In these areas, a family probably met subsistence needs through advantageous marketplace exchanges of their specialized products or through allocations from the state tribute stores.

Outside the concentrated urban areas, chinampa plots were generally larger and resident families smaller. Such a family could probably not only fully support itself from its own chinampa production but also produce sizeable surpluses. This applied particularly to the southern lakeshores of the Valley of Mexico, around Xochimilco and Chalco, which had the greatest concentration of chinampas. Freshwater springs kept the water especially sweet and, compared with the central and northern parts of the valley, this area suffered less from devastating frosts or low rainfall. Here also, compared to the larger urban centers, was a small population of approximately 36,620 persons dependent on chinampa cultivation (Parsons 1976:245–246). According to recent calculations, this population could have produced a maximum annual surplus, above and beyond its own needs, of 19,890,000 kilograms of maize (*ibid.*:250). It has also been suggested that Tenochtitlan, with an estimated population of 150,000–200,000 people, would require 30,000,000–40,000,000 kilograms of maize annually to meet its subsistence needs (all staple foodstuffs being reduced to maize in these calculations).[4] While an estimated 15,200,000 kilograms of maize entered Tenochtitlan annually as tribute from non-chinampa areas, the southern chinampa district would have contributed considerably to the subsistence support of the city. Some of the chinampa surplus was channeled to Tenochtitlan in the form of rents on lands owned by Tenochtitlan nobles (est. 2,535,000 kilograms), and some of the production was demanded by the state in the form of tribute (800,000 kilograms) (*ibid.*). But the vast bulk of the surplus production from this area would have worked its way into Tenochtitlan and other urban households by way of the bustling marketplaces. There the food producers exchanged their surpluses for specialized goods and services provided by the urbanites.

Surplus production from this southern area must have been an extremely important factor in the urban development of Tenochtitlan: It allowed the dense

---

[4] The figure actually should be larger than this. Households of high-ranking nobles consumed vast amounts of food, lavish feasts among nobles and wealthy merchants were common, and the state maintained stores of food surpluses as a hedge against possible famine.

clustering of people in Tenochtitlan on small, probably specialized, chinampas; it provided subsistence goods to the numerous urban specialists—artisans, merchants, priests, military officers, and bureaucratic officials; and it helped underwrite the lavish life-style of the nobility.

Wherever conditions were favorable to chinampa cultivation, lakeside and island cities expanded their settlements by continually dredging new canals and building up the rectangular plots. When a cultivator built a house on the chinampa, the plot took on the added dimension of a residential site. Tenochtitlan grew in this fashion, particularly after the construction of a dike across Lake Texcoco in the mid-fifteenth century. This massive hydraulic construction helped control the salinity of the western part of the lake, as well as moderate changes in the water level; salinity and flooding were ever-present dangers in this internally drained system.

Whatever agricultural techniques were used, the fundamental cultivating tool was the same: the *uictli*, or digging stick. This and other supplementary agricultural and transport implements such as sharp sowing sticks, tumplines, and carrying frames were honored during the month of Etzalcualiztli (May 24–June 12):

> On the day of the feast all these things were placed by the Indians upon a small platform in their homes, and the objects were revered and thanked for their help in the fields and on the road. Food and pulque were offered to them, together with the dish eaten on this day. . . . Incense was offered before them and a thousand salaams, salutations, and speeches (Durán 1971:431–432).

The annual agricultural cycle was similar for all cultivators, although timing varied. The higher lands, for example, were always planted earlier than the valley floors (*ibid.*:397); and chinampa plots were normally under continuous, rather than seasonal, cultivation. The cultivator's cycle involved preparing the soil, sowing the seed, weeding and caring for the growing plants, and harvesting. The tlacolol cultivator usually had the additional initial task of clearing the land of dense, unwanted vegetation; the chinampero normally added a seedbed stage; and the serious canal irrigation cultivator had to pay continuous heed to the condition of his hydraulic constructions. In all these activities, the cultivator was strictly guided by the ritual calendar. This calendar indicated when the proper times had arrived to

> . . . sow, reap, till the land, cultivate corn, weed, harvest, store, shell the ears of corn, sow beans and flaxseed. They always took into account that it had to be in such and such a month, after such and such a feast, on such and such a day, under such and such a sign. . . . If chili was not sown on a certain day, squash on another, maize on another, and so forth, in disregard of the orderly count of the days, the people felt there would be great damage and loss of any crop sown outside the established order of days (*ibid.*:396).

In most cases the cultivator combined his agricultural endeavors with other economic activities. These included gathering wild plants, hunting, fishing, and fowling.

Herbs, fruits, wood products, and salt were especially sought on a part-time (and sometimes full-time) basis. Medicinal herbs were in high demand. There were complicated herbal remedies for most illnesses suffered by the people, including gout, fevers, stomach and intestinal ailments, diarrhea, coughs, sore eyes, skin irritations, and bites (see Chapter 7). Of special interest are peyote and mushrooms. Peyote was used as a fever medicine; sacred mushrooms (*teonanacatl*) were used to remedy fever and gout. Their hallucinogenic properties were well known and exploited on special occasions. They produced many moods and were not to be taken lightly; for example:

> [The mushroom] saddens, depresses, troubles one; it makes one flee, frightens one, makes one hide. He who eats many of them sees many things which make him afraid, or make him laugh. He flees, hangs himself, hurls himself from a cliff, cries out, takes fright. One eats it in honey (Sahagún 1950–1969, book 11:130).

Most medicinal and culinary herbs were widely distributed. Some, however, were found only in specific locales; their wider distribution depended mainly on marketplace exchanges. The many fruits cultivated or collected largely in lowland areas also changed hands in the bustling marketplaces. And the marketplace and tribute systems were used to transfer wood products (notably lumber for building, firewood, and bark for paper) from the forested highlands to non-forested areas. Of course, salt was critical in the Mesoamerican diet, and its collection was a specialized activity concentrated around saline lakes and on the southern Gulf Coast. Regional merchants throughout the empire frequently trafficked in this valuable item.

Hunting was a highly valued enterprise among the Mexica, harking back to their early history as nomadic Chichimecas. Land and water animals were hunted primarily for food and skins, but some were also captured for the rulers' zoos and for taming (notably monkeys). Of the land animals, deer, rabbits, hares, opposum, armadillos, pocket gophers, wild boars, and tapirs were all eaten; their meat, raw or cooked, was regularly available in the major marketplaces. The skins of jaguars and deer were highly prized; rabbit fur was tediously spun, dyed, and applied to expensive capes. For hunting the larger animals, the bow and arrow was the usual weapon; success depended greatly on the stealth and cunning of the hunter. For catching the smaller animals, snares or traps were used.

The lakes and lakeshores teemed with animals, fish, and waterfowl. Turtles, salamanders, frogs, tadpoles, mollusks, and crustaceans were abundant and considered very tasty. Catching these animals required relatively little investment in technology; spears and nets were usually sufficient. In some cases, such as turtle hunting, not even these were needed:

> . . . the fishermen lie in wait as the turtles come out [of the water] arranged in order. When they have emerged, the fishermen quickly pounce upon them to throw one on its back. There it lies. They run; they go to seize another; they run to throw another upon its back. They do nothing but throw each one on its back. Later they gather them without haste, for once they have fallen upon their backs, no longer can they right themselves again. The good fisherman, one who holds night vigil, takes ten, fifteen, twenty of them (*ibid.*:60).

Many varieties of large and small fish were caught in the lakes and streams with the aid of nets and spears. Some persons were full-time fishermen, and they would fish singly or in groups of two or three. As with gathering and hunting, this was largely an individualized or small-scale enterprise.

Edible fowl were also abundant in the lake areas. Sahagún (*ibid.*:25–39, 53–54) discusses over 30 different types of edible birds. Ducks were especially abundant, but geese, cranes, pelican, and a number of lesser varieties were all plentiful and popular. Although fowling was carried on during the entire year, it reached a peak in the winter with the arrival of huge numbers of migratory ducks. Some birds were taken by individuals with the aid of bows and arrows, spears, snares, and nets. When they appeared in great quantities, ducks were often the focus of a communal hunt. The technique "required the setting of large nets on poles at intervals in the water, then arousing the ducks at dusk with shouts and sticks, and retrieving those that became entangled. The *atlatl* or throwing stick was also used" (Gibson 1964:342). Other wild birds graced the tables of the nobility: quail, pheasants, partridges, and pigeons. Fowl probably was rarely enjoyed by the commoners. Birds were prized for both meat and feathers; featherworking was valued by the Mexica as one of their finest artistic skills.

Domesticates were few, but they were very important in the diet. Turkeys were raised for meat and eggs; dogs provided companionship and meat. Dogs and turkeys were occasionally served together, as in the lavish merchant feasts:

> [The host] provided turkeys, perhaps eighty or a hundred of them. Then he bought dogs to provide the people as food, perhaps twenty or forty. When they died, they put them with the turkeys which they served; at the bottom of the sauce dish they placed the dog meat, on top they placed the turkey as required (Sahagún 1950–1969, book 9:48).

The implication is that the turkey meat was more highly esteemed, and the dog meat provided "filler."

Aside from these major cultigens, wild resources, and domesticated animals, a great many other foods were gleaned from the environment. These included locusts, grubs, fish eggs, lizards, honey, and *tecuitlatl*. This last was a green lake scum formed by water fly eggs; the conquistador Bernal Díaz observed that the people made a bread from it which was cheese-like in flavor (1956:217).

The intensiveness and variation in food production had two major consequences in Mesoamerica. First, it stimulated specialization in all areas of food production— from chile peppers or flowers to fishing or fowling. The precise specializations undertaken by members of a community depended largely on the local ecology and on the availability of exchange networks. For example, many farmers in the drier northern part of the Valley of Mexico specialized in maguey production; pulque and textiles from maguey fibers were sold widely in Mesoamerican market-places. And lakeside residents could specialize in lacustrine resources (from fish and waterfowl to salamanders and tecuitlatl) on either a full-time or part-time basis; all of these, fresh or cooked, were popular items in the Valley of Mexico marketplaces. Varieties of certain crops such as maize, chiles, chia, cacao, and cotton each acquired their own special reputation based on their area of cultivation. Each variety was carefully sorted and sold in marketplaces according to its primary area of cultivation. For example, each type of cotton was meticulously separated out: Cotton from irrigated lands was most highly prized, followed by cotton from the tropics, from the west, from the deserts and, finally, cotton grown by the Totonacs (Sahagún 1950–1969, book 10:75). Likewise, chia from Oztoman was separated from Chontal chia, Chalco maize was distinguished from Acolhuacan maize, Tochtepec cacao from Guatemala cacao, and Huaxtepec chiles from Toch-milco chiles (*ibid.*: 65–67).[5]

Secondly, the intensive and highly diversified systems of food production yielded sufficient surpluses to release many people entirely from the food-getting enterprise. These persons channeled their energies and skills into craft production, trade, political administration, military duty, religious service, or a multitude of professional occupations.

DIVISION OF LABOR AND OCCUPATIONAL SPECIALIZATION

Craft Production Craft manufacture was highly specialized in central Mexico, being concentrated in the major urban centers. This specialization must have been on a grand scale, for entire residential sections of Tenochtitlan-Tlatelolco, Texcoco, and other Valley of Mexico cities were populated by full-time artisans and merchants. In the less urbanized areas, craft specialization was less intensive.

Texcoco, for example, distinguished more than 30 occupations, each relegated to its own residential section in the city. This included goldworkers, silverworkers, painters, lapidaries, and featherworkers. In the 1400s the ruler of Texcoco encouraged outstanding artisans to immigrate to the city from distant parts (Alva Ixtlilxochitl 1965, vol. 1:326–327; vol. 2:187). In Tenochtitlan-Tlatelolco, the featherworkers resided in a separate district, as surely did the lapidaries and the gold- and silverworkers.

The artistic creations of the featherworkers, lapidaries, and metalworkers were highly esteemed in Aztec society, and their use was reserved strictly for the nobility. In Mexica lore, the god Quetzalcoatl, as patron of the Toltecs (ca. A.D. 900–1150), is credited with the creation of luxury crafts: "[The Toltecs] cut green stone, and they cast gold, and they made other works of the craftsman and the featherworker. Very skilled were they. These started and proceeded from Quetzalcoatl—all craft works and wisdom" (Sahagún 1950–1969, book 3:13). So admired were the Toltecs in this regard that master craftsmen in the sixteenth century were called *toltecca*, regardless of their ethnic origins. Nonetheless, the archaeological record reveals that at least two luxury arts, stoneworking and featherworking, long preceded Toltec preeminence in central Mexico (Noguera 1971:258–259, 262). The origins of these crafts and the artists who perfected them are somewhat obscure.

Artisans of luxury goods appear to have enjoyed some degree of exclusiveness in Aztec society; in fact, they were organized in a fashion reminiscent of the craft guilds of medieval Europe. Members of these Aztec craft guilds were set apart from the rest of Aztec society by virtue of their separate residence, control over membership, internal control over education and ranking, distinct ethnic origins, commitments to particular patron deities and religious ceremonies, and special relations with the state.

Featherworking had been an ancient art in the Valley of Mexico, where aquatic birds were particularly abundant. Originally the feather artisans worked with

[5] These are only a few examples of the many given.

common feathers such as heron, duck, or turkey. By the late fifteenth century, however, Aztec merchant activity and military conquests brought into the Valley of Mexico plentiful and reliable supplies of precious feathers such as quetzal, cotinga, and parrot. It was probably not until the early sixteenth century that the feather-workers emphasized work with these highly prized feathers, and gained a special status in Aztec society. They created exquisite shields, headdresses, warrior costumes, fans, and insignia—all intricate mosaics of colorful feathers. Use of these valuable and highly esteemed articles was the strict prerogative of renowned warriors and members of the nobility (see Chapter 3; Chapter 7 includes a detailed discussion of the objects).

The featherworkers were early residents of Tenochtitlan and Tlatelolco; in Tlatelolco they occupied an important exclusive calpulli called Amantlan. Indeed, featherworkers generally became known as *amanteca*, or "people of Amantlan." They also occupied separate residential districts in Tenochtitlan and Texcoco, and probably in other cities as well. Amantlan, at least, had its own temple and *calmecac*, or elite school for young men. There were several calmecac in the dual island city. These schools were normally reserved for children of the nobility. The amanteca, as "non-nobles," must have been highly regarded by the nobility to have their own calmecac. Knowledge, skills, and standards of workmanship were passed from parent to child, and both boys and girls were dedicated to the trade (see Figure 2–2*a*). If the child were a boy, they appealed to the gods to endow him with "understanding, artisanship." If the child were a girl,

> . . . one asked that she might embroider well; might dye articles well; might tint rabbit fur; might tint well the varicolored rabbit furs wherever they were placed; or might dye feathers in varied colors: azure, yellow, rose red, light blue, black; (that) she might judge colors, so that she could work her feathers (*ibid.*, book 9:88).

(a)
(b)
(c)

Figure 2–2: Education in the luxury crafts: (a) featherworking, (b) stoneworking, (c) metalworking (Codex Mendoza 1938, vol. 3: folio 70).

The amanteca occasionally acted collectively. For example, during the month of Panquetzaliztli, they bathed and sacrificed an individual set up to impersonate one of their patron gods, Coyotl inaual. If no single individual were sufficiently wealthy to purchase the victim, a number of amanteca would join together and contribute to the costs. Also, during the month of Tlaxochimaco, they especially honored their two goddesses by dancing and celebrating at their calpulli temple.

The amanteca apparently maintained internal ranking. Position and prestige were based on the ability to provide sacrificial victims and conduct religious ceremonies; this in turn was based on wealth. In wealth they were, as a group, comparable to the professional merchants, or *pochteca*. Indeed, the relationships between the amanteca and the pochteca were quite intimate: They lived in adjacent calpulli, their gods were closely associated, and the merchants provided the featherworkers with their precious raw materials.

Featherworkers engaged in both public employ and private enterprise. Those in the public domain worked specifically for the ruler; they created his attire, they fashioned magnificent gifts for his guests, and they adorned the god Huitzilopochtli with feathered cloaks (*ibid.*:91). These artisans had access to the state treasury, which held goods received by the state through tribute and foreign trade. This included great quantities of precious feathers from distant and exotic provinces. In all likelihood, the royal aviary was also a source of priceless feathers for these artisans. The privately employed featherworkers made shields and other plumed devices as a household operation. They must have obtained their raw materials from either the marketplaces, where feathers were always sold, or directly from the long-distance merchants, their close associates. In turn, these artisans sold their creations in the colorful marketplaces.

The skilled lapidaries, like the featherworkers, also appear to have been organized into guilds. The specialized art of stoneworking was probably passed from parent to child, much like the art of featherworking (see Figure 2–2b). Their fine stone manufacture was a luxury craft: The highly ornamented stone objects created by these artisans could be worn and displayed only by members of the nobility. Others who dared wear these precious objects did so on pain of death. The lapidaries worked a great variety of stones, including jade, turquoise, amethyst, obsidian, rock crystal, and amber. With these stones lip pendants, lip plugs, ear plugs, necklaces, and bracelets were fashioned for nobles and gods; intricate mosaics were created, and the ruler's arms were adorned (*ibid.*:80–82; Díaz 1956:211–212).

The lapidaries were most closely associated with the town of Xochimilco, where they carried out their major ceremonies. This town, according to their legends, was their homeland, their place of origin.[6] It is very likely, however, that by the end of the fifteenth century they resided not only in exclusive calpulli in Xochimilco but also in Texcoco, Tenochtitlan-Tlatelolco, and other major Valley of Mexico

[6] However, they probably had an earlier, more distant, origin in the Huaxtec region of eastern Mexico. Three of their four patron deities have Huaxtec attributes: the god Naualpilli was dressed like a Huaxtec, Centeotl as a fertility deity is often associated with the Huaxtec area, and Chantico in many ways appears much like the goddess Xochiquetzal, patronness of the weavers and probably also from the same area.

cities. The stoneworkers engaged in exclusive collective ceremonies to honor their four patron gods. These rituals were organized and supervised by the elders, the master lapidaries of the guild. In all probability, the lapidaries were ranked much like the featherworkers: Skill and wealth formed the bases for prestige.

Master lapidaries were held in special esteem by the Aztec rulers. Lapidaries were among the craftsmen enticed by Nezahualcoyotl to settle in Texcoco; and Moctezuma Xocoyotzin (1502–1520) engaged in conquests on their behalf:

> . . . the lapidaries of the city of Mexico, of Tlatelolco, and of other cities heard that in the provinces of Tototepec and Quetzaltepec there existed a type of sand good for working stones, together with emery to polish them until they became bright and shining. The stone workers told King Moteczoma about this and explained the difficulties in obtaining the sand and emery from those provinces, and the high prices that were asked (Durán 1964:229–230).

According to the chronicle, Moctezuma negotiated with the people of these provinces for the materials; the people took offense at this gesture and hostilities resulted. The Aztec forces summarily subdued the two cities, with the result that the supplies of sand and emery, so important to the stoneworkers, were assured. Lapidaries were both publicly and privately employed; those with enough political clout to incite a war were most likely the palace artisans.

Like the other luxury artisans, the master metalworkers occupied a special position in Aztec society. They resided in separate calpulli, they exercised control over the ranking of their members, and they could transmit the skills of gold- and silverworking exclusively to their children (see Figure 2–2c). During the month of Tlacaxipehualiztli, they sacrificed and flayed a captive in the name of their patron deity, Xipe Totec ("Our Lord the Flayed One"). The metalworkers enjoyed special relationships with the ruling elite; some were employed at the palaces, and no doubt had access to the considerable wealth of the state treasury for their craft manufacture. They created exquisite objects, especially from gold and silver:

> . . . they can cast a bird whose tongue, head, and wings move, and they can mold a monkey or other monster which moves its head, tongue, hands and feet, and in its hands they put little implements, so that the figure seems to be dancing with them. What is even more remarkable, they can make a piece half in gold and half in silver and cast a fish with all its scales, in gold and silver, alternating (Motolinía 1950:241–242).

The royal palaces employed other full-time artisans, particularly painters and sculptors. Little is known of their compensation, except for the perhaps atypical pay received by sculptors who carved a statue of Moctezuma Xocoyotzin. Each received before beginning the work an unknown quantity of clothing for himself and his wife; 10 loads of squashes; 10 loads of beans; 2 loads each of chiles, cacao, and cotton; and a boatload of maize. Upon completion, each worker received 2 slaves, 2 loads of cacao, some pottery and salt, and a load of cloth (Tezozomoc 1975:668–669). This certainly would have raised the sculptor well above the usual commoner in standard of living.

Although the luxury craftsmen enjoyed guild-like seclusion and independence, numerous other artisans mingled more in Aztec society. Specialized crafts such as pottery making, gourd bowl manufacturing, smoking-tube fashioning, mat making, obsidian flaking, and basketweaving were undertaken by commoners on a part-time or full-time basis. As with most production in pre-Spanish Mexico, this craft manufacture was a household enterprise. It was small in scale, used only family members as the labor force, and usually undertook the entire productive activity from start to finish. The mat-makers, for example, collected or sometimes purchased the reeds, prepared them, wove them into mats, and sold the finished products in the marketplace. This means, of course, that many craft specializations were likely to crop up near sites of raw materials, or in major urban centers where vendors brought those materials to sell in the marketplaces.

Some producers of utilitarian manufactured goods, however dispersed they were, did share a common identity and some religious unity: the mat-makers, collectively, worshiped their patron god Nappatecutli, and the sculptors and embroiderers revered the goddess Xochiquetzal. Furthermore, embroiderers born on the days One Flower or Seven Flower were said to be destined to become experts at their crafts. They observed special rites on the latter day: Depending on the degree of their devotion, they fasted and did penance for 20, 40, or 80 days prior to Seven Flower, and offered quail and incense to Xochiquetzal.

Perhaps the most widely distributed craft in central Mexico was weaving. It was a craft undertaken exclusively by women, and all women—regardless of residence, class, or ethnic affiliation—learned to spin and weave cloth. Not all women, however, wove the same materials or elaborated garments with the same amount of decoration. Noblewomen, in the households of rulers and chiefs and serving the gods in the temples, appear to have woven the most elaborate and expensive capes, loin cloths, shifts, and skirts. They wove this finery using imported cotton and embellished their work with rabbit fur embroidery or feather mosaics. Capes were the most highly decorated garments: They graced the idols of the deities, adorned the rulers and chiefs, and were among the most highly prized gifts given from one ruler to another. Women of the commoner class wove garments of yucca and maguey fiber for household use, but also must have produced fine decorated clothing of cotton. Great quantities of ornate capes and other garments were delivered from the provinces to the Aztec Triple Alliance in the form of tribute; such goods must have been produced by women of all classes in the provinces.

Textiles of varying quality and form were used in central Mexico in a multitude of ways. As clothing, they provided modesty and warmth (especially the feathered capes) and served to signal social status. Commoners were strictly forbidden from wearing anything but the coarse undecorated maguey or yucca fiber garments. Nobles might wear any type of clothing, but preferred the most elegant. Nobles were differentiated by the clothing they were allowed, by law, to exhibit: the higher one's status and renown, the more expensive and decorative one's clothing. Strict laws with severe penalties were enacted in the fifteenth century to restrict attire. However, there is some question about the effectiveness of these laws in the sixteenth century (see Anawalt 1980). In addition, large plain cotton capes (*quachtli*) functioned as a medium of exchange throughout central Mexico. Other types of textiles served as (1) religious offerings; (2) awnings or decorative hangings for temples, palaces, and marketplaces; (3) rich adornment for deities; (4) marriage payments; (5) gifts for special ritual and social events, such as the dedication of a youth to the calpulli school, the potlatch-like exchanges by merchants at their flamboyant feasts, or politically inspired exchanges among rulers; (6) household utility items, such as tortilla covers; and, finally, (7) wrappings for mummy bundles prepared, usually, for cremation. In terms of overall output and variety of uses, textile manufacture was the most productive craft of sixteenth-century central Mexico.

Trade and Professional Merchants   Trade in central Mexico could be carried on by virtually anyone: from small-scale producers to large-scale professional merchants (pochteca or *oztomeca*). Marketing the household surplus was simply one aspect of the entire production process undertaken by any family. These producers of small lots of goods, both agricultural products and crafts, constituted the vast majority of the vendors in the marketplaces; their wares may have been of interest to noble or commoner. The professional merchants, on the other hand, dealt in relatively large lots of goods, emphasized the luxury commodities which were the prerogative of the nobility alone, and conducted economic exchanges in both marketplaces and politically neutral ports of trade beyond the bounds of the empire.

These professional merchant groups enjoyed special privileges and a special status in the Aztec state. Merchants were important politically: They entered enemy territory as spies, they could declare and engage in wars, and they could conquer communities. They were also important economically: They provided the bulk of the luxury items so necessary for the nobility as outward symbols of rank. Despite their great political and economic importance, their overall social position appears to have been one of transition. Among the Aztecs, marks of social status included both access to and control over strategic resources (notably land and commoners to work the land), and rights to specific luxury goods as outward displays of rank. In these terms, the merchants were neither nobles nor commoners, but were stationed somewhere between. On the one hand, they paid taxes (though in goods only) and in everyday situations dressed as commoners; on the other, they were greatly esteemed by the ruler, allowed to sacrifice slaves, own land, and permitted to wear certain symbols of noble status at special annual festivals (Sahagún 1950–1969, book 9).

Rather than investing their abundant resources and wealth in overt symbols of rank, the merchants developed a quite different attitude toward resources. They were constantly admonished by their elders to appear humble and dress simply (*ibid.*:29–31). This manner of attire was not necessarily a voluntary choice, as it appears that there were definite social obstacles to luxury consumption on their part (Katz 1972:214). Eric Wolf (1959) has suggested that considerable social tensions were present in sixteenth-century Aztec society; whereas previously some social mobility for commoners existed in the society, now the nobility by birth were restricting commoner access to elite positions. With conspicuous consumption and true nobility status beyond their reach, the merchants became increasingly rich in goods, and used much of their vast wealth to attain prestige and position within the merchant organizations or guilds. Thus, great secrecy might be expected in merchant dealings. Perhaps to avoid the envy or wrath of the nobility, special procedures were followed by a merchant on his return from a successful trading venture:

Not by day but by night they swiftly entered by boat. And as to their goods, no one could see how much there was; perhaps they carefully hid—covered up—all the boats. Not at one's (own) home did one arrive, (but) perhaps at the house of his uncle or his aunt, or of his elder sister. . . . And when he had quickly come to unload what he had acquired, then swiftly he took away his boat. When it dawned, nothing remained (Sahagún 1950–1969, book 9:31).

This practice suggests a necessary avoidance of conspicuous consumption, and the merchants took great care in all contexts except their extravagant feasts. And it was for these feasts that wealth was so assiduously sought and gained.

By the sixteenth century, the professional merchants had formed influential guilds in at least 12 Valley of Mexico cities. These guilds provided their members with exclusive residence and membership rights, specific laws and codes, a system of internal ranking, and an advantageous relationship with the state. The strongest representation of merchants was found at Tlatelolco, which had undergone an extraordinary development of merchant activity. When this city was conquered by Tenochtitlan in 1473, the Tlatelolco merchants became closely tied to the state organization at Tenochtitlan. It is a significant fact, and certainly no coincidence, that the great market of Tlatelolco was located at this center of merchant activity and control.

Entrance into a merchant guild was apparently through hereditary right (Zorita 1963:181). With membership restricted along these lines, the merchants could closely guard the secrets of their trade and their wealth. The guilds were apparently closely knit groups. Whenever a young merchant left for distant parts, he was addressed and admonished by his male and female elders. They warned him that, before he could gain respect as a merchant, he

. . . must first feel and profit by the pain, the afflictions, the privations, the ambushes. Such is exacted from those who go from city to city. . . . Thou shalt be in danger. . . . Thou shalt be long-suffering; thou shalt shed tears. Thy good deeds will not bear fruit, for fatigue will take thy measure . . . (Sahagún 1950–1969, book 4:62–63).

These elders, established merchants referred to as "fathers" and "mothers," also encouraged the neophyte: Success awaited if proper penances were performed. These same "fathers" would inspect the accumulated provisions of a man about to give a lavish feast, to ensure that there would be enough to go around and that the guild would not be shamed by the "stinginess" of one of its members (*ibid.*, book 9).

Not all merchants were equal in rank. At the apex of the merchant hierarchy were the "principal merchants," the "fathers" and "mothers." They played a prominent role in feasts and were responsible for appointing guild members to positions, for dispensing justice, for directing guild activities in general, and for providing a link between the guild and the state. Below the principal merchants, in rough order, were the slave bathers and slave dealers (the wealthiest of the merchants), the disguised and spying merchants (state agents in foreign lands), and the ordinary pochteca or oztomeca. These were followed by the merchant youths, who had yet to prove themselves by daring ventures into hostile lands and clever dealings in marketplaces.

potlatches

Anyone with guild membership could climb the ladder of success in this organization; the keynotes were wealth and generosity. Sponsoring of feasts and ceremonies was the major means by which individual merchants could become esteemed and powerful members of the merchant guild. Accumulation and wise management of wealth—along with the opening of new districts for economic activity—were primary values and goals of the merchants. Success in these areas led to renown, which was cemented into social position by the generous offering of a feast. A typical feast entailed the distribution of food and other goods with ritual precision. Tubes of tobacco were offered, followed by flowers, food (especially tamales), chocolate, and hallucinogenic mushrooms. After the guests had had their fill, the host made offerings of incense and quail to Huitzilopochtli. Through the night the guests sang and danced and experienced wild visions induced by mushrooms eaten the day before. At dawn, and throughout the following day, the host and guests ate great quantities of food, drank the prized and expensive chocolate, and enjoyed the fragrance of flowers and the tubes of tobacco. At the close of a successful feast, the host was severely admonished by his elders not to be proud or haughty, but to return to the everyday life of hardships and tatters. Depending on his fortunes, a merchant entertained lavishly or meagerly. If goods were plentiful, the host distributed the leftovers to his guests and enjoyed high prestige; if goods were limited and none remained to be apportioned among the guests, the host suffered great shame.

The most extraordinary of the feasts were held during the annual festival of Panquetzaliztli. At this time, a wealthy merchant might purchase a slave, ceremonially bathe him or her, and offer the slave for sacrifice. During the course of the festivities, enormous quantities of valuable goods were consumed or given away to high-ranking merchants and nobles: one account enumerates 800–1200 precious cloaks; 400 decorated loin cloths; quantities of skirts and tunics; bins of maize, beans, and chia; 80–100 turkeys; 20–40 dogs; 20 sacks of cacao beans for the chocolate drink and 2000–4000 chocolate beaters; untold quantities of chiles, tomatoes, and squash seeds; and miscellaneous essentials such as sauce dishes, baskets, firewood, and water (*ibid.*:48).

Through this elaborate system of potlatch-like feasts, the merchants were obligated by the guilds to use their accumulated wealth for socially prescribed ends. In this system, the merchant exchanged wealth for rank and position in the guild. This exchange of wealth for position undoubtedly allowed the merchant access to and control over more extensive resources, hence, even more wealth.

The merchants, of all groups in Aztec society, were the only ones allowed to create and enforce their own laws and codes:

And thus did the principal merchants, the disguised merchants, conduct themselves: quite apart did they pronounce their judgements; independently were sentences meted out. A merchant, a vanguard merchant, who did wrong, they did not take to someone else; the principal merchants, the disguised merchants, themselves alone pronounced judgement, exacted the punishment, executed the death penalty (*ibid.*:23).

Merchants could also extend their authority to the marketplace, where they sat in judgment daily over the proceedings of the market of Tlatelolco, enforcing fair prices and ensuring proper conduct: "These same [principal merchants] pronounced judgment upon him who deceived others in the market place, who cheated them in buying and selling. Or they punished the thief. And they regulated well everything: all in the market place which was sold; what the price would be" (*ibid.*:24). Aside from exercising considerable control over their own affairs and opening distant lands to military conquest and economic exploitation, the merchants also apparently were powerful enough in Aztec society to exercise some control over marketplace prices.

Political, Military, and Religious Occupations Beginning in 1430, the rapidly expanding Aztec empire generated complex bureaucratic, military, and religious structures. Increasing numbers of judges, governors, tax collectors, generals, specialized warrior groups, teachers, and priests were required by the state. In all these arenas, the highest positions were invariably occupied by the nobility; some lower positions were open to noble and commoner alike, depending on personal qualifications. Training for important stations in Aztec society was provided by the several calmecac, the elite schools supposedly restricted to the children of nobles. Although "proper" schooling was a necessary condition for high office, it did not ensure any individual success. Valor and bravery on the battlefield—judged by the number of enemy warriors captured—were essential for attaining high positions, but not sufficient. Any person of high status must also exemplify the values of Aztec society: uphold the moral codes, perform the proper penances, and observe carefully the strict rules of social etiquette. (Specific occupations in these realms are discussed in more detail in Chapters 3–6.)

Service and Other Occupations A society as complex as Aztec society contained a host of miscellaneous occupations. Some of these required long and arduous training, such as scribe or astrologer. These persons were undoubtedly well employed. Astrologers, for example, were called upon by virtually everyone for any major event: reading the signs of a newly born child, setting the date for a marriage, fixing an auspicious date for a merchant's feast, or choosing a propitious time for the installation of a new ruler. Midwives and physicians (frequently women) were also extremely knowledgeable, notably in the use of herbs, splints, and other directly physical cures. The "unskilled labor" category would include persons such as porters. With all transport on human backs or in canoes, porters were numerous in central Mexico, moving tremendous quantities of goods from city to city, mountain to valley, capital city to foreign port of trade. And then there were those who lived by gambling or prostitution. Neither of these occupations was viewed favorably, and it was considered that anyone following those paths would surely end in ruin. No legal sanctions were leveled against gamblers or prostitutes, but this description of a prostitute indicates her very marginal social position: "She appears like a flower, looks gaudy, arrays herself gaudily; she views herself in a mirror . . . she goes about with her head high—rude, drunk, shameless—eating mushrooms. . . . She goes about haughtily, shamelessly—head high, vain, filthy, given to pleasure. She lives in vice" (*ibid.*, book 10:55). Prostitutes typically made their services available by parading through the marketplaces, decorated, perfumed, and chewing chicle so that it "clacked like castanets."

Among the Aztecs, a strong work ethic permeated all walks of life. Farmers and artisans, merchants and priests, all were imbued with the work ideals of the culture. In all tasks, one must be diligent, careful, resourceful, and skilled; in all dealings one must be fair, just, and honest. Although these ideals provided strong incentives to work, they were not always met. A carpenter might be nonchalant and wasteful, a farmer lazy and negligent, a featherworker careless and unskilled, and a principal merchant deceitful. Cacao sellers might counterfeit cacao beans, cotton sellers hide cheap cotton inside bolls of expensive cotton, chile sellers sell spoiled and worthless chiles, and bean sellers be "congenital liars" (*ibid.*:27–75). Such behavior, however, was believed to lead a person to ruin, and all people (especially children) were repeatedly admonished and harangued about the virtues of hard work (see Chapter 4).

TRIBUTE AND TRADE

Intense specialization in the production of goods, coupled with large surpluses, generated a need for intricate webs of economic exchange. Specialization always requires exchange channels to enable individual producers to obtain the full range of necessary goods. Surplus production is fruitful only where there are culturally prescribed outlets for the excess produced. Intricate exchange systems serve to tie together the disparate parts of a complex and highly specialized production system, and to channel excess production to special segments of the society. In central Mexico, exchange took three major forms: tribute and taxation, state-sponsored foreign trade, and marketplace transactions.

First, tribute refers specifically to revenue collected by a militarily dominant state from its conquered regions. The payment of tribute serves symbolically to express the dominance of one political entity over another, stimulates production of specified goods in conquered areas, provides revenue for the dominant state, and may also involve certain "contractual agreements" such as protection of the subjugated region from invasion by other groups. Second, foreign trade is a state-sponsored, state-subsidized enterprise. The state relies heavily on the activities of professional merchants, who carry state goods to politically neutral "ports of trade" beyond the bounds of the state. Trade is conducted with the rulers of these trading depots, and the transactions frequently are as political as they are economic. The merchants, in these cases, serve not only as political emissaries but also as private entrepreneurs; they typically conduct their personal exchanges as well as exchanges for the state they represent. Third, marketplace exchange serves to integrate specialized and surplus production on local, regional, and state levels. A wide range of goods is normally available in marketplaces, and buying and selling activities are typically open to anyone. Both supply and demand and administrative controls affect prices, and exchanges may be facilitated by the use of one or more forms of money.

Tribute   Warfare and military conquest were activities central to the Aztec way of life. With each successful conquest, the Aztecs gained territory, subjects, and economic resources. All of these were placed in the service of the conquerors through the institution of tribute. Tribute was an assessment of goods or services or both demanded of each conquered province. By 1519, 38 such provinces gave up sizeable amounts of their production to support the burgeoning Triple Alliance empire.

Goods of all kinds were demanded in tribute: luxury and subsistence items, manufactured and raw materials. Typically, the people of a province surrendered goods which were locally available to them, and which the rulers of the Aztec state deemed necessary to the sustenance of the state. Provinces in close proximity to the Triple Alliance capitals primarily gave goods such as foodstuffs; warriors' costumes; a variety of textiles, wood, bowls, paper, and mats. Cuauhnahuac, representative of such provinces, annually sent to its overlords 12,800 cloaks of various designs, 1600 loin cloths, 1600 women's tunics, 8 warriors' costumes of diverse styles, 32,000 bundles of paper, 8000 bowls, and 4 bins of maize and beans.[7] More distant provinces, usually in ecological zones quite different from the Valley of Mexico, provided goods considered luxuries by the Aztecs: precious feathers, jade, turquoise, gold, cacao, and cotton. One such exotic province, Tochtepec on the Gulf Coast of present-day Mexico, provided the following yearly tribute: 9600 decorated cloaks, 1600 women's tunics, 1 warrior's costume and shield, 1 gold shield, 1 feather standard, 1 gold diadem, 1 gold headband, 2 strings of gold beads, 3 large jades and 7 strings of jades, 40 lip plugs, 16,000 rubber balls, 80 handfuls of quetzal feathers, 4 bunches of green and yellow feathers, 24,000 little bunches of feathers, 100 pots of liquid amber, and 200 loads of cacao (see Figure 2–3).[8]

All in all, the annual revenue of the Aztec state through tribute must have been extraordinary. According to one annual tribute tally (the Matrícula de Tributos), the allied cities received quantities such as the following: 214,400 cloaks, 647 warriors' costumes, 100 bins of foodstuffs (maize and beans), 16,000 bales of cotton, 4800 wooden beams and an equal number of planks and pillars, 32,000 smoking canes, 28,800 gourd bowls, 3200 deerskins, 6400 bunches of quetzal feathers, and 240 gold discs.

The heaviest burden of tribute assessment fell on the provincial commoners. Some toiled on state fields or calpulli lands to cultivate the enormous quantities of foodstuffs demanded in tribute. Artisans delivered a portion of their production to the imperial powers: Items such as turquoise mosaics, copper bells, royal badges, lip plugs, copper axes, jade beads, and objects fashioned of gold were commonly given. Other commoners expended a sizeable share of their surpluses to purchase needed goods in local and regional marketplaces or from professional traveling merchants. Cotton, for example, was widely produced in lowland areas, but vast quantities of finished cotton textiles were given in tribute by non-tropical provinces. Ordinarily the raw cotton was purchased by traveling regional merchants, who carried it from lowland to highland. It was then purchased in marketplaces by commoners of these regions; the women spun and wove it into cloth, and perhaps

[7] These tribute figures are from the Matrícula de Tributos. For more information, see Berdan 1975 and 1980.

[8] This tribute information is from the Codex Mendoza; the page for the same province is missing from the Matrícula de Tributos. For consistency in comparison, the clothing is calculated as having been paid four times a year, as specified in the Matrícula.

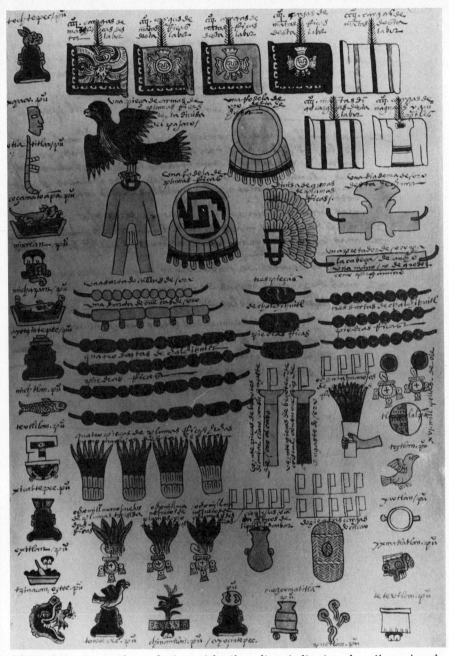

Figure 2–3: A page from the imperial tribute lists, indicating the tribute that the wealthy province of Tochtepec owed to the Triple Alliance powers (Codex Mendoza 1938, vol. 3:folio 46).

embellished it with ornate designs. These garments, cloaks, loin cloths, and women's tunics and skirts were subsequently delivered to the Triple Alliance capitals as tribute.

Although the commoners of the provinces were the predominant contributors to imperial tribute payments, they received little in return beyond vague promises of assistance in the event of famine or military aggression. The commoners situated close to the Triple Alliance capitals, however, received some benefits from the tribute system. Their tribute was largely in the form of labor instead of goods; and this labor, especially on massive hydraulic works, favored them in increased crop productivity. They also served the state as warriors and could gain prestige and honor if valiant; and they probably received allocations of subsistence goods provided by the tribute of more distant provinces. The commoners of the more distant provinces, on the other hand, bore a heavy burden of tribute in goods, and received very little in return; the Aztec state had little interest in investing in the people or the resources of the distant regions.

The Triple Alliance capitals gathered tribute annually, semi-annually, or quarterly, depending on the type of good and the distance of the province from the Valley of Mexico. Tribute collectors (*calpixque*) were stationed in each province to ensure proper and prompt tribute deliveries. A province that failed to meet its obligations, or deliberately defied imperial rule, was severely punished when imperial control was reestablished. As a general rule, tribute assessments were doubled, as in the case of rebellious Cuetlaxtlan. This province, prior to its rebellion, gave cloaks of 10 "lengths," green stones, and skins of spotted jaguars. Following its unsuccessful rebellion, Cuetlaxtlan was required to deliver cloaks of 20 "lengths," white and red stones, white animal skins, live snakes, and 1000 small pieces of cloth. The idea of doubling is interesting, in that a mere quantitative doubling was not involved; rather, the increase was in the value of the goods and their difficulty of supply. Cloaks of twice the size would involve more effort, live snakes would have been difficult to capture and transport, and white animal skins would have been a rare natural occurrence.

Once tribute goods were delivered to Tenochtitlan, they were distributed, in principle, among the Triple Alliance capitals according to the following formula: Tenochtitlan and Texcoco each received two-fifths of the total, while the lesser Tlacopan was awarded only one-fifth. In addition, each capital had its own subject communities nearby that supplied revenue to it exclusively. Sometimes the tribute duties of these communities included provisioning the royal palace with its daily food requirements (as, for example, with Texcoco). Tribute goods were placed in the care of tribute overseers, and stored in central warehouses (*petlacalco*). Here a careful accounting was made of all goods; the careless or dishonest steward was jailed and executed, his family exiled, and his property confiscated. As needed the ruler would call upon the stewards to remove specific items to be distributed for a variety of purposes:

1. Support of Administrative and Military Activities   The enormous imperial bureaucracy, with its multitude of judges, governors, advisors, stewards, and other lesser officials, was sustained through the tribute stores. Warfare, being nearly constant, also placed heavy material demands on the Aztec state: it was imperative to equip and sustain armies in the field, support widows and orphans, and reward warriors who excelled. Additionally, some expenses of warfare were met by the marketplace sellers, who were required to prepare war provisions, and by communities in the path of the marching army, who also contributed provisions, willingly or not.

2. Support of the Royal Palaces   One way in which administrators were supported was directly through the palaces of the rulers. Those included in the Tenochtitlan royal palace were ambassadors, war messengers, judges, high priests, warriors, masters of the youths, keepers of the gods, singers, pages, servants, jugglers, and artisans of fine luxury goods. These, of course, were in addition to the extensive royal family. In terms of sheer quantities of goods consumed at the palaces, the conquistador Bernal Díaz del Castillo (1956:209) estimated that at one time more than 300 plates of food were set before Moctezuma, and more than 1000 for the guard.

The daily food consumption of Nezahualcoyotl's Texcoco palace (1427–1472) reportedly reached extravagant proportions:

> 25 *tlacopintlis* [1100–1200 kilograms] of maize
> 3 *tlacopintlis* [131–143 kilograms] of beans
> 400,000 tortillas[9]
> 4 *xiquipillis* of cacao [32,000 cacao beans]
> 100 turkeys
> 20 loaves of salt
> 20 baskets of large chiles
> 20 baskets of small chiles
> 10 baskets of tomatoes
> 10 baskets of pepitas (Alva Ixtlilxochitl 1965, vol. 2:168).

The obligation of supplying this food rotated among sets of nearby communities subject to Texcoco.

3. Gifts and Commissions   Warriors and administrators and merchants and artisans were frequently rewarded by the ruler for their efforts on behalf of the state. Depending on the number of enemy warriors he captured on the battlefield, a man was entitled to wear a specific style of cloak as a badge of his achievements. Thus, everyone knew at a glance what the man's accomplishments had been. Not only cloaks but also elaborate warriors' costumes were often bestowed on courageous warriors as symbols of their status. All of these visible signs of achievement were drawn from the vast tribute stores of the Triple Alliance rulers. As wars were waged frequently, this process of gift giving was a fairly common activity. But other gifts were given on a more situational basis. Following flood damage to many noble houses in Tenochtitlan, officials and communities who aided in the reconstruction were rewarded with cloaks, badges, cacao, chile, beans, and slaves (Durán 1967, vol. 2:381). Professional merchants, especially when they returned from

[9] The 25 tlacopintlis of maize would have fed as many as 2200 people daily. The number of tortillas, 400,000, is undoubtedly excessive. The source may have exaggerated by the vigesimal figure of 20; 20,000 tortillas per day would then adequately supply 2000–2500 adults (Jerome A. Offner, personal communication).

expeditions which served the state, were given special consideration by the rulers: decorated cloaks, rabbit fur cloaks, loin cloths, maize, beans, chia, and sometimes golden lip plugs. Tribute goods were also used to compensate widows and orphans, and to impress allied and enemy rulers on visits of state.

4. Foreign Trade   Some state goods served in the promotion of foreign trade. In one event during Ahuitzotl's reign (1486–1502), professional merchants from Tenochtitlan were given 1600 large cotton cloaks, which they took to Tlatelolco. These cloaks were then divided equally between the merchants of Tenochtitlan and Tlatelolco and traded for other goods. These goods were then carried to the Gulf and Pacific coastal trading centers, where they were exchanged for still other goods. Throughout all these exchanges, the goods always belonged to the state. This same, or similar, pattern of the use of state goods for trade probably persisted until the Spanish conquest. It is no wonder that the rulers were involved in foreign trade, for the exchanges had a particularly political flavor, and the merchants in their travels often served as state spies in foreign lands.

5. Subsistence Support of Urban Populations and Emergency Storage   As already noted, much of the Tenochtitlan population could not feed itself, so that much everyday support in staples such as maize and beans probably came from the imperial tribute stores. And vast as the noble palaces were, they could not have easily consumed the tremendous quantities of foodstuffs sent to the Triple Alliance capitals as tribute. The state maintained huge bins of foodstuffs which could be used for the urban dwellers, and for emergencies such as famine which were known historically and feared.

In addition to the regular imperial and city-state tribute systems, the Aztec state and nobility commanded other forms of tribute. This included tribute paid at annual festivals and to temples, tribute paid to support extraordinary Triple Alliance events, tribute paid by rural tenants (*mayeque*) to certain members of the nobility, and tribute levied in the form of public work duties.

Five times a year tribute goods were collected to support specific ceremonial activities. The goods included a variety of cloaks, women's clothes, loin cloths, precious warriors' costumes, rich feathers, and gold lip plugs, bracelets, and necklaces. In addition to these recurring levies, the temples were maintained on a daily basis by other means. The temples were given lands to be worked by young men attached to the temple schools, by rural tenants, or by the commoners of specially designated communities. The produce was stored in rooms in or beside the temples; it was then used for the celebration of festivals and religious ceremonies, and the support of the priesthood. The temples of Texcoco had a further luxury: apparently 15 towns were responsible for the needs of the Texcoco temples and royal palace for six months, then another 15 towns provided the service for the remainder of the year. Some of the temples of Tenochtitlan, and probably of Tlacopan as well, were also maintained by certain nearby towns.

Special-purpose tribute was an irregular assessment levied at major state events such as the construction of a new temple or the funeral or installation of a ruler. At the installation of Moctezuma Xocoyotzin as ruler in 1502, each day 1000 commoners reputedly entered Tenochtitlan with loads of animals, birds, chiles, cacao, fish, and fruit, all of which came from within 450 miles around for the celebration of the event (Durán 1967, vol. 2:415). While these special events may sometimes have drawn on the imperial tribute stores, usually they entailed additional assessments.

Another type of tribute levy in the Triple Alliance empire resulted in a decentralized form of tribute payment. Nobles, in their roles as state functionaries and simply as landed nobility, received rights to certain private lands from the ruler, and labor from rural tenants (mayeque). These mayeque were apparently included as part of the land grant. Provincial nobility also possessed lands and associated mayeque. Since these nobles frequently occupied political positions in the imperial administration, the mayeque tribute followed the same pattern as that rendered to administrators sent directly from the Triple Alliance cities. The energies of mayeque were directed toward production for these local nobles and Aztec administrators, rather than for the imperial ruler. In one case, the mayeque of a noble house provided 100 plain white cloaks, 100 bordered cloaks, 100 black-and-white striped cloaks, 100 women's tunics, 400 loads of firewood, 80 women (for household service, most likely), and 800 men for service (AGN Tierras 2692, exp. 16). The mayeque were also responsible for cultivating fields of maize, cotton, beans, and chile. The personal service was rendered daily, and the other tribute was paid annually. With the exception of participation in warfare, the mayeque owed no service to the state. Rather, complete tribute cycles were enacted at the local level, with nobility in administrative positions commanding the tribute production of a large number of conquered rural cultivators. This was an important way in which the state could reward these nobles for their service (see also the section on the mayeque in Chapter 3).

Marketplace Exchange   Foreign trade and the activities of professional merchants have already been discussed in this chapter. Apart from their role in political dealings, the professional merchants also frequented marketplaces in an effort to exchange goods for gain.

The central Mexican marketplace, or *tianquiztli*, was probably the liveliest spot of any community. There people from all walks of life congregated daily, or at least every five days, to enjoy the company of friends, the haggling over the prices of maize or cloaks, and the latest news and rumors of the region. The marketplace, whether large or small, was an outdoor affair. In the larger communities and cities it may have been surrounded by arcades and shadowed by an imposing temple; in the rural villages it may have been a centrally located plaza—relatively quiet and peaceful for four days, wakening as a noisy, bustling, colorful scene on the fifth.

The greatest market in central Mexico was at Tlatelolco. The sight of this marketplace so awed the conquistador Bernal Díaz del Castillo that he later wrote:

> After having examined and considered all that we had seen we turned to look at the great market place and the crowds of people that were in it, some buying and others selling, so that the murmur and hum of their voices and words that they used could be heard more than a league [three miles] off. Some of the soldiers among us who had been in many parts of the world, in Constantinople, and all over Italy, and in Rome, said that so large a market place and so full of people, and so well regulated and arranged, they had never beheld before (1956:218–219).

Typically, the market activities rotated among five communities, each hosting the market one day in five (one Aztec week). Even the Tlatelolco market was on such a schedule. Daily it served as many as 20,000–25,000 people; yet every fifth day 40,000–50,000 people congregated there to buy and sell, talk, and listen (Anonymous Conqueror 1971:392).

On that day, the variety and quantities of merchandise available in any central Mexican marketplace were extraordinary. At Tlatelolco, virtually everything produced and crafted in Mesoamerica was on display—utilitarian goods, luxury items, and services. Utilitarian goods ranged from a bewildering variety of maize and chile to pottery, firewood, mats, lumber, and clothing. Numerous vendors sold cooked food, especially tamales of all kinds. Luxury wares included ornate clothing, tropical feathers, precious gems, gold ornaments, and the prized cacao bean. Services were also for hire: barbers, porters, carpenters, artisans, and prostitutes. Other, smaller marketplaces may have concentrated on utilitarian staples, and had occasional or regular deficiencies of certain goods. The marketplaces typically reflected the local ecology. The forested region of Coyoacan coincided with a marketplace known for wood products and the availability of carpenters; the marketplaces around Cholula focused on locally produced chile and maguey honey. Other specializations, less directly reflecting the local ecology, also appeared in the central Mexican marketplaces. Azcapotzalco and Itzocan were noted slave-trading centers; Acolman was famous for its dogs; Texcoco, for cloth, ceramics, and fine gourds; Cholula, an important merchant center, for its jewels, precious stones, and feathers. So, while some goods were vended by the local producers, many others were carried by merchants from distant regions to these marketplaces/ Professional merchants were indeed the typical purveyors of luxury goods such as those abundantly available at Cholula. And many professional merchants—whether the pochteca of the empire or regionally based entrepreneurs—traveled extensively from marketplace to marketplace buying cheap and selling dear. They trafficked in the whole range of merchandise, but were particularly active in the trade of high-demand, sparsely available goods such as salt, cotton, and cacao beans.

In each marketplace the goods were carefully arranged by type—all of the vegetable sellers were grouped together, as were the clothing sellers, the bird sellers, the tamale vendors, the slave dealers, and so on (see Figure 2–4). This ordering of goods undoubtedly facilitated both actual exchanges and taxation. Prices were established by haggling, and information on price limits was readily available with all the items of a type grouped together. Also, a fairly quick examination would inform any consumer of the types and qualities of merchandise available. Market taxes were probably assessed on dealers according to the objects they sold (AGN Tierras 1735, exp. 2). Where the goods were arranged by type, collection of these taxes would have been facilitated.

Judges and supervisors were commonly present in the large urban marketplaces; similar officials may have reigned over the marketplaces of smaller centers. Marketplace officials (perhaps high-ranking pochteca) had the responsibility of hearing cases of dispute or theft, the power to sentence violators, and the authority to regulate prices and activities in general. Apparently lesser officials wandered about the

Figure 2–4: Reconstruction of the great marketplace at Tlatelolco (Diorama in the Museo Nacional de Antropología, Mexico City; photo courtesy of Public Relations Office).

marketplace, inspecting merchandise and methods of sale and perhaps collecting market taxes.

Reputedly the most common means of exchange in the marketplaces was barter; any good could be exchanged for any other good. Yet certain monies were seemingly used to facilitate the actual exchanges. These monies took the form of cacao beans and large cotton cloaks (quachtli), and perhaps also quills filled with gold dust, copper bells, stone and shell beads, and copper axes. Most of these objects had practical uses as well as exchange functions. Cacao was highly prized as an elite beverage, cloaks were worn as clothing, copper bells were used to adorn representations of deities and to accompany the deceased on their journey to Mictlan, and stone and shell beads were prized articles of ornamentation in the Mayan area.

Cacao seems to have been the most common form of money, and it did, indeed, grow on trees. It was widely accepted as payment for both merchandise and labor. The great importance of cacao in the economy of Mesoamerica is suggested by the common practice of counterfeiting cacao. Sahagún (1950–1969, book 10:65) and Oviedo (1851–1855, vol. 1:316) both describe this practice. Oviedo provides the greatest detail:

> And even in that almond money one finds falsifications in order that one may cheat the other and mix the fake pieces among a quantity of the good ones. These false pieces are made by removing the bark or skin which some of the beans have . . . and [the counterfeiters] fill them with earth or something similar, and they close the hole with such skill that one cannot see it . . . even though a false one is well filled it can be felt by the touch to be different from the real ones (in Tozzer 1941:95).

Fray Bartolomé de las Casas, writing in the mid-sixteenth century, suggested that cacao beans were used to "even out" exchanges effected through barter. Las Casas's statement (1967:vol. 1, 368) suggests an explanation for the recorded presence of both barter and money in marketplace transactions. Perhaps a monetary standard (in cacao or cloaks or both) operated in an abstract sense, while in actual market transactions exchanges looked like barter (for example, chiles for turkey eggs). These items could have been valued in terms of cacao beans, although not exchanged directly for them. For example, 1 strip of pine bark for kindling equals 5 cacao beans; 1 turkey egg equals 3 cacao beans. An exchange may have taken the form: 1 strip of pine bark for 1 turkey egg and 2 cacao beans (the "evening out" mentioned by Las Casas).

The other item commonly used as money was cotton cloaks, or quachtli. Their importance in exchange is indicated by their frequent use in a variety of transactions. Slaves were valued in terms of quachtli; quachtli were used as restitution for theft, for obtaining credit, for ransoming certain slaves, and to purchase land. The standard of living is even expressed in terms of these lengths of cloth: An individual, probably a commoner, could support himself for approximately one year on 20 quachtli (Berdan 1975:224). These cloaks were of a consistently higher value than cacao: depending on the quality of the cacao and the grade of the cloak, values ranged from 65–300 cacao beans for one cloak (Berdan 1974:8). Cloaks and cacao beans may indeed have served as different denominations, "dollars and cents," of the central Mexican monetary system. While the cacao beans survived as a medium of marketplace exchange for many decades following the Spanish conquest, the cloaks rapidly fell into disuse. Undoubtedly, production of cloaks declined; and the Spanish peso, generally equivalent to the quachtli in value, easily took its place in the indigenous exchange system.

Overall, the marketplace was the economic institution which most profoundly affected the central Mexican people in their everyday life. Economically, the marketplaces linked symbiotic regions of production, reinforcing intense specialization in agriculture and crafts. Politically, they were focal points for news and rumor, and havens for spies. Further, merchandise destined for the tribute coffers of the rulers often worked its way into tribute channels by way of the marketplaces. Socially, the marketplace provided an appropriate time and location for enjoyable personal interaction.

Economic activities in sixteenth-century central Mexico were based on intricate systems of specialized production and exchange. While certain products (such as maize) were universally available and consumed, others (such as gold ornaments) were not properly consumed by all members of the society. Whether consumers' habits were dictated by law or the ability to pay, people in the Aztec empire displayed a wide range in their living standards. The ways of life of the different segments of society—from the opulent and privileged rich to the destitute and subservient poor—are the subjects of Chapters 3 and 4.

3 /Social structure and dynamics

Two fundamental principles formed the basis for Mexica social organization: hierarchy and heterogeneity. These two principles were manifested in the Mexica social class system, in the complexities of territorial organization, and in the structure and dynamics of kinship groupings and domestic life. The principles, as well as their manifestations, were reinforced by formal and informal educational systems which conveyed moral instruction and skill training, by the overt marking of critical points in the passage through the life cycle, and by legal and customary means of maintaining social conformity and control. These aspects of Mexica social life are the subject of this and Chapters 4 and 5.

SOCIAL CLASS STRUCTURE

As in other complex, stratified societies, Mexica social organization was characterized by rules which provided for the differential allocation of power, privilege, prestige, and property. The rules identified highly valued positions in the society in conformity with cultural emphases, defined avenues of status attainment, and indicated how rewards were to be distributed to the successful occupants of social positions. The Mexica system of social stratification combined ascription and achievement: Although access to most positions was controlled by birthright, the positions also required validation and allowed some mobility through achievement.

The fundamental social division was between nobility and commoners, with intermediate positions occupied by certain specialists, largely merchants and artisans of luxury goods. Each of these major divisions was divided into several ranks (see Table 3–1). Persons in each of these strata had specific rights and obligations, and carried out particular activities. As will be shown, many of these activities were of a highly specialized nature and were associated with the religious, military, governmental, or commercial hierarchies.

The distinction between nobility and commoners was theoretically established by birth. To be considered of noble birth, Mexica persons were required to trace their biological links to the first Mexica ruler, Acamapichtli. Considering the widespread practice of polygyny among nobles, and the fact that nobility status had traditionally been transmitted through either male or female links, the descendants

45

TABLE 3–1   MAJOR DIVISIONS OF SOCIAL CLASS STRUCTURE

Nobility

Rulers	tlatoani (sing.) tlatoque (pl.)	Supreme rulers of major political bodies (empires, cities, towns)
"Chiefs"	tecutli (sing.) tetecutin (pl.)	Controlled a more restricted area than tlatoque; usually occupied high military and governmental positions
Nobles, "sons of nobles"	pilli (sing.) pipiltin (pl.)	Children of rulers and "chiefs"; occupied governmental, religious, and military positions

Intermediate positions

Merchants	pochtecatl (sing.) pochteca (pl.)	Merchants organized into guilds and trading over long distances; often agents of the state (see Chapter 2)
Luxury artisans	tolteccatl (sing.) toltecca (pl.)	Artisans of crafts such as gold- and featherworking; some were apparently guild organized; others worked for the state (see Chapter 2)

Commoners

"Free commoners"	macehualli (sing.) macehualtin (pl.)	Organized into calpulli, these persons were agriculturalists, fishers, and producers of utilitarian crafts
Rural tenants	mayeque (sing. and pl.)	Commoners who worked on the private lands of the nobility
Slaves	tlacotli (sing.) tlacotin (pl.)	Slaves provided much urban labor for the nobility, and attained their status through gambling, economic necessity, or a criminal act (usually theft)

of Acamapichtli may have "numbered in the tens of thousands by the early sixteenth century" (Calnek 1974:202).

During the reign of Moctezuma Xocoyotzin (1502–1520), however, the identification and perquisites of nobility status became more rigidly defined. Upon accession to the Mexica throne, Moctezuma announced that only nobles and the sons of nobles would serve him personally:

> The king gave orders that no illegitimate boy should be brought before him . . . for he considered that anyone born of a lowly woman or slave might take after his mother and be, therefore, ineligible for his service. All those who served Moteczoma were to be born of lords; all must be legitimate and children of ladies of noble blood (Durán 1964:223).

This notion of legitimacy is also reflected in the writings of Sahagún, who contrasts a legitimate child with a "secret" child, a bastard, the child of a slave (1950–1969, book 10:2). Thus, in the final phase of Mexica history, nobility status was restricted to persons who could demonstrate "noble links" both paternally and maternally. Such a definition of legitimate nobility status, officially promulgated at this time, would have tended to reinforce the practice of endogamy among the nobility.

The importance of consanguineal links is demonstrated time and again in Sahagún's descriptions of noble persons:

> One's father (is) the source of lineage. . . . One's grandmother has noble descendents. . . . A noble person [is] great, superior of lineage. . . . The one of noble lineage [is] one's treasure, one's jewel, one's noble child; a descendent of nobles . . . (*ibid.*:1–22 *passim*).

The elevated position of the nobility was legitimized not only through lineage but also through religious doctrine and legal codes. In the religious realm, all nobles were considered to have been originally descended from the deity Quetzalcoatl. This exclusive ancestry provided an ideological basis for distinguishing nobles from the rest of the population.

The exclusive legal rights of the nobility were specified as early as the mid-fifteenth century. During the reign of Moctezuma Ilhuicamina a number of sumptuary laws were established to visibly distinguish different statuses in Mexica society. For example, in the area of dress and adornment, only the ruler was allowed to wear the most expensive decorated cotton cloaks, high-ranking nobles could wear other decorated cloaks, and lesser nobles were restricted to cloaks of another type. Commoners were allowed to wear only the simplest clothing, that made of maguey or palm fiber. Even the manner of dress was specified: for the commoner, the cloak could not reach below the knee, unless as a warrior he had received wounds on his legs:

> And so it was that when one encountered a person who wore his mantle [cloak] longer than the laws permitted, one immediately looked at his legs. If he had wounds acquired in war he would be left in peace, and if he did not, he would be killed. They would say, "Since that leg did not flee from the sword, it is just that it be rewarded and honored" (Durán 1964:132).

Only the ruler and other nobles were permitted the luxury of such ornaments as gold headbands with feathers; gold armbands; lip plugs, ear plugs, and nose plugs fashioned of gold and precious stones. The laws attained a high degree of specificity: Only the ruler and his second-in-command were permitted to wear sandals in the ruler's palace, while supposedly only certain nobles were granted the right to wear sandals at all. The only exceptions to these edicts on dress involved warriors who had performed great feats in battle; they could wear sandals and certain adornments, yet they must be "cheap and common" in materials and design.

Other visible marks of status involved residence patterns. For example, only nobles could construct houses with two stories. In addition, the royal palace contained separate rooms for nobles and commoners: ". . . in the palaces were special rooms for people of different rank, and when one visited the palace one knew his place and went there directly" (Durán 1964:122). Commoners and nobles were even judged in separate courts (*ibid.*; Sahagún 1950–1969, book 8:41–42). Behind these readily visible symbols of status, more fundamental factors served to distinguish the various classes and ranks. These included differential control over critical resources (particularly land and labor), and rights to occupy important religious and public offices. Through birthright and occupational status, the nobility as a group controlled most of the strategic economic resources of the empire, especially land. The commoners, through their tribute obligations, provided the labor which made these lands productive. They also provided the nobility with other necessary goods such as clothing, status-linked ornaments and paraphernalia, and daily household requirements such as firewood and water.

There were decided differences in expected behavior for nobility and for commoners. One source of information on these differences is the *tonalpohualli,* or "count of days." This day-to-day guide served the Mexica as an astrological handbook, but also provides the anthropologist with a wealth of ethnographic information. It designated every Mexica's lot in life as to success or failure, according to the day of birth. "Good days" such as One Alligator were good for everyone, noble or commoner, male or female. Similarly, "bad days" such as Two Rabbit and Four Water were evil and inauspicious for all born on them. Some other days combined good and evil aspects, still applying to everyone.

Ideal behavior and goals were defined differently for nobility and for commoners in this handbook. For example, a noble born on the day One Alligator "would be a lord, a ruler; he would prosper; he would be rich and wealthy." If a commoner were born on that same day, "he would be a brave warrior—a valiant chief, esteemed, honored, and great. He would always eat." Likewise, a woman born then would prosper: "Successful would be her dealings around the market place . . . it was as if it would sprinkle, shower, and rain her wares upon her" (Sahagún 1950–1969, book 4:2). The count of days abounds in similar examples. The days One Rain and One Wind were associated with the activities of sorcerers. A nobleman born on either day would be "a wizard, inhuman; an astrologer, one who had spells to cast." A commoner would also be a "demon," but apparently of a different order, and clearly not an astrologer (*ibid.*:42, 101). Nobles born on the day One Deer would become rulers, being famous as well as wealthy and generous in food and drink. A commoner would also succeed, but in a more restricted sense: "He lived. He became a brave warrior, a valiant chieftain. He surpassed others" (*ibid.*:9). Nobles—fate and personal efforts allowing—would become important leaders, wealthy, and learned. Commoners would excel on the battlefield and be good providers. Women, few class distinctions being made, would be prosperous in their marketplace dealings, handy in the arts (especially weaving and embroidery), generous and courageous.

"Bad" day-signs generally inflicted misery and suffering on noble and commoner, man and woman alike. Those born under the sign Nine Deer, for example,

> . . . were inconsiderate, not given to silence; impudent; evil talkers, who guarded no secret. They were sowers of discord, of gossip, who spoke with tongue in cheek; spreaders of tales. . . . All (their) acts and efforts were repeated adultery, thievery, absconding with tribute; making off with many things by trickery, coveting, and deceiving (*ibid.*:50–51).

Such persons were also lazy, easy to anger, and in general considered to be a burden on others. This type of behavior cut across both class and sex lines, apparently being found (but not valued) among all types of people.

Expected "favorable" cultural behavior conformed to expected social activities; both were defined differently for nobles and for commoners. A "good" sign for a nobleman would guide him through his high-ranking activities and affluent lifestyle. For a commoner, such a day-sign would promote his success as a warrior, cultivator, fisher, or craftsperson. In either case, "good" signs meant that a person would conform to the rules of behavior appropriate to his position in the society. "Bad" signs meant that a person would fail in such conformity, and fall into disrepute.

Nobles as well as commoners were subject to the strict legal codes and swift justice of the Mexica. Indeed, the higher the rank, the more severe were the penalties. For example, drunkenness in public was a serious offense for all but the elderly. Any commoner discovered in such a state had his head shaven, and was thus publicly shamed. A noble, however, was supposedly put to death for the same offense. Severe sentences were pronounced on judges or other administrative officials who accepted bribes, favored nobles over commoners in court, or otherwise used their public offices for personal gain. There are also many recorded instances of rulers sentencing their own children to death, particularly for adultery or other unapproved relations between the sexes. This included the following case:

> A son of a great lord scaled a wall and entered the house wherein the daughters of the king of Texcoco were reared and spoke to one of them. He stood as he did this, and nothing more happened. The ruler learned of it, but the young man was warned and hid. . . . But the ruler ordered that the maiden, his own beloved daughter, be strangled (Zorita 1963:131).

Nobles and commoners also differed considerably in their standard of living. The elaborate dress and ornamentation allowed the nobility contrasted with the coarse-fibered clothing characteristic of the commoners, as has already been mentioned. Another example sheds even more light on day-to-day differences in living conditions. Consider the following comparison between nobles and commoners in a ceremony held by both: the bathing and naming of a newly born infant.[1] For this momentous event, a ceremony including feasting was held. Among the elite, the banquet began with the serving of copious quantities of tobacco,[2] and the passing of flowers. This was followed by the distribution of large amounts of food and the serving of chocolate, the most highly valued beverage among the Mexica. Entertainment, particularly singing and joking, concluded the festivities for the nobility. The same event was apparently carried out with far less extravagance among the commoners[3]:

> . . . among the poor folk, among the workers of the fields and the water folk . . . only miserably, in poverty and want, were receptions and invitations

[1] A child born on a favorable day would be bathed immediately; but if the day-sign were evil, the parents could wait up to four days for a favorable sign, thus counteracting the effects of the original day-sign. Good and bad days were distributed so that, in any sequence of four days, a reasonably favorable day would appear.

[2] Durán, however, notes that tobacco was normally distributed after meals; he adds that "They say that it was good for the digestion; a feast without tobacco was not a real feast" (1964:102).

[3] Sahagún primarily used aged Aztec nobles as informants. Therefore, this account records the nobles' view of the commoner life-style.

made. . . . Many things were omitted or spoiled. . . . Perhaps only old, withered flowers could he find or come by; perhaps only leftover, bitter sauces, and stale tamales and tortillas were offered them (Sahagún 1950–1969, book 4:124).

Since the occupants of all social levels had different rights, responsibilities, and life-styles, a fuller picture of social life can be gained if each group is considered separately.

Tlatoque, or "Rulers" The *tlatoque* were often called "señores supremos" by the Spaniards. A *tlatoani* was the ruler of a region or town, or perhaps only of a section of a town or city. In some cases a large town with its many subject communities may have been controlled by a single tlatoani, while in others a single community was divided and controlled by more than one tlatoani (Gibson 1964:41–43). The tlatoque of conquered areas recognized and paid tribute to the still more powerful tlatoque of the Triple Alliance capitals, frequently called "señores universales" by the Spaniards.

The tlatoque controlled the tribute of commoners in their jurisdiction, possessed privately owned patrimonial lands, and managed the labor and tribute of their rural tenants, or mayeque. In many recorded cases, the lands administered by a given tlatoani were dispersed over a wide area in noncontiguous plots. Gibson describes this complex situation in detail, providing an example:

> A single town was subject to many service and tribute demands, and its leaders received tribute from many other towns as well. Cuauhtitlan paid tribute in different amounts and principally from separate lands to its own tlatoani, to the tlatoani of Tlacopan, to Montezuma II (who had ten "private" lands in the vicinity of Cuauhtitlan and maintained calpixque [tribute collectors] in two of them as well as in Cuauhtitlan itself), and to other owners in Tlatelolco, Culhuacan, Ixtapalapa, Mexicalzingo, Azcapotzalco and Texcoco (1971:390).

These complicated arrangements make sense when it is understood that obligations to serve the different tlatoque were associated with individual plots of land, each involving the labor of different commoners.

The patrimonial lands of tlatoque were their private property, and could be sold or otherwise disposed of at the discretion of the tlatoani. On his death, a tlatoani's land would be inherited by his heirs. If the tlatoani died without heirs, his patrimonial lands became the property of any ruling tlatoani to whom he owed allegiance, as the lands were considered to have been gifts from that ruler (Torquemada 1969, vol. 2:545–546).

At the apex of the imperial polity were the tlatoque of the Triple Alliance capitals. These rulers claimed extensive patrimonial lands by virtue of their noble birth. Also, as functionaries of the state, they claimed the labor of local commoners (some of whom they allocated to lower level nobles), and the tribute from conquered areas. They sat at the top of the structure which controlled the state resources, the lands in the public domain. These lands included *tecpantlalli* ("palace lands"), *milchimalli* ("lands of the shield," or lands used for military support), and *teopantlalli* ("temple lands"). The appropriation of lands and their produce for state functions, as well as the distribution of lands to lesser nobles, was largely at the discretion of the royal tlatoani.

The responsibilities of any tlatoani encompassed the organization of military activities, the sponsoring of certain religious celebrations, and the adjudication of disputes not resolved at a lower level. The imperial ruler was particularly concerned with warfare. Offensively, he frequently participated in military campaigns: "The ruler was known as the lord of men. His charge was war. Hence, he determined, disposed, and arranged how war would be made" (Sahagún 1950–1969, book 8:51). He also personally saw to the defense of his capital city:

> The ruler was especially concerned with the keeping of watch against enemies and the guarding of the city, all day and all night. Hence he gave stern commands that guard should be kept faithfully . . . the ruler kept careful vigil. He did not become besotted. He himself sometimes set forth by night, circled the city, and beheld what was done (*ibid.*:56).

The ability of the tlatoani to govern his realm successfully depended to a large extent upon his personal qualities. Consider the following ideal qualities of, and demands on, the "good ruler":

> The good ruler (is) a protector; one who carries (his subjects) in his arms, who unites them. . . . He rules, takes responsibilities, assumes burdens. He carries (his subjects) in his cape . . . he is obeyed. (To him) as shelter, as refuge, there is recourse (*ibid.*, book 10:15).

Along with his heavy responsibilities, the ruler enjoyed an extraordinary life-style. His dress was rich and elegant, his dwelling pleasant and extensive, his servants and slaves numerous, and his recreations varied. He particularly was amused by jugglers, acrobats, and jesters kept in his household; he wagered heavily in the ball game (*tlachtli*) and at *patolli*[4]; he hunted game and birds; he sang, and was told proverbs and tales for his enjoyment. He also ate well. Sahagún claimed that each day

> . . . a man, the majordomo, set out for the ruler his food—two thousand kinds of various foods; hot tortillas, white tamales with beans forming a sea shell on top; red tamales; the main meal of roll-shaped tortillas and many (foods): sauces with turkeys, quail, venison, rabbit, hare, rat, lobster, small fish, large fish; then all (manner of) sweet fruits (*ibid.*, book 8:39).

A deceased tlatoani was succeeded in office by a brother or son. By the mid-fifteenth century, Mexica succession appears to have favored brothers, then sons (see Figure 1–3). Succession was not automatic, for an individual was required to have excelled in the martial arts, and to have gained the approval of the rulers of Texcoco and Tlacopan and of the high-ranking Mexica chiefs (see Chapter 5).

Tetecutin, *or "Chiefs"* The numerous *tetecutin* formed the next lower rank of nobility. They apparently controlled more restricted areas and sets of activities than the tlatoque. They attained their impressive titles primarily through success in military activities, although it was usually mandatory that they be *pipiltin*, or nobles, by birth. The manner of acquisition of a *tecutli* title was similar to that faced by a tlatoani's heir:

[4] The patolli game was very similar to the Oriental game of pachisi.

When one of these lords died, the ruler granted his dignity to one who merited it by his services, and a son did not succeed his father unless the ruler promoted him to this dignity. The rulers always inclined, however, to give preference to sons over others, if they deserved it. Otherwise they remained pilles . . . (Zorita 1963:105).

During the reign of Itzcoatl (1428–1440), at least 21 major tecutli titles were established. Those who received the titles were all brothers, cousins, or nephews of Itzcoatl (Durán 1967, vol. 2:99). Among the titles bestowed were *tlacateccatl* ("commander of warriors"), *tlillancalqui* ("keeper of the dark house"), *tlacochcalcatl tecutli* ("chief of the spear house"), *huey tecutli* ("great chief"), and *Mexicaltecutli* ("Mexican chief"). Aside from such long-standing titles, the ruler apparently could create and confirm titles as he saw fit (*ibid.*:100). Some outstanding persons could achieve more than one title. Thus, for example, in the fifteenth century the diplomat Tlacaelel was titled *cihuacoatl* ("Woman–Serpent") and tlacochcalcatl ("Spear House Chief"); along with these titles, he assumed the positions of second-in-command to the ruler and of a chief military commander.

Some of these titles also involved political or military responsibilities (see Chapter 5). Primary among these responsibilities was that of the office of judge. Sahagún (1950–1969, book 8:55) lists 13 judges by titles, and he equates tecutli with judge: "The magistrate [tecutli] (is) a judge, a pronouncer of sentences, an establisher of ordinances, of statutes. (He is) dignified, fearless, courageous, reserved . . ." (*ibid.*, book 10:15). The tlatoani's principal political advisors all carried tecutli titles, as did the high-ranking military commanders and provincial governors. Four of the highest ranking military officers, clad in their ornate symbols of status, are illustrated in Figure 3–1.

Since the tecutli frequently held a political or military office, much of his energy and resources were owed to the state. Whether an administrative advisor or a leader on the battlefield, the tecutli was frequently in attendance at the royal palace, often serving the tlatoani personally. In the fateful meeting between Hernán Cortés and Moctezuma, the latter was attended by numerous high-ranking chiefs, many of them close relatives of the tlatoani Moctezuma. Cortés's own account of the meeting states that Moctezuma was accompanied by some 200 nobles, who approached in two long lines (1928:69).

The status of tecutli brought not only office and honor but also privileges and rewards. A tecutli owned and controlled agricultural lands, and was the head of a "chiefly house" (*teccalli*) to which were attached lesser nobles (pipiltin) and commoners. These nobles were usually close kin of the tecutli, while the commoners may have been more distant kin, local persons granted to the tecutli by the ruler, immigrants, rural tenants, or a combination of these. A chiefly house, then, was internally stratified. Such chiefly houses are described in a series of colonial documents which detail social and economic conditions in indigenous communities just south of Mexico City in the 1530s. They reveal that, at least for that area and time, the number of dependent heads of households of the local chiefs ranged from 7–44 (Carrasco 1976:115).[5] In these cases, the dependents had received lands from the

---

[5] These figures undoubtedly reflect the large-scale depopulation experienced by the Indians under colonial exposure. In indigenous times, the figures were probably larger.

Figure 3–1: The highest ranking military officers: tlacateccatl, tlacochcalcatl, huitz-nahuatl, tiçocyahuacatl. Apparently the first of these normally ascended from the commoner class through outstanding feats in battle; the others were of nobility status by birth, attaining these exalted titles through military exploits (Codex Mendoza 1938, vol. 3:folio 67).

tecutli and in turn were responsible to the tecutli for tribute payments in goods (often clothing) and services (agricultural and domestic labor). The sixteenth-century Spanish judge Alonso de Zorita adds that

> These lords were responsible for the working of the fields, both for themselves and for their people, and they had overseers who saw to this. The lords also had the duty of looking after the people in their charge, of defending and protecting them. Thus these lords were appointed and intended to serve the general as well as their private good (1963:105).

Zorita likens the tetecutin to Spanish *encomenderos*, and emphasizes that the extent of their individual holdings varied greatly. This variation in holdings is clearly evident in the detailed documents discussed above.

The teccalli was, to some extent, integrated through principles of kinship. The kinship system, traced bilaterally[6] but favoring the male line, provided the major link among the nobility of a teccalli. The pipiltin were, in almost all documented cases, close relatives of the tecutli. In addition, persons labeled *teixhuihuan* ("someone's grandchildren") were commonly attached to teccalli. These individuals were probably more distant relatives of the tecutli, and would have been a rung below the pipiltin in the social hierarchy. In addition, some of the commoners may also have been linked genealogically with the tecutli.

The teccalli was also a territorial unit. At times it coincided exactly or almost

[6] Bilateral descent reckons kinship affiliation through both male and female lines.

exactly with a calpulli. Examples of such correspondences have been uncovered in diverse areas throughout central Mexico. The documentary evidence, however, is still fragmentary on this important problem.

Pipiltin, *or "Sons of Nobility"* The pipiltin were, simply, the children of rulers and chiefs. Pipiltin were considered, economically and socially, attached to the house (teccalli) in which they were born. As such they received rights to patrimonial lands and to commoners to work these lands. By the sixteenth century, the pipiltin apparently were a rapidly expanding class of nobles. In the early phases of empire building, polygyny among nobles would have helped provide enough persons of rank for positions in the administration of the rapidly expanding empire.[7] The practice continued throughout the history of the empire, even though the number of positions did not seem to grow at a comparable rate.

Some pipiltin who did not succeed to the rank of tlatoani or tecutli were provided positions in the Triple Alliance capitals or the provinces as bureaucratic officials, tribute collectors, teachers, or military officers. Others entered the priesthood. All of these positions required training in the *calmecac*, a school providing not only training in the martial arts, but also instruction in religion, politics, history, law, astrology, and other esoteric subjects. Attendance at this school was primarily reserved for those of noble birth.

The position of tribute collector was available to the pipiltin. Moctezuma's tribute collectors made a vivid impression on Spanish conquistador Bernal Díaz, who met five of them en route to Tenochtitlan. He describes them as haughty, arrogant, and richly attired (1956:91). In at least this one case, the Mexica nobles inspired a great deal of fear and awe in the local populace; the local leaders "turned pale and trembled with fear" (*ibid.*). (Priests, teachers, and military leaders are described in detail in the following sections and Chapters 4–6).

The pipiltin, as nobles, enjoyed many of the same rights as the rulers and chiefs. They could own land privately. They were allowed to dress in elaborate and finely worked clothing. They were trained in the calmecac and had the opportunity to hold prestigious political and religious positions.

While the children of rulers and chiefs were nobles (pipiltin), the status of the children of pipiltin is not clear. Perhaps they also were pipiltin, or perhaps they were socially demoted to teixhuihuan (grandchildren) status.

During the reign of Moctezuma Xocoyotzin, many pipiltin served that ruler's personal needs in his palace. Cortés mentions that Moctezuma had, in his service, the eldest sons of most of the "lords of the land."

Provincial Nobility The rights and responsibilities of nobles of the Valley of Mexico cities are disclosed in numerous scattered post-conquest documents. These nobles—whether rulers, chiefs, or of lesser rank—were not unaffected by elements of Spanish administration; nonetheless, the type and extent of their claims on resources undoubtedly reflect pre-conquest patterns. The tlatoani and governor of

---

[7] This is illustrated by the following statement, uttered by Moctezuma Ilhuicamina's second-in-command as they prepared for war in the 1440s: "Every time messengers are sent they are chosen from among the nobility. Where will we find enough noblemen to act as messengers?" (Durán 1964:92).

Coyoacan in the mid-sixteenth century, Don Juan de Guzmán, may be taken as an example.[8]

In the mid-sixteenth century, Don Juan de Guzmán received daily household provisions of hens, maize, cacao beans, chiles, salt, tomatoes, gourd seeds, wood, and grass for horse fodder. He also received the services of men to act as guards, and women to grind maize. Only the grass required for the horse, and the hens (probably a substitution for the indigenous turkey) would have surely been Spanish influences.

In addition, as a result of his position as tlatoani, he possessed fields in four nearby locations, which the local people were required to tend. A separate house was provided for him, along with carpenters and stonemasons, and all the artisans and craftspersons were considered attached to his royal household. In total, 380 men from 21 locales were responsible to Don Juan. The market was considered his domain also, and the market tax collected in Coyoacan was given to him.

Don Juan also owned 33 distinct parcels of land scattered throughout the municipality of Coyoacan. This included house plots and orchards as well as plots for subsistence crops. These lands, like the lands mentioned above, belonged to him by virtue of his position as tlatoani.

In addition to the above perquisites, he also owned 23 parcels of private land by virtue of his noble status. These parcels would become the property of his children upon his death.

Don Juan's case was probably replicated among the tlatoque of the Valley of Mexico in late pre-conquest times. It may be inferred that the perquisites followed a fairly consistent pattern, differing mainly in the extent of control over resources, rather than in the type of control.

A glance at the more distant Cuicatec region (in present-day northeastern Oaxaca) sheds additional light on the role of the nobility in the provinces. In this outlying provincial area, also subject to the Triple Alliance, the ruling nobles' (caciques) major responsibilities were associated with the administration and regulation of land and water rights. This contrasts sharply with the urban elite of Tenochtitlan, most of whom were well removed from agricultural administrative activities:

> While the Aztec ruling groups were concerned with warfare, religion, manufacturing, trade, and the control of the periphery as an economic hinterland, the rulers of colonies were more directly involved in the problems of agricultural management (Hunt 1972:227).

Although their responsibilities may have varied, these more distant nobles did have rights similar to those of the Valley of Mexico nobles.

Macehualtin, or "Commoners," and Calpulli Organization Commoners comprised the bulk of the central Mexican population. They were tillers of the soil, fishers, and craftspeople; all paid tribute to some member of the nobility. In addition, they provided the rank and file of the military organization. Much has already

---

[8] AGN Tierras 1735, exp. 2; Anderson, Berdan and Lockhart 1976, document nos. 25, 26. Coyoacan was located on the western shore of Lake Texcoco, just a few miles from Tenochtitlan.

been said about the life-style, rights, and obligations of commoners. A graphic picture of conditions among the Mexican commoners was painted by a Spanish chronicler, Oviedo y Valdés, in the sixteenth century. Drawing on the memories of Spanish conquistadores, and referring to the life of commoners in pre-conquest times, he states that

> In their homes they have no furnishings or clothing other than the poor garments which they wear on their persons, one or two stones for grinding maize, some pots in which to cook the maize, and a sleeping mat. Their meals consist chiefly of vegetables cooked with chili, and bread (translation in Keen 1955:17).

Life conditions among macehualtin were, however, not uniform. They had access to differing amounts of land, and well-endowed persons frequently had mayeque (tenants) as renters to work some of their land. In two documented instances, the plots of commoner land varied in size from 92–8701 square meters (in a section of Texcoco), and from 4–1377 square meters in the chinampa districts of Tenochtitlan (Hicks 1976:72, Calnek 1974:47). Such variation in subsistence base is undoubtedly reflective of some differences in life-style. Although restricted by law in many areas of consumption, some macehualtin must have been more secure and affluent than others. No commoner, unless he had achieved heroic feats in battle, could wear or display precious garments. However, undistinguished commoners could keep or sell such goods if won at contests or received as gifts (Sahagún 1950–1969, book 2:109, 127).

Macehualtin were, for the most part, commoners grouped into calpulli. The precise nature of calpulli organization has been one of the most persistent problems in Aztec studies. Briefly, it appears that the calpulli, as a "ward" or *barrio* of a town or city, was a territorial and land-holding unit through which land was distributed to members for their use. The usufruct of that land was then the possession of the member, but he customarily would not sell or otherwise alienate the plot he worked. Upon his death the usufruct of his plot would be inherited by his children. In contrast to this communal land-holding picture, there are subtle suggestions that some calpulli lands were, in effect, the private property of certain commoners and could be sold (Harvey 1979; Sahagún 1950–1969, book 3:8). According to one popularly quoted source (Zorita 1963), if the holder failed to cultivate his plot for a period of two consecutive years, went to live in another calpulli, or committed a serious crime, the land reverted to the calpulli and was reallocated. The system of reallocation of calpulli lands may have been a fairly rigid process in some areas (Calnek 1974:52), but in other districts, reallocation may have been more casual, with "squatting" a possibility (Anderson, Berdan, and Lockhart 1976: document no. 9).

The calpulli was a territorial unit, but its scale remains a puzzle. Apparently the term could be applied to units of many sizes. Often small units, as well as the larger units that encompassed them, were referred to as calpulli. In Tenochtitlan, the more appropriate term to apply to the territorial unit was *tlaxilacalli*, while calpulli ("big house") may have referred more specifically to the temples of each such unit (Reyes 1975).

Apparently farmers, craftsmen and traders could live and carry out their different activities together within a single calpulli organization. Some other calpulli, however, provided the territorial basis for economic specialization. For example, during the reign of Nezahualcoyotl of Texcoco, special crafts such as gold and feather-working were each established in exclusive calpulli in that city (Alva Ixtlilxochitl 1965, vol. 2:187). Featherworkers (*amanteca*) were concentrated in their own calpulli in Tlatelolco, and professional merchants were the exclusive residents of seven calpulli there (Sahagún 1950–1969: book 9). However, some craftspersons and traders could and did reside in other, unspecialized calpulli. This may have involved the craft production and trading that took place on a relatively small scale, and was part-time rather than full-time activity.

Economic specialists who were concentrated in specific calpulli tended to be either professional merchants or artisans of luxury wares. These groups also seem to have been relatively late arrivals to cities such as Tenochtitlan, Tlatelolco, and Texcoco, being "added on" to already well-established urban complexes. They also appear to have been ethnically different from the general urban population, worshiping their own specific patron deities. For example, the professional merchants, whose origins can be traced to the Gulf Coast area, focused their religious attention on the deity Yacatecutli ("the Long-nosed God"). The lapidaries traced their roots to Xochimilco, and worshiped four deities, to whom they attributed their craft and identity. The gold casters, most likely from south and southwestern Mexico (especially Oaxaca), venerated the god Xipe Totec ("Our Lord the Flayed One").

Each calpulli, whether specialized or not, contained a temple to which the members of the calpulli dedicated themselves. Not only did they share a special identity and ceremonies through the worship of a particular calpulli deity; they also worked plots of land set aside especially for the support of the calpulli temple.

Each calpulli also had its own *telpochcalli* ("young men's house," or school). This educational institution was the responsibility of the calpulli members under the leadership of local distinguished members, usually formally appointed by the state. These leaders were outstanding warriors, and the education in the telpochcalli focused primarily on the martial arts. The young men being trained were responsible for providing the telpochcalli with daily fuel and provisions, making repairs to the building, and cultivating a field for the support of the institution.

The calpulli seem also to have contained elements of social stratification. The vast differences in access to land among the macehualtin imply variations in wealth and life-style. If the same calpulli plots were maintained over generations, each plot being somewhat different in size and productivity, wealth differences among commoners in the Valley of Mexico centers would tend to be exaggerated, thus fostering a system of social differentiation.

In outlying areas, the situation may have been substantially different. This was the case in the Cuicatec region to the east of the Valley of Mexico. This area was some distance geographically, as well as culturally and administratively, from the Triple Alliance capitals.

These peasants were commoners (*Indios naturales*; *macehuales*) and did not own the land privately, nor did they have permanent usufruct of particular parcels. . . . Each year, the individual peasant was assigned a different plot to cultivate. . . . The task of land redistribution was the primary administrative job of the local ruler, who had the power to make the decisions and oversee the annual redistribution of the land among the peasantry (Hunt 1972:203).

Such annual redistribution would have been particularly functional if the areas involved were of unequal productivity, and the purpose were to even out the life chances of all members. It may also have accentuated the importance of the cacique whose right it was to redistribute the lands, and helped him maintain his authority in this provincial area.

The association of a tecutli with a given calpulli, along with his "chiefly house" and related pipiltin, also points to considerable social and economic differentiation among the residents of a single calpulli. In addition, it is easy to see how at least some ranking among macehualtin within a calpulli could occur: A fundamental basis for ranking was achievement in warfare, and virtually all male commoners from the calpulli participated in military activities.

There seems also to have been variation in rank among calpulli. In particular, some calpulli possessed a higher proportion of nobility than others:

> . . . some wards were inhabited by the ethnically dominant groups, included a higher proportion of noble houses, and had as their leaders the leaders of the city-state as a whole; other wards would belong to ethnic minorities, or consist predominantly of commoners . . . (Carrasco 1971:366).

From among its members each calpulli elected a *calpullec*, or calpulli headman. This office had to be occupied by a *principal* who was an "elder," but not necessarily of noble descent. Although the calpullec was elected, it was considered preferable for the position to stay in the same family over generations. In his role as protector of the calpulli, the calpullec was assisted by a council of elders. Although his duties focused on calpulli affairs, he also had important obligations to the state. He was required, for example, to present himself daily to the chief tribute collector of the state to receive any orders.

The calpullec was responsible for maintaining census maps of his calpulli. Since land was a fundamental basis for tribute assessment, such maps served as a current record of tribute payers. Upon the demise of a calpulli member (head of household), his name-glyph was erased from the appropriate section of the map and replaced by the name-glyph of his successor:

> This principal is responsible for guarding and defending the calpulli lands. He has pictures on which are shown all the parcels, and the boundaries, and where and with whose fields the lots meet, and who cultivates what field, and what land each one has. The paintings also show which lands are vacant. . . . The Indians continually alter these pictures according to the changes worked by time, and they understand perfectly what these pictures show (Zorita 1963:110).

The calpulli members were responsible for cultivating a plot of land for their calpullec and assisting him in the performance of his duties as calpulli head. In addition, they paid tribute in both services and goods to a higher authority. In the Triple Alliance capitals, the prime authority was the state (i.e., the ruling tlatoani as a state functionary), and the tribute was largely in the form of services. In lieu of providing state tribute, some calpulli members might be assigned to particular noble houses (teccalli) or temporarily to specific nobles. State-level duties included labor on public works, service in the royal palace, work on emergency projects and, of course, participation in warfare.

The calpulli of the Triple Alliance cities had their own fiscal officers (*tequitla-toque*). These officials were members of the calpulli in which they held office and, along with the calpullec, were responsible for collecting tribute and organizing labor drafts for calpulli or state projects. The organization of such activities was carried out in groups of 100 and smaller units of 20 heads of households:

> . . . these Regidores majores, calpixque, had each one in his barrio other lesser regidores called *macuyltepanpixque* which means centurions because he had charge of one hundred men or houses who obeyed him and responded to his call; and each of these centurions had under his jurisdiction five lesser regidores called *centespampixques* which means *vicenarios* because each one had charge of twenty houses . . . (AGI Patronato 20, no. 5, ramo 22; translation by FFB).

The calpulli was not only a unit for the provision of goods and services to some higher level but was also the occasional recipient of resources external to its own land and labor supply. For example, following the conquest of Azcapotzalco by Tenochtitlan and Texcoco, lands were given to the various calpulli to be used in support of the calpulli temples. It is also likely that the Triple Alliance urban calpulli received subsistence goods from the vast stores of provincial tribute.

Lands belonging to the calpulli could be rented by persons other than calpulli members, the proceeds of rent being used for calpulli needs. Zorita (1963:107) states that these lands were not to be worked by the members of another calpulli, although this rule may not have applied everywhere. Perhaps "displaced persons," lacking both land and community affiliations, were available for this labor. This arrangement, if enforced, would lessen the danger of encroachment on the lands of one calpulli by another, although Zorita phrases the problem in terms of "mixing the lineages." That would suggest calpulli endogamy, a topic to be discussed later in this chapter.

In conquered areas, the local land-holding groups (calpulli or similar units) also provided services for the local ruler and/or Aztec administrator. Furthermore, the massive amounts of tribute in goods provided to the conquering ruler also stemmed chiefly from the labors of the macehualtin, who worked state, military, and temple fields; fashioned cloth; and collected and manufactured other items demanded in tribute.

Mayeque, *or "Rural Tenants"* Rural tenants generally have been described as "serfs." Unlike the macehualtin who lived in calpulli, the mayeque were attached to the private lands of the nobility. Zorita characterizes them as follows:

> These mayeques could not leave the land to which they were attached, nor were they ever known to attempt such a thing. The sons and heirs of the lords of such lands succeeded to them; and the land passed together with the mayeques who lived on it, and with the same obligation of service and rent that the mayeques, their forerunners, had had to pay for their use of the land. The rent consisted in payment of a part of the mayeque's harvest to the lord, or in working a piece of land for the lord, and varied according to the number of mayeques and their agreement with the lord. The same was true of the service, which consisted in the provision of fuel, water, and domestic service (1963: 182–183).

Zorita goes on to relate that the mayeque were not obligated to pay tribute to the "señor supremo" (tlatoani), unless they worked lands owned by him. Rather, the tribute paid to the individual noble was *in place of* the tribute which would have been paid to the tlatoani, with the exception of service in time of war. The mayeque were, however, under the civil and criminal jurisdiction of the tlatoani.

Of all the early sources, it seems that only Zorita uses the term "mayeque," although he also refers to this group as *tlalmaitec* (land-, or farmhands). Variations of this latter term are more commonly found in Nahuatl documents of the sixteenth century, particularly its singular form, *tlalmaitl*. Carrasco (1976:115) found *tequinanamique* and other terms used to refer to such renters, and there may have been considerable variation in terminology. Despite its obscure origins, the term "mayeque" will be used here, since it has become so well grounded in the current literature on Aztec social organization. The sixteenth-century Spanish equivalent appears to be *terrasquerro*.

Table 3–2 compares the two general types of commoners, the mayeque as tenants and the macehualtin as calpulli members. With the exception of resource base, nature and extent of internal organization, tribute recipient, and possibly attachment to the land, the two types appear virtually identical. Instead of different classes, as Zorita presents them, perhaps they should be described as adaptive variations of a single type.

Persons who had been displaced, especially through warfare or economic need, may well have provided the many laborers needed to work the rapidly increasing private lands of the expanding Aztec nobility. Durán describes the displacement of occupants of the lands of Coyoacan (1967, vol. 2:101–102). Following that city's conquest by the Aztecs, its communal lands were divided. Some were allo-

TABLE 3–2   A COMPARISON OF THE TWO TYPES OF COMMONERS: MAYEQUE AND MACEHUALTIN

	Mayeque	Macehualtin
Resource base	Private lands of the nobility	Calpulli lands
Internal organization	No formal organization	Elected leader, council of elders; distribution of land and allocation of public tasks
Inheritance	Dependents inherited use of plot	Dependents inherited use of plot
Tribute payment	Individual nobles	Tlatoani or tecutli, and calpulli
Types of tribute payment	Services, goods	Services, goods
Final jurisdiction	Tlatoani	Tlatoani
Attachment to land	Apparently could not leave nobles' lands, but specific sanctions not documented	Could leave calpulli, but lost calpulli privileges

cated to the Aztec ruler for the support of the royal palace and state functions. Others were distributed among the successful warriors, according to their merit and accomplishments in battle. Durán makes it clear that the residents of Coyoacan were then made "terrasquerros." Since their communal (calpulli) lands had been turned into private lands for the Aztec nobility, their new status was that of mayeque, or tenants.

Tlacotin, or "Slaves" An additional position which could be assumed by a commoner was that of *tlacotli*, frequently translated as *esclavo* ("slave") in the Spanish documents. There were vast differences between these slaves and those captured on the battlefield. The slaves most important to the social hierarchy were those who were required to exchange their services for either the cost of survival or for compensation for some crime committed. A person could sell himself or some member of his family into slavery for subsistence needs. Some literally "lost themselves" by excessive gambling. Others became tied in service to persons against whom they committed crimes (usually theft). Slaves captured in war were, for the most part, sacrificed shortly after their arrival in the Triple Alliance cities.

A person could become a tlacotli through unsuccessful gambling, theft, or other crime; failure to pay tribute; or extreme poverty. Such extreme poverty, reducing persons to beggar activities, resulted in a rather uncomfortable life-style:

> He [in poverty] wore an old cape and threadbare breech clout. He owned no miserable rags, had nothing to cover his hips or spread over his shoulders. He lived in poverty, in his house, exposed to inclement weather. Never was it warm; old, worn mats and seats were strewn about. No one swept. Rubbish was all about and surrounded him (Sahagún 1950–1969, book 4:31).

The transaction involving a change in status to tlacotli had to take place before at least four witnesses (Motolinía 1971:366–367). The price for such servitude is recorded in Motolinía (*ibid.*) as 20 cloaks, which could support the indebted person for approximately one year. After that time he was required to begin his servitude. During the disastrous famine of 1450–1454, the price of a slave was 400 ears of corn (about 1.6 bushels, shelled) for a girl and 500 ears of corn for a boy (Torquemada 1969, vol. 1:158).[9] Any person who failed to pay his tribute was sold into slavery in the marketplace by a *tequitlato* (community-level tribute collector) or other tribute official. The proceeds of the sale were then used to cover the unpaid tribute.

Debts also could be resolved by assuming the status of tlacotli. Motolinía describes such a situation:

> When someone took cloaks on credit, or something of equal value, from some merchant, and died without paying, the merchant had the authority to make a slave of the widow for the debt. If the deceased had left a son, the son was made a slave and not the mother (1971:370; translation by FFB).

[9] These two prices in cloaks and maize should not be taken as equivalents, since both the time periods and the circumstances were significantly different. While the first instance appears to represent general transactions in the Valley of Mexico in the early sixteenth century, the latter describes conditions during a severe mid-fifteenth century famine, when the Mexica had to sell their children for maize to groups on the east coast who were otherwise unaffected by the famine.

It is clear that once debts were incurred, they had to be honored, if not by the debtor, then by his family. Such debts were paid not in currency or kind, but in labor.

A person who acquired a tlacotli controlled his labor, but in some cases was also responsible for providing him with his daily necessities:

> If the slaves were boys, or poor, they stayed at the house of their masters, who treated them almost like sons, and dressed and fed them as sons; and often the masters took women slaves as mistresses; and women, widows, took their slaves in the place of husbands; and there were slaves who managed the house of their master, like a majordomo (Motolinía 1971:371; translation by FFB).

Aside from the obligation of rendering service to his owner, the tlacotli retained most of his personal freedoms, including rights to marriage and property. In some cases, tlacotin amassed considerable amounts of property, even including other tlacotin. And slaves were shown special favor on the day One Death. According to Sahagún,

> None of the slave-owners could scold them, or abuse them with vile words, or call angrily or indignantly to them. . . . They then, first, took from them, struck off, and removed from them the wooden collars, the curved ones in which they were held and with which they went about restrained lest they flee. Then they soaped them and bathed them, and made much of and flattered them (1950–1969, book 4:34).

The status of tlacotli was one which, with one exception, could only be acquired, not inherited; the children of tlacotin were born free. The exception in which persons might inherit tlacotli status was through the system of *huehuetlatlacolli,* or "ancient servitude." This apparently had been abolished by Nezahualpilli of Texcoco in 1505 during a famine, and his lead was followed shortly thereafter by Moctezuma Xocoyotzin. The service involved in this arrangement included especially household chores (carrying firewood, sweeping) and agricultural labor, but the tlacotli resided with his own family rather than in the household of his "owner." The obligation of providing a tlacotli to that household was passed on to the tlacotli's descendants, apparently for an indefinite number of generations. The types of services described were probably provided by all tlacotin (although women also engaged in weaving and served as concubines), regardless of the manner in which their status had been attained.

Specific action could be brought against uncooperative or inadequate tlacotin. The procedure, however, was lengthy and involved. Such tlacotin were given public warnings before witnesses, perhaps judges. If the tlacotli was still incorrigible after two or three warnings, he was fitted with a collar and could then be sold in the marketplace. If he failed to improve, and as a consequence was sold three times in the marketplace, he could then be bought for purposes of sacrifice. Comparatively few such slaves were used for the numerous ceremonial sacrifices, however. Provincial tribute and warfare customarily provided the slaves needed for regular ceremonial events and particularly for special ceremonial occasions (e.g., a royal coronation or funeral or the dedication of a temple).

Although it appears that virtually anyone could acquire tlacotin—even other tlacotin—the greatest numbers were probably found in the households of nobles.

Not only did this group possess the means to acquire additional services but they also had developed a need for such services in their extensive households. Undoubtedly, such "slavery" was more an urban than a rural phenomenon, in that tlacotli labor was not primarily attached to lands (relatively scarce in the urban setting), but was used mainly for household services for the nobility, concentrated in the cities (Zorita 1963:265).

Traffic in tlacotin at the time of the Spanish conquest was a thriving and lucrative business. There was even a specialized group of merchants who dealt in tlacotin. Aside from dealing in slaves in Tabasco on the Gulf Coast, these merchants also certainly frequented the specialized "slave markets" of Azcapotzalco and Itzocan.

Social Mobility Avenues for advancement in the social system were open, in varying degrees, to members of both the nobility and commoner groups. However, members of the former, largely endogamous, category tended to occupy the higher positions in the religious, military, and administrative structures.

Besides the avenues for mobility into prestigious and lucrative positions that have been mentioned for the pipiltin, an additional means was entry into the priesthood. There were numerous ranks within the priesthood, and the temples and deities to which priests were attached were of varying importance. The pipiltin, who attended the calmecac for their education, received training from the priests. Some of these pipiltin would later devote themselves to the priesthood, climbing the religious hierarchy. At times priests engaged in warfare, and as such could attain honors accorded successful warriors (see Figure 3–2).

Figure 3–2: Priests serving in battle, like other warriors, gained status according to the number of prisoners captured. Such feats were rewarded with the warriors' costumes illustrated above (Codex Mendoza 1938, vol. 3:folio 65).

A pilli entered the calmecac as a young boy and served the temple essentially in menial chores. As a youth he was given the position *tlamacazqui*, "young priest," and possibly advanced to that of *tlenamacac*, "fire-giver." From the ranks of these accomplished priests, the two highest positions (*quequetzalcoa*) in the priestly hierarchy of Tenochtitlan were chosen (Carrasco 1971:358). Apparently similar systems were found in Texcoco and Tlacopan.

Some sources suggest that the priesthood was not the exclusive prerogative of the nobility, and commoners could also be dedicated to the priesthood. Attendance at the calmecac, of course, was a prerequisite. It is not clear if commoners could climb the full length of the priestly hierarchy; but they certainly could achieve military honors as members of the priesthood.

Macehualtin could move into prestigious social categories by means other than commitment to the priesthood. The most important of these was through success in military activities; the other, success in commercial enterprises. While a few commoner youths apparently attended the calmecac for training in religious matters, the vast majority attended the telpochcalli of their calpulli. The telpochcalli was militarily oriented in its training, while the calmecac was more religious and esoteric in orientation.

Through the capture of enemy prisoners in warfare, macehualtin trained in their telpochcalli could attain high status, titles, and even access to goods and services otherwise reserved for the nobility. Attainment of progressively higher rank was accompanied by the privilege of wearing particular items of clothing not permitted to other macehualtin (see Figure 3–3). When the warrior had successfully captured four prisoners, he was given the title *tequiua*. Persons of this title attended the war councils and were qualified to serve in important military and civil offices. The

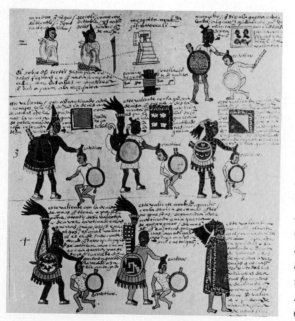

Figure 3–3: Aztecs capturing enemy warriors were rewarded with both cloaks of status-specific design and other elaborate and ornate costumes. At bottom right is a distinguished tlacateccatl, a high-ranking military officer (Codex Mendoza 1938, vol. 3:folio 64).

highest military ranks—*tlacochcalcatl* ("man of the spear-house") and *tlacateccatl* ("commander of warriors")—were apparently then open to the warrior, as well as some civil positions, such as judges (see Chapter 5). Although they could attain high positions, commoners apparently could not achieve full nobility status. The closest approximation to such status was that of the *quauhpilli*. This distinguished warrior group consisted of the generals "whose personal charge was command in war" (Sahagún 1950–1969, book 8:43). They were supported on lands given them by the tlatoani, but could not have mayeque on these lands. The lands could be sold to other nobles by the quauhpilli but probably not to commoners (Torquemada 1969, vol. 2:546). Their position in tribute matters appears to have been comparable to that of the nobility by birth.

Although these commoners could possess economic bases similar but somewhat inferior to pipiltin, occupy special high-ranking military positions, and carry the "-pilli" name suffix, they could not wear certain marks of rank reserved for those of noble birth, and their children did not inherit true nobility status.

Eric Wolf has noted a competitive relationship between the two types of nobility in the sixteenth century:

> As this nobility of service [achieved commoners] grew increasingly important, however, with the expansion of the Mexica domain, it also entered into conflict with the nobility of lineage over the occupancy of bureaucratic positions. During the last phase of Mexica rule an aristocratic reaction curtailed the privileges of the service nobles in favor of a renewed monopoly of power in the hands of the nobility of descent (1959:138).

This conflict may have derived, at least in part, from the increasing numbers of nobility by birth, resulting from the practice of polygyny among this group. Competition for a limited number of administrative, religious, and military positions may have become a serious social problem in the early sixteenth century.

Other occupations of lesser importance open to distinguished warriors included the *telpochtlatoque* (in charge of the telpochcalli), and the *achcacauhtin* (constables, or executors) (Sahagún 1950–1969, book 8:43).

Membership in certain warrior societies (*otomi* and *quachic*) also carried special distinctions. These societies formed distinctive high-ranking military groups, but their unruly members were not considered qualified for administrative posts (Sahagún 1950–1969, book 8; Carrasco 1971:357). Nothing in the sources indicates that these prestigious societies were closed to commoners. Each position had its special symbolic paraphernalia (distinctive insignia, dress, ornaments); and the higher positions had access to certain economic resources. Much as nobles serving in administrative posts received support in the form of goods and services, so persons achieving administrative offices through military success also received similar support while they performed the duties of their offices.

More limited than warfare or religion, commerce also served as an avenue for social mobility. The professional merchants (pochteca) were drawn primarily from specific calpulli in the Triple Alliance capitals and other major Lake Texcoco cities. They constituted a closed group, entrance being by birth. This group received special attention from the tlatoani because of the important economic and military functions it served.

Like priests, the merchants could achieve special honor through participation in military activities (Sahagún 1950–1969, book 9). These long-distance traders had frequent cause to engage in warfare as they journeyed through hostile territories. In addition, the pochteca belonged to hierarchically arranged groups, or "guilds." This internal organization included several positions of high rank and prestige, which could be achieved by the more successful merchants.

Though apparently of commoner origin, the merchant group had achieved an intermediate status—above the commoners, but below the nobility. The pochteca were subject to payment of tribute in goods to the tlatoani, but were freed from obligations in the form of labor. They possessed distinctive attire and paraphernalia, but could display these only at certain festivals. At all other times they were required to dress humbly and were frequently admonished by their elders to avoid public display of their wealth. Apparently, the merchants were wealthy as a group and important to the administration and expansion of the Aztec state, yet unstable and perhaps threatened in their relationships with the nobility. (Chapter 2 discusses in detail the professional merchants and other guild-like specialists.)

KINSHIP, FAMILY, AND DOMESTIC LIFE

In addition to their social class structure, the Mexica defined statuses and regulated relationships through rules of kinship and marriage. Like most indigenous central Mexican peoples, they reckoned descent bilaterally. That is, they traced their significant kinship affiliations through both maternal and paternal lines.

The kinship terminology of the Mexica is clearly bilateral. All terms designate relations from a specific point of reference (ego). Relationships traced through ego's father are equivalent to relationships traced through ego's mother. For example, *tlatli* refers to an uncle, whether father's brother or mother's brother; *citli* means "grandmother," traced through either father or mother (see Figures 3–4 and 3–5).

Significant kin would encompass at the most seven generations, although normally no more than five generations would have living representatives at any time. In ego's own generation, distinctions are made in terms of relative age and sex. That is, older brother is distinguished from younger brother, and older sister from older brother. These same terms are extended to ego's first cousins, maintaining the age and sex distinctions. Relative age appears to have been an important element in defining social relations. Where joint households of married brothers were formed, for example, the elder brother was invariably head of the household, with control of household resources. Sahagún emphasizes this role of the elder brother:

> One's older brother (is) a carrier, a taker, a bearer of all the burdens (of his father's household); one who counsels (his younger brothers), who prepares them for the work of men (1950–1969, book 10:9).

The criterion of relative age blurs for ego in his three preceding and one succeeding generation. However, sex remains an important element in the kinship terminology for members of these same generations (ego's parents, grandparents, great-

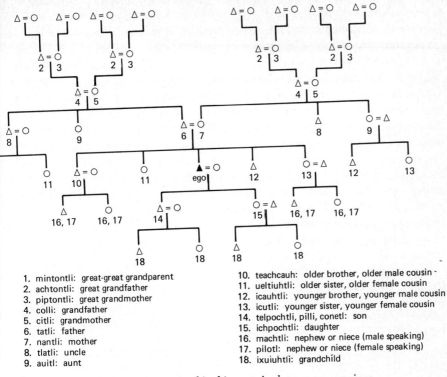

1. mintontli: great-great grandparent
2. achtontli: great grandfather
3. piptontli: great grandmother
4. colli: grandfather
5. citli: grandmother
6. tatli: father
7. nantli: mother
8. tlatli: uncle
9. auitl: aunt
10. teachcauh: older brother, older male cousin
11. ueltiuhtli: older sister, older female cousin
12. icauhtli: younger brother, younger male cousin
13. icutli: younger sister, younger female cousin
14. telpochtli, pilli, conetl: son
15. ichpochtli: daughter
16. machtli: nephew or niece (male speaking)
17. pilotl: nephew or niece (female speaking)
18. ixuiuhtli: grandchild

Figure 3–4: Mexica kinship terminology: consanguines.

grandparents, and children). Beyond them, the terminology generalizes, with single terms referring to any grandchild (*ixuiuhtli*) and any great-great-grandparent (*mintontli*). This far removed from ego, the actual interpersonal relationships were perhaps vague; the terminology does not, therefore, provide the finer distinctions found for more closely related kin.

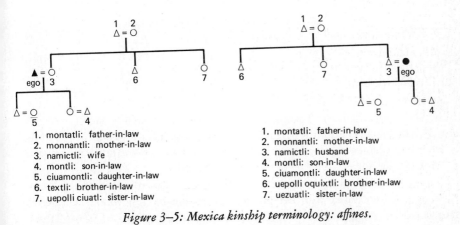

1. montatli: father-in-law
2. monnantli: mother-in-law
3. namictli: wife
4. montli: son-in-law
5. ciuamontli: daughter-in-law
6. textli: brother-in-law
7. uepolli ciuatl: sister-in-law

1. montatli: father-in-law
2. monnantli: mother-in-law
3. namictli: husband
4. montli: son-in-law
5. ciuamontli: daughter-in-law
6. uepolli oquixtli: brother-in-law
7. uezuatli: sister-in-law

Figure 3–5: Mexica kinship terminology: affines.

In the context of these kinship networks, the early Mexicans carried out their day-to-day activities. Kinship rules served as the foundation for certain important behavioral relationships: marriage, post-marital residence, and inheritance.

Marriage Rules   Marriage patterns are most abundantly documented for the nobility, where marriages were frequently made with the express aim of establishing or strengthening political alliances. For example, the ruling houses of both Texcoco and Teotihuacan maintained fairly consistent relationships through marriage during the fifteenth and sixteenth centuries (Carrasco 1974). The typical pattern here involved the marriage of a royal female of the dominant Texcoco to a royal male of the subordinate Teotihuacan. The mode of succession was from father to son, and the next ruler of Teotihuacan would be the son of parents from both Teotihuacan and Texcoco. In particular, the heir's father was from Teotihuacan, maintaining father-to-son succession. This rule would help solidify Texcoco's political control in this subordinate provincial area. Continued consolidation and control was assured typically by the marriage of this new Teotihuacan ruler to his mother's brother's daughter (*icutli* if she is younger, *ueltiuhtli* if older), a royal female cousin from Texcoco. Their heir married in the same manner, and so on. Although the ruler of a subordinate city normally had several wives, his successor was most assuredly the son of a wife from a higher-ranking dynasty. This occurred even at the highest levels. Thus, Nezahualpilli (son of Nezahualcoyotl and a Mexica princess) succeeded his father to the Texcocan rulership, as did Cacama (son of Nezahualpilli and, again, a Mexica princess). It is likely that similar techniques of establishing and maintaining political relations were widespread in central Mexico.

No fixed rules of exogamy beyond nuclear family prohibitions have been found. As a rule, individual nobles married their cross-cousins; but examples abound of marriages uniting close kin of all categories. Marriage patterns, at least by the sixteenth century, were probably roughly consistent with social class divisions, with class endogamy being the rule. It also appears that the calpulli tended toward endogamy. This would have special significance for the many specialized calpulli. Merchant and craft guilds, by means of endogamy, could maintain fairly exclusive rights over important resources and knowledge, thus enhancing their positions in the overall state structure.

Polygyny was practiced among the nobility, but apparently not among the commoners. This custom tended to produce a great many pipiltin, and by the sixteenth century they may have outnumbered the positions available to them. For example, Nezahualpilli, ruler of Texcoco (1472–1515), reputedly had more than 2000 wives (or perhaps concubines) and 144 children. Eleven children were considered legitimate, although the remainder were granted substantial wealth and lofty positions. Nezahualcoyotl, reigning in Texcoco from 1418 to 1472, apparently fathered 60 sons and 57 daughters. The sons were granted lands and villages to serve them. While one wife was commonly designated "legitimate," children of the other wives were not shunned socially or neglected in inheritance matters.

Once a marriage was established, the bride and groom—whether nobles or commoners—were faced with the problem of setting up residence as a married couple.

Residence and Household Composition   An important feature of bilateral kinship systems is flexibility in post-marital residence. This flexibility is normally made possible by the absence of any strict rule of residence. Such appears to have been the case in central Mexico. Drawing on extensive early colonial census documents from two barrios of communities just south of Mexico City, Pedro Carrasco has compiled statistical data on actual residence patterns (which, within certain limits, would reflect residence rules). In one barrio (Molotla, probably in Yautepec) he discovered that, of 128 families, about one-third were nuclear and the other two-thirds were joint families (see Carrasco 1976 for data). Nuclear families consist of parents and sometimes children, while joint families have at least two married couples residing in the same household.

The situation is quite different in Carrasco's second case, that of Tlacatecpan, the main barrio of sixteenth-century Tepoztlan. Here just over half of the 549 households consisted of nuclear families, and the remaining households involved joint families (see Carrasco 1964). From these data at least, it appears that there was no strict practice emphasizing either independent or joint residence.

The Tlacatecpan data provide some additional insights into residence patterns. Carrasco studied two subdivisions of this barrio: the "ward people," or macehualtin resident in the calpulli, and the "cacique's subjects," or people attached to the tecutli's house (teccalli). The "ward people" were predominately organized in nuclear families, with only one-third of the households being joint. Quite the reverse was the case for the "cacique's subjects"; nearly two-thirds of the latter's households were joint, one-third were nuclear. Perhaps in this provincial area there was a slight adaptive advantage in forming nuclear households in the calpulli context; in particular, there would be a strong incentive to form independent households if rights to land were assigned on the basis of "head of household." Similarly, the adaptive advantage of the joint household under the teccalli arrangement may have been in consolidating the labor force obligated to serve the local tecutli.

Where joint households were formed, the head of the household was invariably a married male. Such units were most commonly based on agnatic ties among males (e.g., brothers, father-son, uncle-nephew). However, there is sufficient variation from this to suggest that no firm rule was observed. For example, there are several instances of a married daughter (with her husband) residing with her parents, or of households being formed by the addition of relatives of the wife of the household head.

In Tenochtitlan itself, there was a tendency for joint families to be formed. In particular, married children continued to reside with either the groom's or the bride's parents. There was considerable flexibility in residence; apparently couples could reside with a wide range of relatives on either the husband's or wife's side. These patterns of forming joint households and of flexibility in residence held for nobles as well as commoners. The households of nobles characteristically were more extensive than those of commoners. Certainly the household of the cacique of Tlacatecpan in Tepoztlan was the largest single household of the barrio, containing 23 persons. Normally, however, joint households contained 2–6 nuclear families.

A number of factors may have contributed to the formation of either nuclear or joint households. These may have included the nature and extent of the household subsistence base, tribute assessments, and population mobility. Where resources were scarce relative to population, flexibility in household formation may have been an adaptive strategy. It allowed the population constantly to realign itself relative to available resources, especially land, thus evening out the pressure on these resources.

Some of the data cited above may reflect temporary, rather than permanent, residence. Bride service, for example, might account for some of the cases where a married daughter continued to reside with her parents. In the Tepoztlan case, Carrasco has suggested that married sons may have resided only temporarily with their parents, eventually splitting off to form nuclear households.

The usual site occupied by any household was an enclosed *calli* ("house"). It frequently contained many separate rooms, each opening onto a patio, the focus of household activity. Among the rooms was often a *cihuacalli* (woman's house). This was probably a common room, perhaps containing the "kitchen." In addition to residential rooms, house sites also frequently contained storage bins for maize and cisterns for water collection. There was considerable variation among residences in size and layout, depending on the size, composition, affluence, and needs of the resident household.

Inheritance   It is usual in human societies for kinship to provide the basis for the transfer of rights to titles and possessions. This was the case among the Aztecs. However, achievement also played a significant role in determining actual chains of inheritance.

With regard to titles, what was inherited was membership in a particular social category (e.g., pilli) which made an individual eligible for political, religious, and military titles and positions. Records of achievements, especially military achievements, provided the means by which fine distinctions among eligible title-holders were made. For example, the title of tecutli did not necessarily pass directly from father to a particular son, but from father to an eligible son. If there were no qualified successor, the title would have to be relinquished by the family. There were numerous pipiltin, but few titles to be doled out among them. At the loftiest political levels, titles and rights to wield power were jealously guarded and customarily maintained by a single family line. By the sixteenth century one could easily speak of dynasties in central Mexico.

The most common forms of inheritance were father to son and brother to brother. In areas where father-to-son inheritance was the rule (e.g., Texcoco and Tlacopan), the procedure for selecting successors for the highest political positions was as follows:

> The son chosen was the eldest son born of the ruler's principal wife. . . . If the eldest son was not qualified to rule, his father selected from his other sons the one who seemed the most competent to succeed, always giving preference to the sons of his principal wife in this and all else. If the ruler had no male heir, but had daughters, and one of them had sons, the ruler chose as his successor that grandson whom he regarded as best qualified to rule. If he had grandsons by his sons, however, he preferred them to grandsons by daughters (Zorita 1963:90).[10]

---

[10] The bilateral nature of inheritance is clearly pointed out here; although daughters could not succeed to office, their sons could.

When a ruler left no qualified heir, succession was determined by the nobility. Following well-defined rules, they first assessed the virtues and achievements of the ruler's brothers, then other kinsmen if necessary. If none of these persons was considered eligible, they would resort to some member of the nobility outside the traditional royal family. If a ruler of one of the Triple Alliance cities were being chosen, confirmation by the rulers of the other two cities was critical, and added to the new leader's legitimacy to rule (see Chapter 5).

The goal in Aztec succession was not only to find a legitimate heir but also to select a competent successor. This dual goal applied at all political levels. The resulting fluidity in succession rules led to some internal conflicts and a certain amount of "palace intrigue." Take the example of Nezahualpilli, who succeeded to the throne of Texcoco in 1472 at the young age of seven; his father had designated him as legitimate heir. However, Nezahualpilli had at least four older brothers, the eldest being instated as regent for the new ruler. The three other brothers coveted the rulership, and plotted to depose the child. The plot became serious enough to require the rapid intervention of the rulers of Tenochtitlan and Tlacopan. Taken quickly to Tenochtitlan, the young Nezahualpilli was confirmed by the two Triple Alliance rulers as legitimate ruler of Texcoco, with his older brothers looking on sadly and hopelessly (Alva Ixtlilxochitl 1965, vol. 2:241–250).

Inheritance of property was undoubtedly more broadly defined than inheritance of title or position. Although not well documented for pre-Spanish times, there is an abundance of documentation, primarily wills, for colonial Indians (see Anderson, Berdan, and Lockhart 1976:44–83). These wills, involving both commoners and nobles, probably closely mirror pre-conquest patterns.

Inheritance by relatives of the most critical resources, land and house sites, took at least the following forms:

> father to son
> father to daughter
> mother to son
> mother to daughter
> husband to wife
> brother to older and younger brothers
> grandfather to grandson
> grandfather to granddaughter
> grandmother to grandson
> grandmother to granddaughter
> aunt to nephew
> father-in-law to daughter-in-law
> mother-in-law to son-in-law

Usually, where there were several close relatives, lands and house sites were divided among them, rather than being vested in a single individual. There is no clear difference between nobles and commoners in any of these matters. Especially notable is the wide range of possible heirs; distributed across three generations, land could pass from male to male or female, female to female or male, and even to in-laws. While such broadly defined inheritance patterns probably were present in pre-

Spanish times, the massive Indian depopulation in colonial times perhaps made the actual inheritance of land by distant relatives a more common event.

Household possessions were passed at least from mother to daughter, and luxury status symbols such as feathered military devices from brother to brother. Apparently, tribute from dependent labor also could be inherited. In a 1566 will, a nobleman passed the rights to such tribute to his legitimate wife. The tribute included regular payments in turkeys, cacao beans, tamales, chiles, and wood (*ibid.*: 51).

In sum, rules for transmitting titles, property, and rights were based on kinship. Where fine distinctions within kinship categories were made, they were ideally on the basis of achievement and personal qualities: among sons, the most promising; among brothers, the most capable.

4/Daily life

CULTURAL CODES, DAILY LIFE, AND INTERPERSONAL RELATIONS

Embedded in social classes and surrounded by their kinfolk, the Mexica undertook a variety of daily activities. The interpersonal relations and the content of these daily activities were governed by explicit cultural codes. These codes defined appropriate (as well as inappropriate) behavior, and set out rules for mutual rights and obligations. The codes were in many ways common to all members of the society, but there was also substantial variation according to class, sex, age, and special positions and occupations.

One commonality was the ideal of the "exemplary life." For everyone, it was highly valued to be a follower of this ideal, whose hallmarks were obedience, honesty, discretion, respect, moderation, modesty, and energy. These abstract ideals were translated into more concrete behavior through a number of rules. For example, a nobleman advised his son to live in accordance with eight rules:

First: . . . Thou art not to give thyself excessively to sleep . . . lest thou wilt be named a heavy sleeper . . . a dreamer. . . .

And second: thou art to be prudent in thy travels; peacefully, quietly, tranquilly, deliberately art thou to go. . . . Do not throw thy feet much . . . nor go jumping . . . lest thou be named fool, shameless. . . .

Third: thou art to speak very slowly, very deliberately; thou art not to speak hurriedly, not to pant, nor to squeak, lest it be said of thee that thou art a groaner, a growler, a squeaker. . . .

Fourth: . . . thou art not to peer at one, not to peer into one's face, not to stare at one.

Fifth: Guard, take care of thy ears, of that with which thou hearest. Do not gossip; let what is said remain as said.

Sixth: when thou art summoned, be not summoned twice . . . thou art to do things at only one bidding, for if thou art twice summoned thou wilt be considered as perverse, lazy, languid, negligent, or thou wilt be regarded as one disdainful of orders, as a haughty one. This is the time when the club, the stone should be broken on thee.

Seventh: . . . thou art not to dress vainly, thou art not to array thyself fantastically. . . . Thus art thou to tie on thy cape: do not tie it on so that thou goest tripping over it; neither art thou to shorten thy cape. Moderately art thou to tie it on. Nor art thou to expose thy shoulder.

Eighth: Listen! Above all thou art to be prudent in drink, in food. . . . Thou art not to eat excessively of the required food. . . . Thou art to drink, to eat slowly, calmly, quietly. Thou art not to stir up the pieces, not to dig into the sauce bowl, the basket (Sahagún 1950–1969, book 6:121–124).

These eight rules speak directly of the ideal attributes of moderation and discretion. The Mexica viewed themselves as traveling, in life, along a mountain peak. On each side of the peak was a deep abyss. Any deviation from the "straight and narrow" would result in a fall into the crevices; only moderation and discretion in all things would prevent one from tumbling.

With these ideal attributes and rules as guides, just what did it mean to be a proper Mexica father or mother, ruler or peasant, priest or prostitute? How should these different persons act out their roles in everyday life? For the majority of persons in Mexica society, the primary unit of social interaction was the household. As already seen, this unit, nuclear or joint, varied in both number and types of persons. Consider the various persons in Mexica households.

The Mexica father/husband was responsible for the well-being of his household. He served as provider and administrator of the household's property, and as advisor and teacher of his children (particularly his sons). If he had nephews or nieces who had been orphaned, he also cared for them. It was especially important that he be thrifty and "future oriented," energetic and compassionate. Much of his energy, however, was expended outside the household itself, in field or palace, on battlefields or temple platforms.

The Mexica mother/wife, on the other hand, devoted most of her time and energy to the smooth running of the household. Ideally, she was an attentive mother: diligent, careful, and energetic. She concerned herself with the early education of her daughters. Whether noble or commoner, it was critical that a woman be skilled in weaving and food preparation. A noble girl, upon entering womanhood, was advised of her future duties:

What wilt thou seize upon as thy womanly labors? Is it perhaps the drink, the grinding stone? Is it perhaps the spindle whorl, the weaving stick? Look well to the drink, to the food: how it is prepared, how it is made, how it is improved . . . look well, apply thyself well to the really womanly task, the spindle whorl, the weaving stick (*ibid.*:95–96).

This same noble girl was admonished not to concern herself with "the herbs, the wood, the strands of chile, the cakes of salt, the nitrous soil" (*ibid.*:96), for these were not the province of the noblewoman, but of the commoner. A noblewoman had servants to perform these chores, including travels to the marketplace for provisioning the household. She was a manager, coordinating the activities of a large household, and spending much of her time perfecting the art of weaving (see Figure 4–1a). The commoner woman, described as robust, vigorous, and energetic, would have undertaken the entire spectrum of household chores herself: cleaning, cooking, marketing, and caring for children, as well as doing the spinning and weaving expected of all women.

In a joint household, the married woman frequently resided with in-laws. The potential for conflict in such households may have been considerable, for the "good in-law" is frequently described as one who is a peacemaker and appeaser, while the "bad in-law" is one who sows discord. In addition to the frequent admonitions given to the youths, and the explicit cultural ideals of moderate and tranquil interpersonal relations, there may also have been "avoidance rules." A brother-in-law and sister-in-law addressed each other by special formal terms; the "bad brother-in-law is one who lives in concubinage with his sister-in-law, who lives in concubinage with his mother-in-law. He is covetous" (*ibid.*, book 10:8). Rules demanding that persons in these relationships avoid one another would have reduced the potential for conflict within the extended household.

The ideal child was always respectful, obedient, and humble. Although great emphasis was placed on the training of children, this ideal was not always achieved. For example, a "bad son" may be

. . . one who ignores commands; a fool, lewd, gaudy, vain, untrained; a dunce who accepts not, who receives not the counsel of mother (and) father. Training, teachings, reprimands, corrections go in one ear and out the other (*ibid.*:2).

By the same token, the "bad girl" would be

. . . full of vice, dissolute, proud; a whore, she is showy, pompous, gaudy of dress, garish; she is a loiterer, given to pleasure (*ibid.*:3).

Such women, who would frequent the marketplace for business, were described as vain, gaudy, destitute, and usually drunk (see Figure 4–1*b*). None of these qualities was esteemed in Mexica culture. In a more concrete vein, consider the problem of a wayward son as stated in his father's colonial period will. In addition to taking money owed to some carpenters, the son

. . . took a horse, he just stole it, I am not giving it to him nor have I absolved him; it was worth 5 pesos . . . I his father have not absolved him, for there is a great deal of badness in him. If sometime his badness diminishes, he is to pay me back (Anderson, Berdan, and Lockhart 1976:61).

Children resided in their parents' household; boys later moved out to live in the telpochcalli ("young men's house") of their calpulli, or in a calmecac (elite school); and girls often moved out at marriage. If children were orphaned, they were most commonly reared by uncles and aunts. The orphan's status in the household may have been a rung below that of the other children. A nephew or niece is described as one who "serves in another's house, a servant; one who lives with others." Specifically, a nephew or niece "sweeps the streets, serves, cleans the house, places things in order, arranges things, carries things, accepts reprimands patiently" (Sahagún 1950–1969, book 10:4). At an early age children began to bear the burden of household work; as they became adolescents they would begin to orient more and more of their time and energy to demands made by the state and the many deities.

All relatives had culturally defined duties toward one another. They also had responsibilities and activities outside the household bounds, involving nonkin, the

Figure 4–1: Illustrations of everyday Mexica people and activities, showing Spanish stylistic influence: (a) noblewomen chatting (Historia General de las Cosas de Nueva España 1926:lámina LXIX, illus. 83); (b) a harlot (ibid.:lámina LXXI, illus. 108); (c) a fisherman (ibid.: lámina LXXII, illus. 133); (d) good, diligent farmers (ibid.:lámina LXVIII, illus. 70); (e) a lazy farmer (ibid.:lámina LXVIII, illus. 71).

state, and the deities. This was particularly the case for male members of the society. For priests especially, each day was divided into nine units, providing a temporal frame for their everyday activities. The divisions were of unequal length, and were marked in the temples by the offering of incense to the sun god:

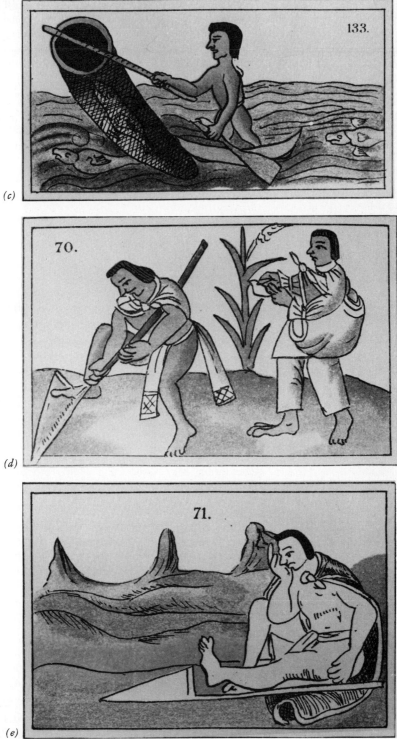

(c)

133.

(d)

70.

(e)

71.

And thus was incense offered four times during the day, and five times during the night: the first time (was) when the sun burst forth. The second time (was) when (it was) time to eat (the first meal). And the third time (was) at midday; and the fourth time (was) when already the sun had set.

And at night, thus was incense offered: the first time, when it was dark; the second time, when it was time to sleep; the third time, when the shell trumpets were sounded; the fourth time, at midnight; and the fifth time, near dawn (*ibid.*, book 2:202).

The degree to which these divisions were significant to people other than priests is not known. However, Soustelle (1961:162) suggests that the temple activities may have signaled times for other events, such as council meetings or court proceedings.

Roughly associated with these periods, the usual Mexica daily round consisted of arising at dawn and setting immediately to work. In midmorning it was customary to have a light meal, consisting of a bowl of *atolli* (maize gruel) for commoners, and the highly prized chocolate for nobles. Following this break, the Mexica returned to work or play, enjoying the main meal at midday. During the heat of the day people would relax, and return to work or diversions for the remainder of the afternoon. It is likely that they enjoyed a brief evening meal, and then retired shortly after sunset. However, during the night, priests arose frequently to offer incense and devotion to the deities, and to sound shell trumpets from temple platforms. Also during the night, close watch was kept over the cities for any possible military threat. The cities around Lake Texcoco were active places by both night and day.

Depending on one's social class, occupation, and age, there were some variations in this daily round. The activities of farmers and fishermen would have been particularly sensitive to the change of seasons (see Figure 4–1c–e). Although they did not meet every day, the high-ranking judges

. . . would seat themselves at daybreak on their mat dais, and immediately begin to hear pleas. The judges' meals were brought to them at an early hour from the royal palace. After eating, they rested for a while, then returned to hear the remaining suitors, staying until two hours before sundown (Zorita 1963:126).

The daily life of priests and their students living in the calmecac also varied from the customary round. Before dawn, all would arise and sweep the temple and its courtyard. Still before dawn, the elder youths went to gather maguey thorns, important in the late-night rituals in the temple. And just before dawn, some of the young men went to gather wood for the fires which burned throughout the night for the priests as they kept vigil. During the day youths worked at making adobes, cultivating fields, or constructing canals, while a few were left behind to guard the calmecac and to take food to those working outside the calmecac. At some unspecified time in the afternoon, all the calmecac residents engaged in penances and other religious devotions. It was undoubtedly at this time that much of the esoteric training associated with the calmecac went on. Beginning at dusk the priests took the maguey spines and carried them several miles to offer them as penance. Continuing from sunset to midnight, the priests, carrying pine torches and incense, offered their maguey spines and blew shell trumpets. At midnight everyone sleeping in the calmecac awoke and prayed, and the highest ranking priests bathed at that time.

In addition to the work involved in making a living, the Mexica enjoyed a number of diversions on a fairly regular basis. Most popular were *tlachtli* (the ball game) and *patolli*. The ball game was an extremely versatile sport played for entertainment as well as for gambling and ritual purposes. The game was played on a ball court that was 100, 150, or 200 feet long, with a line drawn across the center and two rings on either side (see Figure 4–2*a*). The game was played with a hard rubber ball and it was necessary for players to wear gloves, girdles, and hip guards made of deerskin. Even so, players were often badly bruised, and sometimes fatally injured, by the impact of the ball. The players would hit the ball back and forth, being sure to use only their knees and buttocks; the use of any other body part constituted a foul. Fouls were also counted if the ball entered a team's back court, or if a team failed to hit the ball across the center line. However, a team that managed to hit the ball through a ring won an immediate victory. The game required considerable dexterity and adroitness. It was particularly popular among the nobility, who were active players and wagered everything from precious gems to clothing, feathers, cacao, houses, fields, and slaves. Some persons, paupers, played and bet as a means of livelihood, and were rarely if ever prosperous:

> . . . they were forced to gamble their homes, their fields, their corn granaries, their maguey plants. They sold their children in order to bet and even staked themselves and became slaves . . . (Durán 1971:318).

Patolli (see Figure 4–2*b*) was an extremely popular game and was played much like pachisi. Beans, which served as dice, were marked with white dots to indicate numbers. Each player had six pebble counters which were moved on a board according to the throws of the dice. Some persons were apparently addicted to the game and to the gambling which usually accompanied it:

> The gamblers dedicated to this game always went about with the mats under their armpits and with the dice tied up in small cloths . . . it was believed that they [the dice] were mighty . . . they spoke to them and begged them to be favorable, to come to their aid in that game . . . (*ibid.*:304).

It is understandable that patolli players would encourage the dice for, as in the ball game, very costly goods were wagered on this game: fine stones, feathers, elaborately worked clothing, fields, houses, and slaves. For extra luck, a serious player might turn his household grinding stone and griddle upside down and hang his pestle in a corner of the house (Sahagún 1950–1969, book 5:109).

The customary daily routines were occasionally interrupted by special secular and religious events. The secular activities were geared mostly to adult males and consisted mainly of construction projects and daily services to rulers. Commoners, alternating among themselves, provided the labor for these projects and services on a regular basis (see Chapter 2). Warfare was the lot of all men, noble or commoner, and it could take men from their homes for years at a time. This, of course, involved adjustments on the part of all household members (see Chapter 5).

Also punctuating the daily life of all Mexica were ceremonial activities. Some

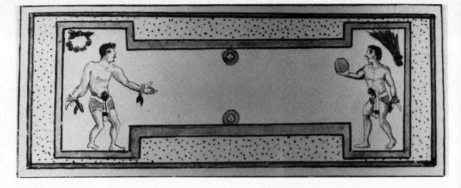

Figure 4–2a: Aztec diversion: A colonial representation of the ball game. Note the jade necklace and precious feathers which were wagered (BOOK OF THE GODS AND RITES and THE ANCIENT CALENDAR, by Fray Diego Durán, translated and edited by Fernando Horcasitas and Doris Heyden. Copyright 1971 by the University of Oklahoma Press, publishing division of the University, plate 34).

Figure 4–2b: Another Aztec game—patolli. The four beans were used as dice, and stones were moved along the board. Costly goods such as necklaces and feathers were bet on the game (Historia General de las Cosas de Nueva España 1926:lámina XLVIII, illus. 63).

of these, like the 18 monthly ceremonies of the solar year, were predictable. These events generally involved fasting followed by singing, dancing, feasting, and offerings (including sacrificial victims) to the deities. Not everyone participated in all these ceremonies with equal intensity. For example, children were especially important in the ceremonies of the third month, merchants were most active in rituals of the ninth month, and young warriors and harlots took center stage by singing and dancing in the eighth monthly festival.

Besides the monthly festivals, less elaborate rituals were associated with the 260-day ritual calendar, or *tonalpohualli* (see Chapter 7). Like the monthly ceremonies, most of these rituals consisted of some fasting, dancing, singing, and feasting. But the focus of these rituals was on offerings to the deities. Gods were offered incense, flowers, perfumes, ornaments, and quails; their images were adorned with papers; and amaranth likenesses of them were made. Human sacrifices and bloodletting were also common aspects of these rituals. In some rituals everyone participated, such as the one on the day Four Movement, when all persons offered blood drawn from their ears to the sun. Other days emphasized certain occupations: Painters and weavers celebrated the day Seven Flower, merchants openly displayed their wealth on Four Wind, and those who gained their livelihoods from water (fishermen, water sellers) revered the goddess Chalchiuhtlicue on the day One Water (see Chapter 6).

Certain special unscheduled events also changed the pace of daily life. The dedication of a temple or the funeral or installation of a ruler required special ceremonies and services. These events normally took several days and involved elaborate, exciting, and time-consuming ceremonies. Extensive special provisions also were required for these occasions. For instance, to supply the banquets associated with the installation of the *tlatoani* Moctezuma Xocoyotzin in 1502, great loads of many types of animals, wild and domesticated birds, chiles, fish, fruit, and cacao were brought to Tenochtitlan daily by 1000 *macehualtin*. These provisions were drawn from the empire as a whole, and producing and transporting them would have required many people to take on additional activities.

Life cycle events also caused pauses in everyday routines. The major events celebrated were birth and the naming ceremony, entering and leaving the calmecac or telpochcalli (for males), marriage, old age, and death. The manner in which the Mexica passed through these crucial stages in the life cycle is treated in the next section.

LIFE CYCLE AND EDUCATION

Pregnancy and Birth   Childbearing was the essence of Mexica womanhood. As the man gained honor and renown by going valiantly into battle, so the woman gained honor and respect by bearing children. Her battle was comparable to the man's battle. If each battle was courageously fought and won, the prizes were handsome: special status and regalia for the man, the baby and respect for the woman. If the battle was lost, and each died honorably, outstanding rewards awaited them in the afterlife: The man followed the sun in its daily rise to the zenith; the woman accompanied the sun from its zenith to its descent in the west.

At the first realization that conception had taken place, a banquet was arranged. Numerous relatives of the father- and mother-to-be attended and enjoyed much eating, drinking, and displays of flowers and tubes of tobacco. This banquet was the setting for extensive orations and eloquent responses among the elders, the pregnant woman, her husband, her parents, and her parents-in-law. The pregnant woman was especially reminded that she should thank the gods for the gift they had given her:

> And speak not to thyself; say not: "Already I am carrying something; already I am this way; already I am pregnant." And do not become proud, do not become arrogant! Our lord will know of that within thee; he knoweth of things, he seeth within the rock, the tree. Soon something will befall thee; our lord will bring about for us the death of our child (*ibid.*; book 6:141–142).

Because the gods had favored her, she should take care to not in any way endanger or abort "the precious necklace, the quetzal feather" within her womb. A great deal of practical advice was transmitted on this occasion. The pregnant woman was not to lift heavy things, nor overdo enjoying the sweatbath, nor overindulge in sex. This last was considered particularly dangerous by the Mexica, for

> . . . it is said: "Thou wilt die in childbirth. For this will cause the baby to be stuck . . . for it [the semen] exceedeth glue in adhesiveness. It is so adhesive, so viscous, that thou wilt thereby perish" (*ibid.*:143).

Additional precautions were advised for the duration of the pregnancy. The expectant mother was not to eat tamales that had become stuck to the cooking pot, for the baby would likewise adhere to her womb. She was not to walk about at night; but if she must, she was to place some ash, a pebble, or wormwood in her bosom to protect the child from night-wandering apparitions. She was restrained from gazing at a hanged person, lest her baby be born with the umbilical cord wound around its neck. Nor was she to look at an eclipse of the sun or moon, or at the rising moon, since this would cause the child to be harelipped. An obsidian knife placed in the woman's bosom, however, would provide protection from this last threat.

In the seventh or eighth month of pregnancy, the woman's relatives reassembled and again feasted. The purpose of this occasion was to hire and consult with a midwife. The midwife prepared a sweatbath for the pregnant woman, and massaged her abdomen to arrange the baby properly in the womb. In addition to the precautions already related, the midwife issued stern commands to the mother-to-be and her relatives: The expectant mother was to eat well and not to be denied anything she desired; she was not to sleep in the daytime; not to chew chicle; nor look at anything frightening, offending, or red. The Mexica felt that failure to observe these rules could result in a difficult birth, birth defects, stillbirth, or the death of the mother.

When the woman went into labor, the midwife tried to speed the process by bathing her in the sweatbath and having her drink an herbal expellent (*ciuapatli* root, *nopalli* leaves, or chia). If this did not succeed, some ground-up opossum tail, reputed to be a powerful expellent, was given to her. If this also failed, the midwife suspended the woman, shaking and kicking her in the back. In some cases, this also failed to induce delivery, and the baby died in the womb. When this happened

> . . . the midwife inserted an obsidian knife within the woman. There she dismembered the baby; she drew it forth piece by piece. Thus the parent was yet relieved (*ibid.*:157).

If the mother died trying to give birth, she was revered as a goddess. When her relatives went to bury her, they had to guard her carefully, since young warriors eagerly sought her middle finger and locks of her hair. These they would place on their shields when they went into battle to assure themselves of courage and success in capturing enemy warriors. Similarly, thieves tried to steal her left forearm, which reputedly assisted them in their "business."

When a baby was born, the midwife cut the umbilical cord and buried the afterbirth in a corner of the house. The umbilical cord of a baby girl was buried by the hearth, symbolizing her lifelong attachment to the home. A boy's umbilical cord was dried and later left on a field of battle, thereby dedicating him to service in warfare. The midwife then bathed and swaddled the infant. During all of this she spoke softly to the baby, welcoming it and introducing it to the Mexica view of life:

> Precious necklace, precious feather, precious green stone, precious bracelet, precious turquoise, thou wert created in the place of duality, the place (above) the nine heavens. . . . Thou hast come to reach the earth, the place of torment, the place of pain, where it is hot, where it is cold, where the wind bloweth. It is the place of one's affliction, of one's weariness, a place of thirst, a place of hunger, a place where one freezeth, a place of weeping. It is not true that it is a good place; it is a place of weeping, a place of sorrow, a place where one suffereth (*ibid.*:176–177).

Shortly thereafter the infant and mother were visited by relatives, who welcomed the child with eloquent greetings and proclamations, and admonished the mother to be careful with herself and the baby (see Figure 4–3*a*). This visiting lasted up to 10 or 20 days. Also immediately following the birth the parents consulted with a soothsayer, who read the child's fate in the astrological "book of days," or *tonalamatl* (see Chapter 7). He assessed the child's future according to the day and time of its birth, predicting whether the child would be honorable or disreputable, wealthy or destitute. The soothsayer also determined the day on which the infant should be bathed and named; particularly "good" days were chosen for this important ritual event.

The bathing ceremony took place in the early morning, with relatives of the baby present (see Figure 4–3*b*). While uttering speeches of dedication, the midwife ritually bathed the infant in the courtyard of the house. If the child was a boy, the midwife then offered him the paraphernalia of a warrior: a little shield, bow, and four arrows, along with a cloak and a loin cloth. If the child was a girl, the midwife gave her items symbolizing her future duties: a little spindle whorl, batten, basket, spinning bowl, skeins, shuttle, as well as a skirt and tunic (*ibid.*: 201). The child was then given a name and dressed. Young children went running off, shouting the new name to the community at large. The baby was carried inside to its cradle, and the adults enjoyed a great deal of feasting and drinking. If the household was a wealthy one, the event was done on a grand scale; if a poor one, the feasting was more modest (see Chapter 3).

Children were frequently named after the day of their birth, especially children of commoners. Names such as Ome Coatl ("Two Serpent"), Macuilli Tochtli ("Five Rabbit") or Naui Cuetzpallin ("Four Lizard") were prevalent. Other names might be given, particularly among the nobility. For example, a girl might be named Miauaxiuitl ("Turquoise Maize Flower") or Quiauhxochitl ("Rain Flower"); a boy might bear a name such as Itzcoatl ("Obsidian Serpent"), Quauhcoatl ("Eagle

Figure 4–3a: An elderly relative visits a new mother and child. The speech scrolls indicate that the visitor is offering greetings, admonitions, or other formalized speeches (Historia General de las Cosas de Nueva España 1926: lámina XXXI, illus. 85).

Figure 4–3b: The bathing ceremony (ibid.:lámina XXVI, illus. 41).

Serpent"), Quauhtlatoa ("Talking Eagle"), or Moctezuma ("Angry Lord"). Fray
Diego Durán speculates that the child who later became the ruler Moctezuma
Xocoyotzin displayed a scowling countenance when being named and so was
dubbed "Angry Lord" (1971:424). When the Spanish friars arrived in Mexico,
they baptized Indians and gave each a Christian name. The Indians usually maintained at least part of their original name as a surname. In the colonial period, this
syncretism produced names such as Juan Icnoyotl ("John Misery"), Francisco Xico
("Francis Bee"), Juan Tzonen ("John Hairy"), and Pedro Tochtli ("Peter Rabbit") (Anderson, Berdan, and Lockhart 1976:84–85).

Childhood   In their earliest years of life, little was expected of children. They
remained close to home in their parents' care. The "good child" is simply described
as healthy, strong, and happy; the "bad child" as sickly, maimed, and violent in
temperament. However, at about age five or six, overt attempts were begun to
educate and train children. It was crucial that nobles and commoners alike acquire
the qualities of obedience, respect, and honesty. When walking about, noble boys
were always to be accompanied by "pages" whose duty it was to assure the proper
conduct of each noble child—to see

> . . . that his conversation should be proper; that he should respect and show
> reverence to others—(when) perchance he somewhere might chance to meet a
> judge, or a leading militia officer, or a seasoned warrior, or someone of lesser
> rank; or a revered old man, or a respected old woman; or someone who was
> poor. He should greet him and bow humbly. He said: "Come hither, my beloved
> grandfather; let me bow before thee." . . . And when the young boy thus
> saluted others, they praised him highly for it (*ibid.*, book 8:71).

In addition to cultivating obedience, respect, and honesty, commoner boys were
admonished to work diligently:

> Do what pertains to your office. Labor, sow and plant your trees, and live by the
> sweat of your brow. Do not cast off your burden, or grow faint, or be lazy; for
> if you are negligent and lazy, you will not be able to support yourself or your
> wife and children (Zorita 1963:145–146).

These boys' duties and chores began early in life: At age four they were expected
to help by carrying water, at age five by carrying bundles to market and by toting
firewood, at age six by continuing to carry goods to the market and to assist by
collecting grains of maize in the marketplace,[1] and at age seven by fishing with a
net. These types of activities apparently continued through age fourteen, for at
ages thirteen and fourteen boys are at least still carrying firewood and fishing, as
well as paddling canoes (see Figure 4–4). Under other conditions, a boy might
have concentrated on cultivation techniques or the art of featherworking, rather
than fishing.

---

[1] Sahagún says that "if they saw or came upon dried grains of maize lying scattered on the
ground, then they quickly gathered them up. They said: 'Our sustenance suffereth: it lieth
weeping. If we should not gather it up, it would accuse us before our lord'" (1950–1969,
book 5:184).

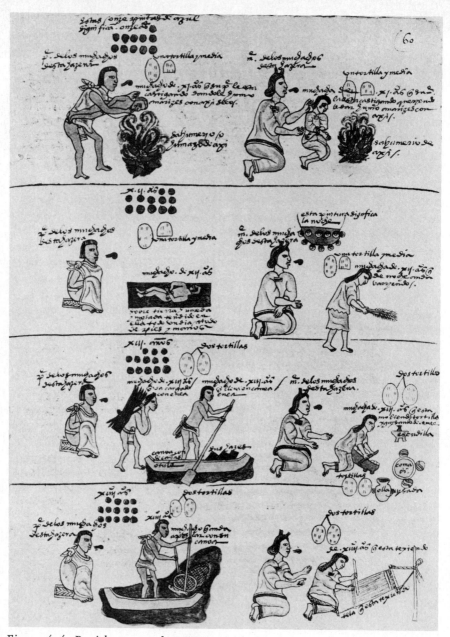

Figure 4–4: Punishments and training of children, ages eleven through fourteen (Codex Mendoza 1938, vol. 3:folio 60).

An important way of instilling moral codes and practical knowledge was through admonitions. These lengthy orations inculcated the child with the Mexica view of the world as a painful and dangerous place, and offered advice on how to cope in such a world: Proceed always with moderation, humility and diligence. The specific rules of etiquette described at the start of this chapter were also emphasized to the child to provide him with guidelines for behavior and survival in a world that offered only fear and pain.

Punishments for misbehavior were severe. The mildest punishment took the form of a scolding. The child might be compared to an Otomí, a people held in very low regard by the Mexica:

> Now thou art an Otomí. Now thou art a miserable Otomí. O Otomí, how is it that thou understandest not? Art thou perchance an Otomí? Art thou perchance a real Otomí? Not only art thou like an Otomí, thou art a real Otomí, a miserable Otomí, a green-head, a thick-head, a big tuft of hair over the back of the head, an Otomí blockhead . . . (Sahagún 1950–1969, book 10:178).

If scolding failed to produce the desired results, more direct measures were employed. At age eight, a boy was warned about the use of maguey spines for punishment, and at age nine, the spines were used; at age ten, a boy might be beaten with a stick; at age eleven, he might be held over a fire and forced to inhale "chile-smoke"; and at age twelve, he might be tied hand and foot and required to lie on a wet mat (see Figure 4–4).

A young boy's training, whether on a moral or practical plane, took place in a family context. Among the nobility, this instruction involved not only the polygynous family but also a wide array of nursemaids, pages, and servants. Whether noble or commoner, the father and grandfather were especially charged with the responsibilities of teaching, advising, admonishing, and punishing.

When a boy reached the age of ten, he began to allow a tuft of hair to grow on the back of his head. He continued to wear this long tuft of hair until he succeeded in capturing an enemy warrior in battle, usually not at least until his teen years. It was considered shameful for a youth who had competed in several battles to still be wearing the tuft. At the very least, a youth risked being insulted by girls during the monthly celebration of Uey Toçoztli. If a youth spoke to a girl in the ceremonial procession, she might retort by saying:

> Verily, he with the long (tangled) hair of a youth also speaketh! Dost thou indeed speak? Be thou concerned over how may be removed thy tuft of hair, thou with the long hair! Thou with the evil-smelling, stinking forelock, art thou not only a woman like me? . . . (*ibid.*, book 2:61).

These jeerings sparked the boys to more daring action on the battlefield, for it was painfully insulting to be called a "big tuft of hair over the back of the head."

The pattern for rearing girls was similar to that for boys, although the girls' activities were quite different. Beginning at age four, girls were instructed in spinning, which apparently continued through at least age ten. By age twelve, a girl's duties included the sweeping of the house and street at night. At thirteen, she was taught how to grind maize, make tortillas, and prepare other foods; at fourteen she was instructed in the essential task of weaving. Certainly, by the time she was fourteen years of age, a girl had gained considerable practice and proficiency in the essentials of her life's work: spinning, weaving, and cooking.

Girls, like boys, were also instructed in the moral codes of Mexica culture. A girl was advised to be obedient, discreet, and chaste. Admonitions were the primary means of instilling these virtues; these were generally offered by her mother and other, elderly, female relatives. Her father, however, also took some responsibility for instructing his daughter, emphasizing prudence, chastity, and dedication to her future husband, and pointing out the skills she must acquire as preparation for marriage.

Between twelve and thirteen, some noble girls spent a year of service in the temples:

> They lived in chastity and seclusion as maidens who had been assigned to the service of the god. Their only work was sweeping and sprinkling the temple and cooking the daily food for the idol and for the ministers of the temple . . . (Durán 1971:83).

As with boys, punishments for girls were severe. At age eight, a girl was warned about the use of maguey spines as punishment; at age nine, maguey spines might be applied to the girl's hands for some misdeed; at age ten, she might be beaten with a stick for spinning cotton poorly; and at age eleven, she might be required to inhale "chile-smoke" (see Figure 4–4).

Formal Education   In Mexica society, education outside the home was primarily geared toward males. However, girls did attend the *cuicacalli* ("house of song"), and some noble girls underwent training as priestesses.

Apparently, males and females, nobles and commoners, all attended a cuicacalli between the ages of twelve and fifteen (see bottom of Figure 4–5).[2] The cuicacalli were adjacent to temples, and served both as the residences of instructors and as the "school" building. They were large buildings, elaborately decorated, with rooms surrounding an open courtyard where dances were performed.

At the cuicacalli, "Nothing was taught there to youths and maidens but singing, dancing, and the playing of musical instruments" (*ibid.*:289). Attendance and activities were highly regulated. Instruction began an hour before sunset; boys and girls were assembled in their calpulli by elderly men and women, and all proceeded to the cuicacalli. There the students danced and sang long into the night, under the watchful eyes of the instructors. Instruction in the cuicacalli served as an important means of transmitting knowledge and beliefs. Not only were song and dance essential to the proper performance of most religious rituals and ceremonies, but a vast amount of information was contained in the songs themselves. Religious in content, the songs praise the deities and tell of creation, of life and death, and of the relationship between mortals and the deities.

All noble boys, at least by age fifteen,[3] attended the calmecac for their formal education (see top of Figure 4–5). The calmecac were attached to temples, and there were at least seven of them in Tenochtitlan alone. It is possible, however, that every major temple had a calmecac associated with it. Some of the calmecac pro-

---

[2] Durán (1971:290) gives the ages of attendance as twelve to fourteen; the Codex Mendoza (1938, vol. 3:part III, folio 61) gives age fifteen.

[3] The sources disagree on the age at which boys entered the schools. The Codex Mendoza (1938, vol. 3:part III, folio 61) indicates age fifteen; Sahagún (1950–1969, book 8:71) gives age ten, twelve, or thirteen; Zorita (1963:135) mentions age five; and Torquemada (1969, vol. 2:222) age five or six. Perhaps the age of entrance varied with the specific calmecac or course of study.

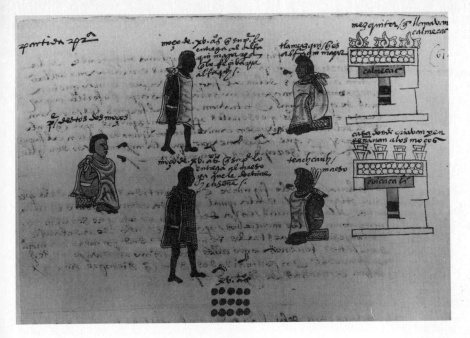

Figure 4–5: At about age fifteen, boys entered the calmecac (top) or the cuicacalli (bottom) (Codex Mendoza 1938, vol. 3:folio 61).

vided highly specialized training. For example, the calmecac associated with the temple of Camaxtli (hunting deity) trained youths as skillful hunters; education at the temple of Tezcatlipoca (an omnipotent deity) was oriented toward preparing noble and common youths to become priests. In other calmecac youths were trained for a variety of futures, including the priesthood. The specific education received by a boy undoubtedly varied according to the calmecac he attended: Each deity had its own special set of ceremonies and ritual paraphernalia, and each placed different demands on the mortals dedicated to its worship. As a general idea of calmecac duties and activities, the account given earlier in this chapter may be taken as a guide. Much of the day and night were spent in hard physical work and penances. However, it was critical that the boys acquire a great deal of esoteric knowledge as well. They were taught

> . . . the songs which they called the gods' songs. They were inscribed in the books. And well were all taught the reckoning of the days, the book of dreams, and the book of years (Sahagún 1950–1969, book 3:65).

Orations, songs, histories, calendrics, and the interpretation of dreams and omens were committed to memory in the calmecac. It was essential that the student learn the hieroglyphic writing system, for books were used in teaching the many arts—military, mechanical, astrological, religious, and legal (Durán 1971:293).

The martial arts were included in the calmecac curriculum. This instruction was critical, since a nobleman was expected to be skilled, courageous, and successful on the battlefield. This instruction began by at least age fifteen, and included some direct experience:

> And then they took him to the wars. The seasoned warriors went taking great care of him, lest somewhere he might be lost. And they taught him well how to guard himself with a shield; how one fought; how a spear was fended off with a shield. And when a battle was joined . . . they taught him well and made him see how he might take a captive (Sahagún 1950–1969, book 8:72).

Deviations from the approved pattern of activity were severely punished. Students were admonished by the priests, whose exhortations on a good and proper life sometimes failed:

> If at times it appeared that one perhaps drank wine, or was given to women, or committed a great (fault), then they went to apprehend him. No mercy was shown. He was burned, or strangled, or cast into the fire alive or shot with arrows. And if he sinned only lightly, they drew blood from his ears, his flanks, or his thighs with maguey spines or with a (sharpened) bone (*ibid.*, book 3:64).

Faults deserving of the latter punishment would be failure to speak well or to greet others properly.

Formal education was also compulsory for commoner boys. By age fifteen, a boy was working and sleeping in the telpochcalli ("young men's house") of his calpulli. The major instructional emphasis of this school was military, for adult male commoners formed the backbone of the imperial military force. As in the calmecac, these boys spent a great deal of time at physical labor. They worked either in the telpochcalli itself, sweeping and laying fires, or in the community at large:

> And they went about together where they had anything to do—perchance (preparing) mud (for adobes, making) walls, cultivating the soil, (digging) canals; they did these going all together, or they divided up. And they went into the forest, and gathered and carried on their backs . . . torches for the song house (*ibid.*:54).

When a noble or commoner youth reached the age of twenty, he was considered sufficiently educated to assume adult roles. He left his calmecac or telpochcalli and prepared for marriage.

Marriage   The establishment of marriage ties, in its ideal form, necessitated an elaborate and time-consuming procedure. The youth's parents took the first step in arranging the marriage. Among nobles,

> . . . (The father) said: "Poor is this, our youth. Let us seek a woman for him, lest he somewhere do something. He may somewhere molest a woman; he may commit adultery. For it is his nature; he is matured" (*ibid.*, book 6:127).

A feast was then prepared by the parents, consisting of tamales, chocolate, and various sauces. Those who had been the youth's teachers were invited, and they ceremonially released the youth from their care. Only then, apparently, was there discussion by the youth's kin of the appropriate choice of wife. In actual practice, this may have been discussed at length prior to the initial events. Discussions may or may not have included the youth himself, whom the documents consistently omit from any role in this ideal decision-making process.

Once a decision was made, elderly women who served as matchmakers went to the home of the chosen girl, arguing their case to the girl's parents. This procedure was repeated for several days, with no response expected (nor received) from the girl's parents. When (and if) an agreement was reached, the elderly male relatives of the young man consulted the soothsayers. These learned specialists determined the most appropriate day for the ceremony. Days labeled Reed, Monkey, Crocodile, Eagle, and House were considered good days for any marriage ceremony (see Chapter 7). Elaborate preparations for the event were then made at the bride's home:[4]

> . . . ground cacao was prepared, flowers were secured, smoking tubes were purchased, tubes of tobacco were prepared, sauce bowls and pottery cups and baskets were purchased. Then maize was ground. . . . Then tamales were prepared . . . perhaps three days or two days the women made tamales . . . (*ibid.*:129).

Invitations to the feast were offered to high-status, established persons, as well as to the groom's peer group. Etiquette at the ceremony appears to have been rigidly defined. First the "masters of the youths" from the schools arrived and ate and drank; then old men and women arrived and were provided with food, drink, flowers, and tobacco. Women then arrived carrying gifts of cloaks and maize. All day the guests ate and drank, and drank, and drank.

Toward sunset, the bride-to-be was bathed, decorated with red feathers and dyes, and placed on a reed mat in front of the hearth. The old men of the groom's family then spoke to her:

> Forever now leave childishness, girlishness; no longer art thou to be like a child. . . . Be most considerate of one; regard one with respect, speak well, greet one well. By night look to, take care of the sweeping, the laying of the fire. Arise in the deep of night. Do not embarrass us; do not reject us as old men, do not reject thy mothers as old women (*ibid.*:130).

After humbly enumerating her own inadequacies, the girl was carried by the groom's female relatives to his house. The procession included kin of both the bride and groom, walking in two rows with some carrying torches (see bottom of Figure 4–6). This part of the ceremony gave the event a particularly public aspect, and has some appearance of "bride capture" by the groom's relatives.

Arriving at their destination, bride and groom were placed on a mat in front of the hearth, the groom's mother presenting gifts of clothing to her new daughter-in-law, the bride's mother giving gifts, also of clothing, to her son-in-law. The matchmakers then reappeared, tying the couple together by their garments (see top of Figure 4–6). After being solemnly fed tamales, they were led by the matchmakers to a private room. The couple remained alone in this room for four days, guarded outside by the matchmakers, who did not refrain from indulging in copious quantities of pulque. The bride's parents apparently also remained at the home of the groom during this period. The couple were not to consummate their marriage until the end of these four days. On the fifth day, elaborate festivities again took place, with feasting, dancing, and exchanges of gifts by in-laws. Both bride and groom were admonished and reminded of their new duties and responsibilities.

---

[4] This quotation undoubtedly describes the nature and extent of preparations for a marriage between nobles; marriages involving commoners would have been on a less extravagant scale.

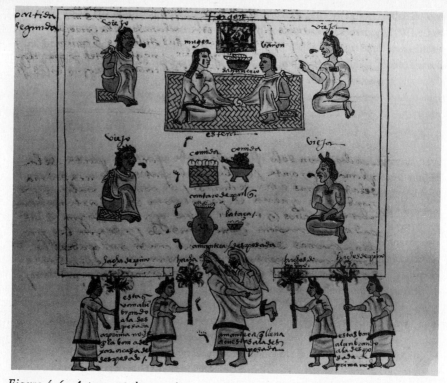

Figure 4–6: Aspects of the marriage ceremony. Above, the tying of garments before the hearth, accompanied by the admonitions of elders. Below, the groom's female relatives carry the bride to the groom's household (Codex Mendoza 1938, vol. 3: folio 61).

The documents do not indicate how often or to what extent these ideal arrangements were met. Undoubtedly, it often would have been difficult for many persons to strictly adhere to all the formalities. Surely commoners, having less wealth, had a more troublesome time than nobles in meeting the ideal requirements. Also, young pipiltin, or nobles, were allowed to have concubines before they married, with no obligation to marry a concubine. If a child were born under such an arrangement, the youth had to decide either to marry or to leave the girl. Some of these relationships, then, could result in marriage; whether the events and ceremony took the same form as the one described above is not at all clear.

With marriage bonds established, the young couple undertook expected adult responsibilities. Primary among these were the establishment of a household and the raising of children. Almost all women spent most of their adult lives maintaining home and hearth. Adult men served as heads of households and as leaders and participants in community activities. Their lives proceeded much as described in the opening section of this chapter. If a person survived the dangers of war and the sacrificial stone, the threats of illness, and the vagaries of accidents, he or she entered a stage in the life cycle which offered special rewards and responsibilities.

Old Age With the onset of old age, a Mexica became white-haired, wrinkled, decrepit, and was frequently portrayed as acting childishly. At extreme old age, a great-great-grandparent was "one who trembles with age, a cougher, a totterer" (*ibid.*, book 10:5). It was important that, on reaching old age, a person leave behind a respected legacy. The honored great-grandfather, for example, "leaves a good reputation, a good example," and the respected great-grandmother "is accorded glory, acclaim by her descendants" (*ibid.*). The elderly did not just look back at past deeds, but devoted themselves to managing households, teaching, advising, and punishing the young. For example,

> The good old man (is) famous, honored, an advisor, a reprehender, a castigator, a counselor, an indoctrinator. He tells, he relates ancient lore; he leads an exemplary life (*ibid.*:11).

Most of the admonitions delivered to young people were indeed offered by old men and women. Not all of these persons, however, took their responsibilities to heart. The "bad old man," for example, was "a gaudy old man, a luxurious old man, an old fool, a liar. He invents falsehoods" (*ibid.*).

Important in a great many ceremonies, the elderly were accorded special privileges. Paramount among these was the right to drink to excess. Public drunkenness was strongly prohibited among the rest of the population, but old men and women could become intoxicated with no fear of reprisals (see Figure 4–7).

Death and Conceptions of the Afterlife If a Mexica suspected the immediacy of his or her own death and had committed some serious undetected crime in his or her lifetime, this person would offer a confession. Since confession could be made only once, a Mexica was careful not to confess prematurely, for there would be no chance for forgiveness of any future misdeed. The ritual was arranged by and conducted in the presence of a *tlapouhqui*, or reader of the sacred books. The confession itself was directed toward two deities: Tezcatlipoca, the omnipotent, and Tlazolteotl. Tlazolteotl was also called Tlaelquani, for while she instilled im-

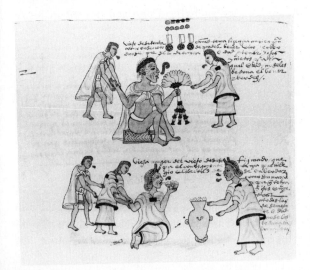

Figure 4–7: Elderly men and women were allowed the luxury of drinking to the point of inebriation (Codex Mendoza 1938, vol. 3:folio 71).

proper desire and love in mortals, she also was the "eater of filth" and forgave them:

> It was said: evil and perverseness, debauched living—these Tlaçolteutl offered, inflamed, inspired. And likewise she forgave. At her whim, she removed the corruption; she cleansed, she washed (*ibid.*, book 1:8).

After the penitent admitted the misdeeds, the tlapouhqui would order some punishment, usually fasting and piercing the tongue with maguey spines. The penitent was now properly prepared for death.

Both the funeral rites and the future of the person in the hereafter depended on the manner in which he or she died. Burial was the lot of persons who died in the realm of the water deities: by drowning, being struck by lightning, or suffering leprosy, dropsy, or gout. For one who drowned,

> . . . they [the priests] accorded the dead one much honor as they took him. They bore him away upon a litter to bury him at Ayauhcalco. They went blowing their flutes for him; they built him a covering of reeds (*ibid.*, book 11:68).

Women who died in childbirth were also buried. Since parts of their bodies were ambitiously sought by young warriors and thieves, their funeral processions and graves were closely guarded by their families.

If a high-ranking person was buried, he was set upon a chair (*icpalli*) and surrounded by his spear, shields, and precious gems and metals (Anonymous Conqueror 1971:398). Likewise, if a merchant was buried, he was accompanied by his wares and wealth; poor commoners had more meager burials.

Cremation, however, was more usual. The body was carefully and thoroughly wrapped in cloth, making a compact bundle. Depending on the status of the deceased, the "mummy" might also be ornamented with paper adornments and feathers (see Figure 4–8). After the body was burned, the remains were placed in a container and buried. Along with the ashes, the deceased's possessions were also buried.

Other aspects of the funeral rites, both for burial and cremation, were roughly similar for everyone. First the corpse was carefully washed and dressed in his or her finest clothes. Then,

> Dirges . . . were chanted, and (the dead) were mourned, great ceremonies taking place in their honor. At these funerals (people) ate and drank; and if (the deceased) had been a person of quality, lengths of cloth were presented to those who had attended the funeral. (The dead man) was laid out in a room for four days until (mourners) arrived from the places where he had friends. Gifts were brought to the dead man (Durán 1971:122).

If a person died in distant parts—a merchant, for example—his family mourned him for four days. At the end of this period, the family members "washed their heads with soap. Thus it was said, the deceased was bathed; and thereby they destroyed and banished their grief" (Sahagún, 1950–1969, book 4:69). They then made a statue of bound pine logs in the deceased's likeness, decorating it with paper ornaments. If he had died in battle, the statue was displayed in the calpulli temple for one day and then burned at midnight. If he died in some other, less

Figure 4–8: A deceased merchant wrapped in cloth and ornaments and accompanied by his precious gems, gold, feathers, and jaguar skins (Codex Magliabecchiano, in the series CODICES SELECTI, vol. XXIII, Akademische Druck- u. Verlagsanstalt, Graz 1970, folio 68).

glorious fashion, they displayed and burned his statue at his home, and just before sunset (*ibid.*:69–70).

A variety of futures awaited the Mexica in the hereafter, again depending on the way in which they had died. The most exalted afterlife went to warriors and to women who had died bearing children. Warriors who died in battle or who had been sacrificed accompanied the sun on its journey from its rising to the zenith. After traveling with the sun for four years, they returned to earth as hummingbirds or butterflies. Women who died in childbirth carried the sun on a feathered litter from the zenith to its setting. At sunset they delivered the sun to those who dwelt in Mictlan, the place of the dead (see Chapter 6). These same women then roamed about as *cihuapipiltin* or *cihuateteo*, women goddesses. They were greatly feared, for they might suddenly appear, especially at crossroads, and cause serious fright and bodily harm (*ibid.*, book 1:6).

Those who had been singled out by the water deities also enjoyed a happy afterlife. They lived in the comfortable and verdant gardens of Tlalocan, a divine place of happiness and ease (see Chapter 6).

Most Mexica, however, descended to Mictlan, a place of dark emptiness. This underworld was divided into nine layers, through which the deceased had to travel. The journey took four years, and the deceased was assisted by a yellow dog, his worldly possessions, and plenty of food, all cremated with him. Aid was also given by survivors, who made periodic offerings for the deceased. If the deceased was a nobleman, supposedly his servants were killed and cremated in order to prepare his food and serve him in the underworld. The deceased traveled through mountains, past a serpent and a green lizard, across eight deserts, over eight hills, through the "place of the obsidian-bladed winds," and across the "place of the nine rivers," finally arriving at the deepest layer. The place of the obsidian-bladed winds was believed to be the most difficult part of the journey. The deceased gained some measure of protection by covering themselves with the worldly possessions burned with them; this included everything from shields to spindles. Those who were destitute and poor in life had little protection here and suffered a great deal.

On the whole, nobles and those who upheld the ideals of Mexica life were given proper funerals and had relatively easy journeys through the land of the dead. Less funerary attention was given to those who were indigent, committed serious unforgiven crimes, or lived shameless lives; these suffered very painful journeys.

SOCIAL CONTROL AND LAW

Not all Mexica were always humble, hard working, and law abiding as the statements on ideal behavior might suggest. While old men were charged with relating ancient lore, some lied. Farmers were to be diligent and productive, but some were lazy and negligent. Women, who were admonished to be chaste and virtuous, occasionally became harlots. And judges and officials were at times dishonest or accepted bribes. Some people committed adultery, became thieves, or committed homicide.

In general, wayward behavior was discouraged and controlled through the enculturation process. The frequent admonitions and exhortations served to instruct and remind individual Mexica of their roles, responsibilities, and proper behavior. When these means failed, the elders and other instructors might resort to threats of supernatural or physical punishments.

Threats of punishments from the supernatural invariably meant physical chastisement during the person's lifetime. No threat of punishment after death could be invoked in Mexica culture, since the type of afterlife was determined primarily by how a person died, not by how he or she lived. Threats of punishments from the gods were most commonly used for religious affronts. For example, the god Macuilxochitl ("Five Flower") would punish those who broke the rule of sexual abstinence during fasting by visiting them with venereal diseases, hemorrhoids, boils, and piles. Or if the god Omacatl ("Two Reed") was not properly cared for and revered, he became angry and visited the offender with physical discomfort: ". . . food stuck in his throat; the water wound about the roof of his mouth like a snake. His gullet was troubled when he ate. And if he walked, he stumbled and fell" (*ibid.*:14). Or if the Tepictoton ("Little Molded Ones") were offended by improper ceremonial observances, they would cause lame and misshapen limbs, or trembling feet, eyes or lips. If a person were afflicted with these ailments, it was clear to everyone that he or she had irked the "Little Molded Ones." And for the rites venerating the goddess Xochiquetzal ("Flower–Quetzal Feather"), all were to wash themselves in the rivers. The priests warned

. . . that those who did not would suffer ills and contagious diseases, such as pustules, leprosy, and malformed hands. It was thought that these ills appeared because of sin and that the gods sent them as a vengeance. Through fear (of these ills) everyone, whether a child or a grown man, went to bathe at dawn (Durán 1971:245).

The Mexica also had secular laws defining acceptable and unacceptable behavior, and legally sanctioned punishments for breaking the laws. The law was rigorous and strict, the punishments swift and severe. For seemingly mild misdeeds, such as improper speech or disrespectful behavior, a Mexica would customarily be pierced with maguey spines. If a Mexica sang poorly, danced out of step, or played a musical instrument out of tune, he would be imprisoned, and perhaps die there (Sahagún 1950–1969, book 8:56).

Drunkenness was believed to be at the root of much improper and criminal behavior. It caused quarrelling, boasting, and poverty. It led one to commit adultery and to steal. No wonder, then, that public drunkenness was severely punished. A known drunken priest or official could suffer the death penalty. If a high-ranking official became drunk, but without public disgrace, he merely forfeited his titles and office. Commoners were punished less severely for first offenses: Their heads were shaved in public and their houses demolished. A second offense resulted in the death penalty. Drunkenness was viewed as a serious offense, one that could lead to social discord and criminal behavior. Yet drunken behavior was explained fatalistically, being associated with the ritual day Two Rabbit: "It was said: 'So is his rabbit. Thus was his day sign; in this way did the wine gods manifest themselves on him'" (*ibid.*, book 4:16).

Other serious crimes were adultery, thievery, and homicide. If a man and woman were caught in an adulterous act by the woman's husband, both were summarily stoned in the marketplace. If the adulterous couple was accused by hearsay, which was later verified, they were hanged rather than stoned. No one, noble or commoner, was spared these severe penalties. In one recorded case, Nezahualpilli, a ruler of Texcoco, sentenced one of his wives and her three current lovers to death. Rank had no privileges here, even though the woman was a daughter of Axayacatl, ruler of Tenochtitlan, and her lovers were all high-ranking nobles.

Stealing was less severely penalized, depending on the place and extent of the misdeed. If a person stole from a dwelling, he was placed in slavery to the person from whom he stole. If the victim did not wish this additional labor, he could sell the offender to someone else for the amount of the theft. If the theft took place in the countryside, or if a person repeatedly stole, the designated punishment was death (Alva Ixtlilxochitl 1965, vol. 2:188–189).

The act of killing or planning to kill another person was usually met with the death penalty. However, a person committing this crime might also be placed in bondage to the family of his victim: "The murderer was turned over to the widow or to the relatives of the deceased, (to be) forever a slave. He was to serve them and to earn a living for the children of the deceased" (Durán 1971:96). Additionally, if someone overpowered and kidnapped a child, selling him into slavery, the offender was hanged (Alva Ixtlilxochitl 1965, vol. 1:237).

Other laws applied to land jurisdictions, the maintenance of status symbols, the responsibilities of high-ranking officials, and the duties of soldiers in battle. According to Texcoco law, which was generally accepted in the Valley of Mexico, land rights were closely guarded. Should someone move boundary markings on private lands, or take possession of some land, the stated penalty was death.

The laws were very specific with regard to status-linked rights. The use of clothing, ornamentation, and housing was all carefully regulated by law. Only the ruler could wear the finest cloaks; others wore specific styles of cloaks according to their rank. No undistinguished commoners could wear cotton cloaks; theirs must be made of maguey fiber. Likewise, commoners could not wear their cloaks below their knees unless their legs bore battle scars. Only nobles could wear ornate and expensive jewelry: lip plugs, ear plugs, nose plugs, bracelets, and necklaces. Only nobles could build houses of two stories. That is, no one could pretend to be of a status he was not, and all statuses were legally defined and protected. The law stated that any violation of these statutes met with the sentence of death.

While high rank was protected, it also carried onerous responsibilities. As already seen, punishments frequently were more severe for the offending noble than for his peasant counterpart. Additional crimes and punishments were associated with prestigious occupations. The priest who lived in concubinage was executed; a tribute collector who collected too much also met with execution; and the judge who took bribes or provided special favors also received the death penalty.

Special laws applied on the battlefield. It was particularly important that a warrior obey a commander's orders; any disobedience resulted in death by beheading. Also, if one warrior took another's captive or gave his own captive away, the punishment was death by hanging (*ibid.*, vol. 2:189). A major goal of Aztec warfare was the capture of enemy warriors, and high rewards and status awaited those who were successful on the battlefield. It was considered important, therefore, that there be no abuses of this system.

These laws and their associated penalties were an essential part of a complex governmental and legal bureaucracy. This political system, along with the extensive warfare and human sacrifice which accompanied it, is the subject of Chapter 5.

5/Imperial politics and warfare

During the century-long process of empire building, the Aztecs developed complex governmental and military structures. At the core of these institutions was the city-state, the prevailing mode of political organization in central Mexico during at least the fourteenth through early sixteenth centuries. The city-state was composed of a large community and its surrounding dependent areas. In most cases, the community was of considerable size, some in fact being true cities. Each served as the political, economic, and religious center of its city-state. Typically, the dependent districts were politically and militarily subject to such a center, providing considerable amounts of tribute in goods and services. It has been estimated that by the early sixteenth century the territory of central Mexico was divided into some 50–60 city-states (Bray 1972:165). These city-states varied greatly in size and importance, and each engaged in an involved web of alliances and hostilities with neighboring city-states.

Each city-state was the domain of a ruler, or *tlatoani*. Some of these rulers were autonomous and did not owe allegiance or service to any other tlatoani; others were under the domination of powerful imperial rulers, such as those of the Triple Alliance cities. Domination, subjugation, and alliances shifted continually throughout the fourteenth and fifteenth centuries. But by the early sixteenth century the Triple Alliance had brought large numbers of city-states under its control, creating a vast imperial network. Still, other regions lay beyond its control. The Aztecs treated some of the independent city-states as allies, others as enemies. They and one of their most committed enemies, Tlaxcalla, engaged in periodic ritualized warfare which trained the combatants and provided human victims to be sacrificed to the gods. This chapter considers the manner of rulership and government among the Aztecs; the adventures of warfare and conquest; and the practice of human sacrifice, so often a result of warfare and conquest.

RULERSHIP AND GOVERNMENT

The affairs of state were conducted by a complex political body. Each city-state was ruled by a tlatoani who was ultimately responsible for events within his realm; he conducted wars, meted out justice, and supervised the major rituals. He was at the same time the supreme advocate of the rights of the nobility, defender of the commoners, and benefactor to the poor. Depending on his circumstances, he might form alliances with other *tlatoque,* administer conquered city-states and exact tribute from them, or personally serve in the court of a dominant tlatoani.

The tlatoani was fundamentally a monarch. On the eve of the Spanish arrival, dynasties had entrenched themselves in several of the central Mexican city-states. In Tenochtitlan, the Mexica had established one. Inheritance of the supreme Mexica position was the exclusive prerogative of members of a single family, believed to have descended from the god Quetzalcoatl. The rulers were the earthly counterparts of celestial deities; their rule was by divine right. Upon his coronation, the new ruler was introduced to his new status by a great dignitary:

> . . . now thou art deified. Although thou art human, as are we, although thou art our friend, although thou art our son . . . no more art thou human, as are we; we do not look to thee as human . . . he [the god] is within thee; he speaketh forth from thy mouth. Thou art his lips, thou art his jaw, thou art his tongue, thou art his eyes, thou art his ears (Sahagún 1950–1969, book 6:52–53).

Mexica inheritance typically passed from brother to brother before descending to the eldest son of the eldest brother. In either case, the precise line of inheritance could be bypassed if the heir were ineligible. It was critical that each new tlatoani had been tried in battle. He must also be elegant in speech; even his title meant "speaker." He must be both warrior and diplomat, as well as the earthly representative of a god.

Since the right to rule was not automatic, but required some deliberation and choice to arrive at the most capable ruler, the privilege of selection carried great power. Precedent was set by the first Mexica ruler, Acamapichtli, who declined to name a successor, but left it to election. This tradition continued until the Spanish conquest, although it appears that the numbers of persons allowed to participate in selecting the ruler narrowed considerably during the 90 years of imperial growth. The elite sixteenth-century electors included only the highest chiefs, the representatives of the districts, various groups of renowned warriors, and exalted priests. Together, this august gathering reached accord as to who would be the new ruler, and who would constitute his supreme council of four advisors. Although an election did take place, the eligible candidates were all from the same family: the ruler and his council of four advisors, which included his second-in-command, the *cihuacoatl* ("Woman-Serpent"),[1] were all close relatives. It was a dynasty in which the specific family member who would rule was determined by an elite group of nobles, warriors, and priests.

It was always from the Council of Four that the next Mexica tlatoani would be selected. Another close and tested relative then rose to fill the vacant post on the council and assume the important title. Although this selection process appears to have been largely an internal event, it was apparently important and expected that the rulers of the other two Triple Alliance capitals affirm the selection and give their assent. This was the case whether the new ruler was to govern Tenochtitlan, Texcoco, or Tlacopan.

---

[1] Although given a female name, this individual was always a man. The office seems to have been hereditary, from father to son.

The critical events surrounding the coronation of a Mexica ruler were deeply religious, but also cleverly political. The initial series of events was religious. High priests summoned the new ruler and presented him before a group of nobles congregated at the temple of Huitzilopochtli. The ruler was dressed in priestly garb and was taken by the priests to the idol of Huitzilopochtli. There he offered the god incense while the populace looked on and shell trumpets were blown. The new ruler's four advisors were also religiously dressed and offered incense. Then all five were led down the 120 steps of the temple and taken to a house of fasting. Here, dressed in "fasting capes" with a design of bones, they fasted and did penance for four days. At the end of this period, the priests came for them and they repeated the incense rite at the temple of Huitzilopochtli. Finally, they ate and again ascended the steps of the great temple. There, by piercing the fleshy parts of their bodies, they offered blood, and again incense. Descending from the temple and bathing, they fasted for an additional four days, again offering incense and blood after their fast. The ruler was then escorted to his palace, while his four councilors were led to their homes.

It was customary for the new ruler to then depart on a war of conquest. This war proved his mettle on the battlefield, and also provided prisoners for the human sacrifices which would honor his inauguration. When the successful ruler returned triumphantly from his campaign, drums were beaten and shell trumpets blown throughout the city.

As with all critical events, a propitious day was chosen for the ruler's official installation. Ahuitzotl, for example, was installed on the day *ce cipactli* (One Alligator) in 1486. This was a most favorable day, according to the 260-day ritual calendar, or *tonalpohualli*.

Rulers from both hostile and friendly lands were invited to attend the grand coronation. The enemy rulers and their retinues entered the city at night, so as not to be discovered. During their entire stay in Tenochtitlan, they were sequestered in secret quarters of the palace, surreptitiously attending ceremonies. The most spectacular event of the ruler's coronation was his feast. The ruler provided his foreign guests with sumptuous gifts: elegant clothing, sandals, warriors' costumes with shields, precious jewels, and priceless jewelry. They, in turn, offered him presents of great wealth and beauty. The ruler also gave presents to those who served him, the gods, and the state: the nobles, warriors, judges, singers, and priests. This "potlatch-style" event was punctuated by splendid orations, dancing, colorful processions, sacrifices of war prisoners, and the eating of hallucinogenic mushrooms.

In part, this expensive and conspicuous activity was designed to impress the foreign visitors—to convince the subjugated rulers not to rebel, to reaffirm to the allies that the alliance was to their advantage, and to strike terror into the hearts of the enemy.

Following his official installation, the ruler was addressed and admonished in eloquent speeches by high-ranking persons skilled in the art of discourse. Through the use of intricate metaphors and extensive examples, the speakers defined the royal role and the new ruler's relationships to others. The dignitaries warned him that his new burden was heavy: ". . . the rulership is not a peaceful place, a good place, for things slip, things slide" (Sahagún 1950–1969, book 6:63). He was reminded that he was now deified, and he must work diligently to maintain the order of the universe. He must be wise, capable, and accomplished in speech; he must not frighten, ridicule, scandalize, or take advantage of his subjects. To the people he was now father and mother: "On thy back, on thy lap, in thy arms our lord placeth the governed, the vassals, the common folk, the capricious, the peevish. For yet a while thou wilt fondle them as children . . ." (*ibid.*:48–49).

After a series of discourses emphasizing these royal ideals, the ruler himself responded. First he addressed the noble gathering, humbly and modestly accepting his exalted position. He then turned his attention to the populace, warning them to beware of the vices of drunkenness, theft, and adultery; encouraging them to seek the renown and prosperity which awaited those who were diligent and brave in religious and secular activities. Finally, a high-ranking dignitary admonished the people to heed the words of the new ruler.

Once properly installed in office, the ruler turned his attention to affairs of state. The political arena in which he operated may be divided into three segments: diplomacy, warfare, and justice. All these political matters were supervised by a supreme council, the *tlatocan*, which lent advice to the ruler and his Council of Four. The tlatocan was composed of 12–20 distinguished members (Davies 1973:80).

In matters of diplomacy the Mexica ruler was directly advised and assisted by his "vice-ruler" (cihuacoatl) and the other members of his Council of Four. The ruler turned to these advisors, all his close relatives, for counsel on important matters of state: establishing and maintaining diplomatic relations with friendly and hostile lands, the initiation and conduct of warfare, and the management of the empire in general. The cihuacoatl took much of the burden of day-to-day governance off the tlatoani, handling official finances, organizing military campaigns, determining rewards for warriors, serving as supreme judge, and acting as ruler in the ruler's absence. Durán reports that in the fifteenth century one Mexica cihuacoatl, named Tlacaellel, exercised considerable political power. Living more than 80 years, his control extended through the reigns of three Mexica rulers; after his death the position of cihuacoatl was rarely mentioned. It seems that no subsequent cihuacoatl had the force of personality of Tlacaellel, but the position retained its high esteem, privilege, and authority. On the whole, in the sixteenth century the cihuacoatl and the Council of Four were more involved in carrying out the decisions of the tlatoani than in influencing them.

Each new personality surely brought a somewhat different flavor to the position of tlatoani or cihuacoatl. The cihuacoatl Tlacaellel is a case in point. While he supposedly dominated Mexica politics in the fifteenth century, much by force of his own personality, his successors appear to have simply been high-level administrators doing the bidding of the tlatoani. Each tlatoani likewise brought a distinct quality to the throne: Ahuitzotl (1486–1502), at least outwardly, was generous and loving to his people; Tizoc (1481–1486) was comparatively weak and less than courageous on the battlefield (and his early death may not have been an accident); Moctezuma Xocoyotzin (1502–1520) was austere and severe, feared rather than loved by his subjects. The personal preferences of influential rulers were, in some cases, more than passing fancies and encouraged certain already existing tendencies in their city-states. During the rise of Mexica military might, the Mexica ruler Moctezuma Ilhuicamina (1440–1468) extolled warfare and conquest; the Texcocan ruler Nezahualcoyotl (1418–1472) favored law, engineering, and the arts. Although many additional factors were involved, it was no accident that by the sixteenth century Tenochtitlan had gained military supremacy in the Triple Alliance, while Texcoco had become the site of the highest court and the center of the arts.

The outlines of the administration of empire were established by the end of Itzcoatl's reign (1440), and an increasing consolidation of power in the hands of the Tenochtitlan ruler took place during the brief history of the empire (Davies 1973:132, passim). Notwithstanding this centralization of power and consolidation of resources, the empire was loosely organized. Regional and provincial rulers, after being conquered by the Triple Alliance, frequently were maintained in their traditional positions; only rarely was an Aztec governor assigned to a conquered province. In essence, the imperial administration consisted of the establishment of certain high-ranking Aztec officials in the provinces (usually tribute collectors, or *calpixque*), the imposition of specific tribute levies, and threats of reprisals if these duties were not met. There were some variations in the pattern to accommodate unique provincial conditions: Military garrisons were established along hostile borders and in troublesome districts, and on rare occasions colonists were sent to settle underpopulated areas.

In affairs of war, the tlatoani was advised by a war council composed of all warriors who had attained the status of *tequiua* (a seasoned warrior who had successfully captured at least four enemy warriors). This council met in a chamber of the royal palace and offered advice and received orders on military affairs only.

There was no large-scale standing army in pre-Hispanic Mexico; the bulk of the warriors were *macehualtin* who were trained in the martial arts and mobilized in times of war.[2] But there were some professional and semi-professional military officers, and these officers constituted the military council. While success on the battlefield was the criterion for elevation into this organization, it appears that among the Mexica the top officers, the "generals," were usually also members of the royal family; ascription as well as achievement entered into these status designations. The Mexica also rewarded their most valiant warriors (tequiua) by allowing them admission into one of a number of "knightly orders." Although only nobles were eligible for the most prestigious orders (the Eagle and the Jaguar), eligible commoners could enter the other, less prestigious ones. Members of two military orders, the Otomí and the *quachic*, vowed never to retreat in battle; they were, however, considered too unruly to occupy administrative posts. Members of these elite army corps were exempt from tribute payment, and apparently were supported by the state in their material needs. In actual warfare they fought as a unit, usually undertaking the most dangerous assignments. And as with virtually

---

[2] Some full-time military men also must have manned the occasional garrisons which dotted the imperial frontiers.

all Mexica organizations, they had specific religious patrons and obligations. The tequiua, nobles and commoners alike, also formed part of the military councils that met periodically at the "eagle house" in the Tenochtitlan royal palace.

Justice was the third major segment of political rule. Each city-state of central Mexico had developed a complex centralized court system by the sixteenth century. For the Mexica, the lowest courts were at the *calpulli* level, but the judges were appointees of the state, not the calpulli. Minor cases were treated at that level, more serious cases were directed to the state courts: the *tlacxitlan* or the *teccalco*. It appears that the less serious cases involving commoners were sent to the teccalco, where

> Every day the common folk and vassals laid complaints before [the judges]. Calmly and prudently they heard the plaints of the vassals; in the picture writing which recorded the case, they studied the complaints. And when they tested their truth, they sought out and inquired of informers and witnesses who could size up the plaintiffs, (who knew) what had been stolen and what was charged (Sahagún 1950–1969, book 8:42).

The more serious cases, and all cases involving nobles, went to the tlacxitlan, apparently composed of 13 senior judges. This was the high court. For noblemen as well as commoners justice was swift and, for those judged guilty, the stated sentence was often death (see Chapter 4). In criminal cases, appeal could be made to the cihuacoatl, who served as the supreme judge. In making his judgment, he was assisted by the 12 other high judges. In civil cases, no means of appeal existed (Torquemada 1969, vol. 2:352). Apparently no death sentence was to be carried out without notifying the ruler (Durán 1964:132), and the tlatoani did involve himself in the more unusual or politically sensitive cases.

The officials of the Aztec bureaucracy were extremely numerous. Of the Mexica alone, Durán comments: "The nation had a special official for every activity, small though it were. Everything was so well recorded that no detail was left out of the accounts. There were even officials in charge of sweeping" (1964:183). The ordering of state and empire required a vast number of officials; and the state, largely through tribute revenues, supported these persons in their material needs. As servants of the state, these officials' functions were either political, economic, or military. For example, the Mexica legal system alone employed numerous judges at various levels, scribes to record each case in detail, bailiffs to summon individuals involved in each case, and executioners to carry out the most extreme punishments. Jails existed, requiring even more officials to supervise them. Other political officers included ambassadors, a multitude of royal palace officials such as messengers and tutors, and the heads of the wards of the city. While the highest positions among the Mexica were normally reserved for nobles, in Texcoco commoners were well represented, particularly on the war council (Alva Ixtlilxochitl 1965, vol. 2:178).

Officials were also employed by the state to oversee economic affairs. There were tribute collectors in each conquered province, tribute supervisors in each Triple Alliance capital to guard and dispense the tribute on order of the ruler or the cihuacoatl, and scribes to maintain detailed and accurate financial accounts. In addition, the organization of the city of Tenochtitlan was suited to efficient tribute collection and the allocation of public works duties. According to one source, the division of the populace was as follows:

> As soon as a child is born he is registered with the heads and captains of the wards. One man had in his charge twenty households, another forty, another fifty, others had a hundred, and thus the city and its wards were divided. He who had a hundred houses in his charge would appoint five or six of his subjects and divide them among the hundred homes. If he received fifteen or perhaps twenty households, he was obliged to govern them, collecting tribute and men for public works. And so the officials of the Republic were innumerable (Durán 1964:183).

These many officials had to appear daily at the royal palace to receive orders for the day regarding the public works obligations of their charges.

The state also supported the military professionals: officers and members of the elite army corps. These dedicated individuals provided the backbone of the Mexica army. The effectiveness of the army was crucial in the achievement of a paramount Mexica goal: military conquest and its rewards of economic control, sacrificial victims, and individual honor and renown.

WARFARE AND CONQUEST

Warfare was a dominant theme in the pre-Hispanic central Mexican cultures, and it reached its zenith as a cultural preoccupation with the Mexica. Warfare touched virtually all aspects of Mexica life: social, political, economic, and religious. At birth an infant boy was dedicated to the battlefield, and a mother who died in childbirth was likened to a warrior. The schools for both noble and commoner boys emphasized the martial arts. A man slain on the battlefield or on the sacrificial stone, as well as the woman who died in childbirth, was granted a glorious afterlife. Fine distinctions in social status, and the attainment of superior positions in the society, were defined for men by their success in warfare. And one of the primary ideals of the tlatoani was that he be an able military leader. In fact, the Mexica political structure revolved around warfare, which frequently resulted in political and economic control of new lands. Since Tenochtitlan was not economically self-sufficient, it required external material support which was most reliably supplied as tribute (secured through conquest). Material needs included not only staple foodstuffs but also luxury goods. An abundance of these expensive and exotic items was essential to the maintenance of the Mexica state—they were used as rewards to valiant warriors and others who contributed to the military and administrative successes of the empire. This system of rewards, then, provided substantial motivation for even more daring military enterprises. And warfare was always entwined with religion. The troops were justified in their conquests by their patron deity Huitzilopochtli, who spurred them on; and the enemy warriors they captured would provide food for the gods, to keep the universe intact. In short, the culture nurtured ideals that were best realized on the battlefield. It was thus essential that warfare be a fairly continuous activity.

Warfare must be distinguished from conquest. The most straightforward goals of warfare were the capture of enemy warriors for sacrifice and battlefield experience for the troops. For the neophyte war was a training ground, for all warriors it was an arena for the hopeful achievement of honors. Conquest entailed an added goal: economic control over land and production. Most of the wars initiated by the Mexica had this added goal of conquest. Another type of war—labeled "war of flowers" (*yaoxochitl*)—apparently did not have conquest as an immediate goal.

The Mexica felt justified in initiating warfare operations upon any affront to Mexica people, or upon the reticence of autonomous lands to cede to special Mexica demands. Assault on traveling Aztec merchants is the most commonly recorded stimulus for Aztec military action, and was the usual pretext for conquering the distant provinces. But outrages to Mexica marketwomen set off a war with Coyoacan; and the mistreatment of a Mexica ruler's sister, wife of a Tlatelolcan ruler, prompted violence between these two city-states. However, these kinds of events seem to have triggered wars already anticipated. Coyoacan was marked for Mexica conquest, for it controlled abundant supplies of needed freshwater. Tlatelolco likewise was too close and too powerful economically to remain free of the Mexica yoke for long. And the war against Toluca in 1474 was sparked by a Mexica demand for wood supplies, and refusal by Toluca. Yet this was merely an excuse; the fundamental reason for conquest was revealed by the cihuacoatl Tlacaellel who said that "since the time of his brother, Moteczoma, he had been convinced that that province should be conquered, since he feared that its inhabitants might ally themselves to Michoacan" (Durán 1964:161).

Frequently, the Mexica would instigate wars with independent city-states by making unusual demands which would symbolize the subservient position of the independent state. So, when the Mexica requested that Xochimilco supply stone and wood for the construction of their great temple, the Mexica messengers were greeted with this inflammatory reply:

> What do you say, O Aztecs? What do you seek? Are you drunk? Are you out of your minds that you have come here with such a demand? Are we your vassals or slaves that we must provide you with stone and wood and everything you need? Are those who sent you our lords and masters? Go home, Aztecs, and tell them that it is not our will to grant them what they demand! (*ibid.*:74).

Similarly, the Mexica tested the subservience of neighboring Cuitlahuac by inviting its ruler and noble maidens to a feast, requesting that the virgins sing and dance. This request was summarily dismissed by the Cuitlahuac ruler; the result was warfare and subsequent conquest by the Mexica.

Whatever its goals and pretexts, all central Mexican warfare was highly standardized and ritualized. Even warfare aimed at conquest involved lengthy negotiations and bargaining. Initially, the errant city or city-state would be given an opportunity to submit voluntarily to Triple Alliance domination. In such instances, goods and services rendered resembled a moderate gift more than tribute. However, were the gift ever stingy or withheld, military repercussions would surely follow. If a city did not agree to submit voluntarily, a series of negotiations followed. Where all three Triple Alliance powers were represented on the field, the negotiations looked like this:

1. Tenochtitlan ambassadors approached the leaders and elders of the recalcitrant city, impressing on them the devastation that would result from a full-scale war. They reminded the leaders that they still had time to submit as "friends of the empire," with the obligation of allowing Aztec traders access to local markets, submitting certain gifts to the imperial capitals, and permitting an image of Huitzilopochtli to reside in their city. In the customary central Mexican fashion, the ambassadors offered the elders gifts of shields and *macquauitl* (clubs inset with numerous sharp obsidian blades), and then retired for 20 days.

2. If the city offered no favorable response by the end of this period, the Texcocan ambassadors were sent to negotiate. This encounter was much like the previous one, except that the "reminders" became warnings and threats. The leaders of the city were presented with more gifts of weapons, and allowed an additional 20 days to surrender peacefully.

3. If the city still did not yield, Tlacopan ambassadors were sent, again bearing gifts of weapons, and they especially appealed to the warriors of the city, who would suffer the most if the city persisted in resisting the Triple Alliance powers. In a game of intimidation, the ambassadors enumerated the devastating consequences to the city if it insisted on being subdued by force—"the entire province will be destroyed with fire and blood and all the captives taken as slaves" (Alva Ixtlilxochitl 1965, vol. 2:192; translation by FFB). With the passing of another 20 days, the states were officially in a state of war.

This formal set of events was not always followed. For example, when the Mexica opened hostilities in 1466 with the unfriendly city-state of Tepeaca (where Mexica merchants had been killed), Moctezuma Ilhuicamina merely sent symbolic presents of shield, macquauitl, and feathers to the ruler of Tepeaca. This indicated that they were now in a state of war.

While the negotiating stages allowed the enemy to obtain information on troop strength and armament, and even provided the enemy with weapons, the actual warfare was conducted with ferociousness, cunning, and stealth (see Figure 5–1). Although surprise attack was virtually impossible, enemy warriors were frequently enticed into clever ambushes and traps. The battle against the Matlatzincas of Toluca in 1474 is a fine example of these military tactics. The young Mexica ruler, Axayacatl, ordered the bulk of his troops to cross a river and then retreat; meanwhile, he and some of his warriors lay hidden in ambush. Axayacatl hoped that the enemy would advance on his main body and be caught in the trap. However, the Mexica were not the only people to use this clever strategy, and in this case both sides had set an identical snare. After a temporary stalemate, the Matlatzincas finally erred and fell into the Mexica trap (Durán 1967, vol. 2:271–272). Military prowess was also evident in the manner in which the Triple Alliance powers deployed their troops. A typical war of conquest included not only warriors from Tenochtitlan, Texcoco, and Tlacopan but also from the numerous previously conquered cities. In these military operations, the people of Xochimilco and Chalco appear as the most consistent allies of the Triple Alliance. On distant campaigns, troops from conquered provinces were frequently assembled during the course of

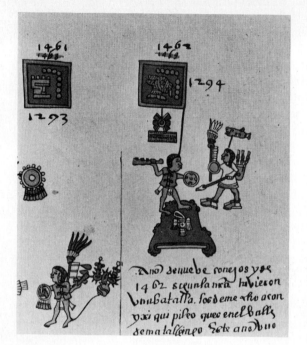

Figure 5–1: War in which the Aztecs conquered Xiquipilco. Note the accoutrements of battle: the cotton armor, shields, macquauitl, and ornate feathered devices (Codex Telleriano-Remensis 1964: folio 37v).

the march. On the battlefield these different allies and the special military orders were deployed separately, fighting as units. Members of the Otomí military order, having vowed never to flee in battle, always fought in pairs. The Mexica typically placed themselves in the most dangerous situation. By doing so, they allowed themselves the greatest opportunity to capture enemy warriors and gain honor and renown. However, when wars were lost by the Triple Alliance, the Mexica also often suffered the greatest losses. In the tragic war with Michoacan, the Mexica returned home with a mere 200 warriors of the uncounted thousands they had sent (Durán 1964:167).

Spies were commonly used in central Mexican warfare, and they sometimes employed clever tactics to obtain valued information. Aztec merchants disguised as provincial inhabitants frequented the marketplaces of conquered and unconquered provinces. In conquered provinces they could assess the local political climate, important intelligence since rebellions were frequent. In unconquered areas they evaluated the riches of the land, as well as its military strength. For their dangerous missions, these merchant spies were generously rewarded by their rulers. But spies were also used at the site of the battle. When the Triple Alliance forces reached Michoacan, the Mexica ruler sent spies into the Tarascan camp to obtain vital information. The spies approached the enemy camp by way of a tunnel, and listened to the Tarascan conversations through a crack in the ground. In this case, the Mexica ruler was dismayed to hear from his stealthy spies that he was outnumbered by 16,000 well-armed and well-trained men! (*ibid.*:166).

Despite their military prowess, the Aztecs suffered some major defeats, and powerful states such as Michoacan, Tlaxcalla, and Meztitlan remained unconquered by the Triple Alliance forces. However, a great number of cities and city-states did fall. Battlefield victory for the allied forces was officially signaled by the burning of the enemy's major temple (see Figure 5-2). This symbolized the supremacy of the Mexica god Huitzilopochtli over the local patron deity. With the obvious defeat or surrender of the enemy, negotiations again took center stage. The vanquished approached the victors and asked to be pardoned, enumerating the goods and services they would willingly offer as tribute. The conquerors normally shrugged that the tribute offered was insufficient and insisted on more, detailing their demands. The conquered delegation might offer something different; and so the bargaining went on until an agreement, a kind of contract, was reached. Aside from the specifics of tribute levies, it was understood that the conquered district would no longer act autonomously in political affairs, would honor and respect the god Huitzilopochtli, and would provide military troops when required. For its part, the new province was normally allowed to retain its traditional rulers, mode of government, and language and traditions. Rarely were cities razed or populations destroyed.

Although this was the usual, and ideal, manner of ending a war, some pillaging and looting did apparently take place. After a tedious march from the Valley of Mexico to Tehuantepec (about 775 kilometers), and a military engagement in which the Triple Alliance forces overwhelmed those of Tehuantepec, the Aztec warriors could not seem to control their desire to loot and destroy the city. They were finally brought under control, but complained bitterly that the booty was rightfully theirs, especially after such an exhausting campaign. Such looting and destruction was counterproductive to the imperial Aztec goals: they needed the provinces to provide them with continuous and assured supplies of goods through tribute, not the spoils of a one-time sacking.

Some wars were not fought for conquest. The most notable of these "wars of flowers" was carried on between the Triple Alliance and the Tlaxcallans and Huexotzincos. It was initiated in the mid-fifteenth century during the reign of Moctezuma Ilhuicamina. Under this mutual arrangement, planned wars were periodically fought between the two opposing forces. The goal was not conquest, but the capture of enemy warriors for sacrifice to the gods. By capturing enemies, warriors also earned prestige; and when this custom began the Mexica ruler informed his warriors that "they were now to fight in a military market place where they would buy honor and glory with their blood and their lives" (Durán 1964: 141). Each side, Aztec and Tlaxcallan-Huexotzinco, had a convenient arena for securing sacrificial victims and individual honor; neither (particularly the Aztecs) had to engage in distant wars to provide these needs for their gods and their warriors. In fact, these prisoners were the most highly prized: beyond his basic four captures, a seasoned Aztec warrior could capture a great many Huaxtecs or others and gain no special honor; but if he captured one or more warriors from the Tlaxcalla-Huexotzinco area, he gained great renown and prestigious goods. With greater rewards awaiting them in these wars, the Aztec warriors were sparked into especially ferocious fighting. The Aztecs believed that victims from these Nahua-speaking groups were the most palatable to their gods when offered for sacrifice.

There is some question if it would have been worthwhile or even possible in the

Figure 5–2: Some conquests of Moctezuma Ilhuicamina. The dates of his rule border the page. Note the burning temples as symbols of conquest (Codex Mendoza 1938, vol. 3:folio 7).

sixteenth century for the Aztecs to have conquered Tlaxcalla. Certainly, the potential tribute that could be extracted from Tlaxcalla would have paled against the luxurious tribute the Aztec empire received from many other provinces.

The Aztec-Tlaxcalla wars in the sixteenth century were furiously fought, and there is some suspicion that more Aztecs than Tlaxcallans were captured and sacrificed. During the reign of Moctezuma Xocoyotzin, it appears that the Aztecs would have liked to subdue their powerful neighbors. But they repeatedly suffered tragic setbacks. One defeat at the hands of Huexotzinco was so heartbreaking that "When [Moctezuma] heard this mournful news he began to weep bitterly. The tidings spread throughout the city and everyone sobbed in sadness and despair" (*ibid.*: 235).

That more was involved than recurring ritual battles is also suggested by the fact that Tlaxcalla, in the sixteenth century, was virtually cut off from any external trade routes. The situation was so serious that the people suffered a severe shortage of the staple salt. But, on the whole, each side held its own in this bitter periodic war. When the Spaniards arrived, the advantage finally went to their allies, the Tlaxcallans (see Chapter 8).

HUMAN SACRIFICE

The practice of human sacrifice was of intense importance to the central Mexican peoples. Consequently, an understanding of the cultures of the Mexica and their neighbors involves a clear grasp of their beliefs, attitudes, and behavior pertaining to human sacrifice and cannibalism. The Mexica explanations for these customs are presented here, followed by some controversial scientific explanations currently debated by twentieth-century anthropologists.

The Mexica bore a heavy burden. According to their beliefs, they had to ensure the continuation of the universe. The only way this could be successfully accomplished was with the continual offering of human blood. This practice had a long-standing religious foundation, focused on the sun god Tonatiuh.

According to Aztec mythology, the birth of the present sun set the stage for human sacrifice. This sun was the fifth to be created by the gods (see Chapter 6), who assembled at Teotihuacan to decide which of them would cast himself into a fire and emerge as the sun. There were two volunteers, one capable of making expensive and valuable offerings (Tecuciztecatl), the other wretched and impoverished (Nanauatzin). When it came time for the well-endowed god to cast himself into the flames, his courage foundered. Four times he tried and four times he failed. Then the wretched god gathered his courage and leaped quickly into the fire. As the remaining gods waited anxiously in the darkness, Nanauatzin finally rose in the east as the sun, abruptly followed by Tecuciztecatl as the moon. But the ostentatious moon rose as bright as the sun, which seriously offended the gods. To remedy this problem, one of them hurled a rabbit onto the face of the moon, thus dimming its brightness. It was the image of this rabbit which the Aztec people saw on the moon. But the work of the gods was still not finished, for the sun and moon now sat together, unmoving in the sky. To set them in motion and put them in their proper relationship, the gods offered themselves as sacrifices, providing an example for human beings. It then became the solemn duty for mortals to continually provide the sun with human blood, thus sustaining the sun's daily movements.

A different myth, with the same sacrificial consequence, recounts the birth of the Mexica patron god, Huitzilopochtli (a sun deity). Huitzilopochtli was miraculously conceived when his mother, the goddess Coatlicue (sometimes called Tonantzin), was busy sweeping. As she swept, a ball of feathers appeared and she put it in her bosom. Later, she found that the feathers had disappeared, and she was to bear a child. As mother goddess, she had already borne the Centzonuitznaua ("Four Hundred Southerners," or stars) and their sister Coyolxauhqui (representing the moon). These offspring, angered by their mother's impropriety at becoming pregnant, set out to kill her. When Coyolxauhqui and her brothers arrived, bedecked in battle array and marching in columns, Huitzilopochtli suddenly emerged, born fully armed with shield, dart thrower, and darts, and decorated with feathers and paint. With an ignited serpent he destroyed Coyolxauhqui,[3] and with his other weapons he overpowered her four hundred (in other words, innumerable) brothers. The dawn of each Aztec day saw the reenactment of this conflict: The sun Huitzilopochtli fought off the moon and the stars to bring day to his people. In order to nourish him and give him strength for this battle, mortals must supply human blood through sacrifice.

As was pointed out in Chapter 4, the Aztec perception of the world stressed uncertainty: The present was tenuous, the future was fragile. In this forbidding, precarious situation, the people's only recourse was to maintain proper moral conduct and strictly observe religious duties. In the abstract, the most critical duty was to ensure the continuation of the universe; in the concrete, the most critical activity was to guarantee the human blood required for cosmic preservation. Not only religious beliefs but also cultural proclivities demanded that the Aztecs practice human sacrifice.

Everyone was a potential candidate for sacrifice; fate determined which individuals would be so honored. In terms of numbers, prisoners captured in battle led the list. Following a major battle with Tlaxcalla-Huexotzinco or a war of conquest, mass sacrifices were performed. These sacrifices always commemorated a special event such as an important religious ceremony, the coronation of a new ruler, or the dedication of a new temple. There are great discrepancies in the reporting of actual figures. For instance, at the dedication of the great dual temple in 1487 in Tenochtitlan, Durán (1964:194, 199) reports the highly suspicious figure of 80,400 captives sacrificed over a four-day period, Torquemada (1969, vol. 1:186) is close behind with 72,344, and the Codex Telleriano-Remensis (1964:lámina xix) pictographically records 20,000. These figures are all high compared with the numbers reported for other major festivals. But whatever the actual count, the circumstances of this temple dedication are intriguing: A large host of enemy rulers was invited to witness this event, an event at which they saw many of their own

---

[3] In 1978, a mammoth sculpted stone disc portraying the dismembered body of Coyolxauhqui was unearthed in downtown Mexico City.

people sacrificed to the Aztec gods. Following the sacrifices, luxurious tribute from the many conquered provinces was delivered ceremonially and ostentatiously to the Mexica ruler. All of this was done so that "the enemies, guests, and strangers were bewildered, amazed. They saw that the Aztecs were masters of the entire world and they realized that the Aztec people had conquered all the nations and that all were their vassals" (Durán 1964:195).

A common feature of many of the monthly religious rituals was the sacrifice of one or more deity impersonators. The individual selected as the impersonator was dressed and decorated in the likeness of the god or goddess, and performed various ritual activities such as keeping vigil, making short pilgrimages, dancing, and singing. At the culmination of the ceremonies, when the impersonator was sacrificed, the god, not the mortal, was honored. The rituals associated with the impersonation of the important god Tezcatlipoca were particularly elaborate. For this special role, a handsome young man free from physical flaws was chosen. He assumed the identity of Tezcatlipoca for a full year, walking about in godly regalia and playing a flute. One month before he was to be sacrificed, he was married to four women who represented goddesses. As his sacrificial day approached, he and his wives journeyed from place to place, singing and dancing. Arriving at his designated temple, he voluntarily and alone ascended the steps. At the top the priests threw him on the sacrificial stone and cut out his heart, offering it to the sun (Sahagún 1950–1969, book 2:68). As with virtually all those sacrificed, he was then decapitated, his head taken for display on the skull rack, or *tzompantli*. In some instances, the symbolism of deity impersonation continued following the sacrifice. For example, after the impersonator of the goddess Toci died, her skin was flayed and worn by a priest. This priest, then, richly adorned as the goddess Toci, went about participating in a variety of rituals—singing, dancing, and honoring valiant warriors.

At some ceremonies, certain groups or individuals had the privilege of offering for sacrifice one or more "bathed slaves." The merchants were one such group. A merchant or cohort of merchants underwent a great deal of practical and ritual preparation for this special offering. First a slave, man or woman, was purchased in the marketplace; particularly prized were comely slaves skilled in song and dance. Then the merchant built two or three houses, on the roofs of which the slave would later be required to dance. He then assembled his worldly goods and presented great quantities of gifts to high-ranking military officers and those who had already gained distinction by bathing a slave. Journeying to the merchant headquarters of Tochtepec, near the Gulf Coast, he made offerings to the merchant god Yacatecutli, and feasted the most prominent merchants. These formalities in Tochtepec indicated his slave-bathing intentions to both the merchant guild and its patron deity. The merchant affirmed that he was capable of performing the ceremony in proper style; they, in turn, legitimized his right to do so. Returning to the Valley of Mexico, he received a propitious day-sign from an astrologer, and began his preparations in earnest. In a series of ceremonial feasts, he invited guests from other cities in the valley, offering them food and gifts. All the while, his bathed slave(s) danced, adorned in good clothing and ornaments. For the merchants, this was an important rite of passage which displayed their accumulated wealth, wealth symbolizing their skill as merchants. As for the slaves, they were looked after carefully, dressed well, fed well, and bathed in sacred water. After undergoing a set of rites, they were offered for sacrifice by their owners, who climbed the temple steps with them and delivered them into the hands of the priests. Each body was then returned to its owner, whose relatives cooked it in a pot. "Separately, in an olla, they cooked the grains of maize. They served (his flesh) on it. They placed only a little on top of it. No chili did they add to it; they only sprinkled salt on it. Indeed all (the host's) kinsmen ate of it" (*ibid.*, book 9:67).

The most commonly practiced form of human sacrifice was autosacrifice. The priests, in particular, often drew blood from the fleshy parts of their own bodies— earlobes, tongues, thighs, upper arms, chests, or genitals. Sharp maguey thorns were most commonly used, and occasionally for greater penance cords or reeds were passed through the wounds. Virtually everyone, at some ceremonial event, was required to draw blood to demonstrate religious devotion. Even very young children were not exempt, although adults performed the rite for them, most typically piercing the child's earlobes.

Abstractly, all human sacrifices were dedicated to the sun. But this idea was generalized to all aspects of the natural world. The central notion was that without sacrificial death there could be no life. Sacrifices were offered to many deities in the pantheon, some of whom had special appetites. The solar deities preferred captives from Tlaxcalla and Huexotzinco, and the rain god Tlaloc thrived on children.

In addition to different tastes, different sacrificial techniques were used to propitiate the many gods and goddesses demanding sacrifices. The techniques, in fact, were varied and imaginative. In the vast majority of the sacrifices, an incision was made in the person's chest and the heart torn out (see Figure 5–3). Still palpitating, the heart was offered to the god and usually placed in a sacred vessel (*quauhxicalli*).[4] Most war captives, the bathed slaves, male deity impersonators, and some of the female deity impersonators were sacrificed in this manner. Female deity impersonators were sometimes sacrificed by having their heads severed before their hearts were removed. Children were offered to Tlaloc through drowning, their copious tears serving as a good omen for abundant rain.

Other techniques were used in special ceremonies. Captives were cast into a fire and their hearts removed as an offering to the fire god Xiuhtecutli; some men were ceremonially shot with arrows during the month Ochpaniztli; and in honor of the god Xipe Totec, the bravest captives, faintly armed with "feather-bladed" wooden cudgels and tied to a stone, fought a mock gladiatorial battle with fully armed Aztec warriors before reaching the sacrificial stone. But no matter the technique, the heart was typically removed and the head cut off and displayed on the skull rack. On occasions the skin was flayed and worn ceremonially by a priest; more frequently the limbs were detached from the body, stewed, and ritually eaten by rela-

[4] Dr. Francis Robicsek, cardiovascular surgeon and Maya scholar, has stated that an experienced surgeon could perform the operation in approximately 20 seconds, and that once removed, the heart may continue throbbing for perhaps as long as five minutes (Dumbarton Oaks Pre-Columbian Center Conference on Ritual Sacrifice, October 13–14, 1979).

Figure 5–3: Portrayal of a ritual heart sacrifice (Codex Magliabecchiano, in the series CODICES SELECTI, vol. XXIII, Akademische Druck- u. Verlagsanstalt, Graz 1970, folio 70).

tives of the victim's captor, by priests, or by other designated persons. The torsos were reportedly thrown to the carnivores in the royal zoos (Díaz del Castillo 1956: 213).

All of these sacrifices took place in a highly religious context. The event they commemorated always had a religious component, the sacrifices were always offered to some deity, and they were always performed by priests or persons acting as priests. The attitudes expressed toward the sacrifices were likewise sacred. A captor could not eat the flesh of his own captive, explaining " 'Shall I, then, eat my own flesh?' For when he took (the captive), he had said: 'He is as my beloved son.' And the captive had said: 'He is as my beloved father.' And yet he might eat of someone else's captive" (Sahagún, 1950–1969, book 2:52–53). The person about to be sacrificed was a sacred offering, a messenger to the gods. No malice or hatred existed between a captor and his captive; rather, a sense of kinship prevailed. Fate had determined who should be offered to keep the sun strong, the rains sufficient, the maize plentiful, and the wars successful. It was considered an honor to provide sacred nourishment to the supernatural and natural worlds. When people died in sacrifice, they died as gods, and a glorious afterlife awaited them. Their fate was reportedly borne willingly and resolutely. Stories abound of men captured in battle who, when offered life, insisted on their destined death through sacrifice. For example, when the renowned Tlaxcallan warrior Tlahuicole was captured by the Aztecs, he was offered life and a military position. He served valiantly for the

Aztec forces in a campaign against the Tarascans, but upon his return he insisted on being sacrificed (Torquemada 1969, vol. 1:219–220). Once having been captured, his fate was sealed and he must honorably abide by it. The same attitude is illustrated by stories of a young Tarascan prince who was ordered killed by his enraged father because he had evaded sacrifice (Craine and Reindorp 1970:225–227), and of two Aztec warriors who were captured by Cortés's men and insisted on being sacrificed even when offered release (Davies 1973:172).

The peoples of fifteenth- and sixteenth-century central Mexico practiced human sacrifice on a scale unparalleled in the history of mankind. What were the motivating forces behind this practice, and the ritual cannibalism that often followed the sacrifices? Hypothesized answers to this question have stirred considerable debate among twentieth-century anthropologists. In general, the controversy rages between those who prefer a religious explanation and those who advocate an ecological-nutritional explanation, usually referred to as cultural materialism.

The religious explanation places the motivations behind sacrifice and cannibalism in the Aztec symbolic and belief systems. Briefly, it was generally accepted in pre-Hispanic central Mexico that human sacrifices were essential to the continuation of the universe. This belief was fundamental in explaining the mysteries of life and death; specific patterned behavior—human sacrifice and cannibalism—was in complete harmony with that belief. Those who were sacrificed became divine; those who consumed the flesh of a sacrificed person were consuming the flesh of a sacred entity. As Durán put it, "The flesh of all those who died in sacrifice was held truly to be consecrated and blessed. It was eaten with reverence, ritual, and fastidiousness—as if it were something from heaven" (1971:191). In this vein, Ortiz de Montellano (1978:614–615) has suggested that many of the sacrifices were offered to the gods as a ritual thanksgiving. While supporters of the religious position feel that belief systems can be the prime mover of behavior, the materialists argue that the religious explanation is not a scientific explanation for a real-world phenomenon. They assert that belief systems beg for explanation and cannot singly generate customs such as human sacrifice and cannibalism.

The ecological approach searches for a natural, rather than supernatural, explanation. As formulated by Michael Harner (1977), this position claims that the central Mexicans had to resort to human sacrifice and associated cannibalism because of a dietary deficiency of proteins and fats. Harner's thesis rests on the relationship between human populations and resources available to feed them. He claims that among the Aztecs increased population seriously reduced the amount of wild game available as a source of protein. Lacking a domesticated herbivore, the Aztecs had to find other means to meet necessary protein requirements. The answer, continues Harner, lay in cannibalism, a food source supplied through human sacrifice. He suggests that this need for meat was clothed in rich ritualistic garments, which disguised its real raison d'être. Recognizing that only distinguished and/or high-ranking persons could consume human flesh, he argues that this could be an incentive to greater efforts on the battlefield, since distinction was won in this fashion.

To be explanatory in an ecological sense, this thesis must establish sound evidence for, and links between, the following: (1) protein- and fat-deficient diet, (2) cannibalism to alleviate this problem, and (3) human sacrifice as the means to provide the general population with food (relying mainly on warfare for the supply of sacrificial victims). In the first place, it is doubtful that the Aztec diet was protein and fat deficient. In one sixteenth-century source alone, 32 different types of fowl are mentioned as being edible; some are noted as being very abundant, others as being very fatty (Sahagún 1950–1969, book 11:25–39, 53–54). A large variety of edible fish was also available to the lake populations, as well as numerous edible water and lagoon animals (*ibid.*:59–65). Aside from fish, fowl, wild game, and domesticated animals (turkeys and dogs), the maize-beans complex as a supplier of protein should not be underestimated. Although cultivated food plants were produced on a seasonal basis, these foods would have been available to the central Mexican populations in large quantities year round. Harner makes no mention of the durability of these foods, and the fact that they were stored in large bins (not only in the major central Mexican cities but also throughout the empire). These bins were filled not only from local *chinampa* cultivation but also from conquered provinces, which provided these staples in tribute. Combined, the four grains paid in tribute alone (maize, beans, chia, and amaranth) could provide a balanced diet "exceeding the daily protein requirements" for 60,000 to 150,000 people annually (Ortiz de Montellano 1978:612). The durability of these foods and the ability of the imperial centers to draw on wide areas of foodstuff production would have significantly lessened the impact of possible famine.

If cannibalism were functioning to supplement a protein-deficient diet, it is peculiar that the greatest amount of cannibalism coincided with harvesttime (*ibid.*: 614–615). The carnivores in the royal zoos were indeed fed human torsos, but they also were given domesticated dogs, thus competing with the people for a common source of protein (Díaz del Castillo 1956:213). During Cortés's siege of Tenochtitlan, people were starving on the streets and eating anything from adobe to leather, but human bodies lay all about, uneaten (Ortiz de Montellano 1978:613). It is unlikely that protein shortages were present in the Aztec diet, and equally unlikely that simple nutrition was a driving motivation behind the custom of cannibalism.

In addition to these nutritional and economic arguments, the problem of distribution greatly weakens Harner's hypothesis. He acknowledges that the upper echelons of Aztec society, who had access to a variety of protein sources, also had almost exclusive rights to cannibalism. The commoners, who he observes had limited access to general protein sources, also had the least access to cannibalism. Only through achievement on the battlefield could they gain rights to human flesh; little such protein would have entered the mouths of children and adolescents, who would have needed it the most (*ibid.*:615). If cannibalism were causally tied to protein deficiency in the central Mexican population, it would have been at best a limited remedy for the least needful segment of the population.

Harner has presented the view that some 250,000 persons were sacrificed annually in central Mexico in the fifteenth century (based on the unpublished figures of Woodrow Borah). This is an astonishing figure, far exceeding any estimates based on known data. Typical estimates for annual sacrifices hover around 20,000, and that may also be somewhat high. How many of these persons were also the subject of cannibalism is unknown; but certainly not all were consumed.

While human sacrifice and cannibalism were integral parts of the religion and justified through the belief system, human sacrifice was also demographically and politically relevant. Demographically, human sacrifice may have functioned as one means of population control. If the population was reaching its limits relative to the means of production, then human sacrifice may have served to check the population growth. However, if overall population size were the problem, it would certainly have been more efficient to sacrifice women of childbearing potential than mature males. In a society where polygyny was practiced (albeit only among nobles), reducing the male population would have had only a small temporary effect on the overall population growth.

A greater problem may have been the distribution of the population. With the expansion of the Triple Alliance empire, increasing human sacrifices tended to depopulate outlying provincial areas more than the dense urban districts; activities of warfare and human sacrifice tended to deplete the adult male component of the provincial population. By reducing the military strength of a conquered province, the Triple Alliance also temporarily reduced the possibility of rebellion in that province. This practice undoubtedly facilitated the loose administrative structure characteristic of the Triple Alliance empire (Berdan 1975:304). It is notable that the great increases in human sacrifice coincided with the era of greatest imperial expansion; the demographic effects of this custom may indeed have had important political ramifications.

It should be kept in mind that neither human sacrifice nor cannibalism were simple customs without variations. Not only "ultimate" sacrifice, but also auto-sacrifice, must be explained. And while virtually all cannibalism was highly ritualized, there are suggestions that a more straightforward cannibalism was practiced directly on the field of battle (Wagner 1944:317). A more abstract "eating of flesh" took place during certain religious ceremonies, where images of deities made of amaranth dough were eaten with the belief that the essence of the god was being ingested. Whichever explanation is ultimately best supported—ideational, materialistic, demographic-political, or some other—all of these complexities must be taken into account.

Politics, warfare and human sacrifice all had a profound impact on every Mexica's life. Each of these arenas was supported by strong cultural ethics, and perpetuated by intense religious beliefs and demands. Religion, which penetrated every aspect of Mexica life so profoundly, is discussed in Chapter 6.

6/Religious organization
and beliefs

Once every 52 years, the people of central Mexico joined in a solemn religious event. On the designated day, all fires were extinguished, and all household idols thrown out. The cooking implements and the three traditional hearthstones of each household were also discarded. The houses and surrounding areas were meticulously swept and cleaned of all debris. As night fell, everyone climbed to housetops and walls, pregnant women taking care to cover their faces with maguey-leaf masks. Children were similarly masked and not allowed to doze, for if they did, and the critical cosmic rite about to be performed failed, it was believed they would be transformed into mice.

Then, in the darkness, priests personifying the most important deities ascended the summit of Uixachtlan.[1] At precisely midnight, one of the priests slew a captive in the traditional fashion. With a fire drill, he then proceeded to kindle a new flame in the open chest cavity of the sacrificed captive. If the fire were successfully drawn, all would be well with the universe for another 52 years. The swiftest runners spread this new flame to each temple, school, and household. Meanwhile every man, woman, and child would bleed his or her ears in penance. If the fire did not light, the ceremony failed. This signaled the impending end of the present sun, believed to be the fifth to have reigned in Mexica mythological time. Darkness would then overcome the earth, and the *tzitzimime*, celestial monsters, would descend to earth and devour all human beings.

This drama, so charged with anxiety and fear, symbolized the most salient features of the Aztec belief system. The cultural mood of uncertainty was overwhelmingly present. The perception of time as cyclical and repetitive provided the mythological foundation for the ceremony, whose ritual implied that it rested with the Mexica to attempt actively to delay the eventually inevitable. They took an active, rather than passive, posture in relating to the supernatural. This is nowhere more marked than in the custom and meanings behind human sacrifice, and in this "new fire" ceremony. In short, this ceremony epitomizes the Mexica's view of the universe: its structure, content, dynamics, and the human role in its preservation.

---

[1] Today called Cerro de la Estrella ("Hill of the Star"), this mountain is located on the outskirts of Mexico City.

These beliefs provided a philosophy, a backdrop, against which a multitude of gods and priests assumed special personalities and acted out their designated roles. Religious positions, whether in the natural or supernatural world, were arranged according to two principles prominent in other aspects of Mexica life: heterogeneity and hierarchy. Deities were pervasive and diverse. The gods were linked to virtually all natural phenomena, with different gods claiming different realms and, at the same time, exhibiting unique personalities. The complex priesthood closely mirrored this supernatural variety. The deities and their associated priesthoods were not only diverse but also were arranged hierarchically: Some realms were considered more important than others.

Among attitudes, fate was prominent, but humanity was not left in despair. Through dedicated and active participation in rituals and careful attention to astrology and divination, any Mexica could help mold fate. In the large-scale ceremonies it was critical that the Mexica perform penances and other acts of devotion properly and sincerely. If a man was to be sacrificed, for example, the gods would be pleased if he bore his fate willingly. In individualized rites involving the interpretation of one's astrology or other forms of divination, the Mexica attempted not only to discover fate but also perhaps to manipulate it.

All of these beliefs and activities are part of the Mexica religious system, and are included in this chapter: ideas about the nature and dynamics of the universe; the vivid mosaic of deities; the complex religious priesthood; the colorful and awe-inspiring ceremonies; and the realm of astrology, divination, and omens.

MYTHOLOGY AND LEGEND:
THE STRUCTURE OF THE UNIVERSE

The Dynamics of Creation   All known religions contain mythologies that explain the creation of the universe and its inhabitants. These mythologies also delineate the relationships between the natural and supernatural worlds. Among the Aztecs, one version of these explanations, embedded in an ancient mythology, took the following form:

At the source of all creation were two primordial deities, Ometecutli ("Lord of Duality") and Omecihuatl ("Lady of Duality"). As the initial creators of all life, this twosome produced four quite different sons: the Red Tezcatlipoca (Xipe Totec), the Black Tezcatlipoca (Tezcatlipoca), Quetzalcoatl (presumably the White Tezcatlipoca), and the Blue Tezcatlipoca (Huitzilopochtli). Each of these new gods was associated with a different cardinal direction, color, tree, animal, and other natural and cultural phenomena. Two of these gods, Quetzalcoatl and Huitzilopochtli, were charged with the further creation of life, including gods, humanity, environments, and all living substances. Among the creations attributed to these gods were fire, the first human beings, the calendar, the underworld and its presiding gods, the heavens, water and its reigning deities, and the earth (Historia de los Mexicanos por sus Pinturas 1941:228–229). This last was formed from an alligator monster, or *cipactli*, within the great waters already created (Nicholson 1971:398).

Once these fundamentals had been arranged, a series of four separate ages, defined as "suns," ensued. In total, they lasted 2028 years. Each was ruled by a separate deity, peopled by different types of humans, and terminated by a cataclysmic event, in which the people of the age were destroyed or transformed into other beings. Miguel León-Portilla (1963) posits that these ages represent a kind of cosmic battle among the four sons of the Duality deities. Table 6–1 summarizes the most typically documented sequences, and includes the fifth and current sun.

Not all central Mexican traditions agreed with this Tenochtitlan sequence of solar ages. One set of variant sources essentially placed the first four sons in reverse order; others documented three, rather than four, sons. Despite these variations, which were most likely regional, the essential cosmic theory was the same. Prior ages had existed, and the pattern of these ages tended to be repetitive. The gods made successive attempts to create humanity, with each attempt ending in full-scale disaster. The current age was to be no exception to this pattern, and would also end in destruction. And no future, or sixth, sun was predicted: The world would simply fall into deep darkness at the end of the fifth sun.

Following the destruction of the fourth age, heaven, earth, and its inhabitants had to be reassembled. The first chore, that of terrestrial re-creation, fell to two unlike gods: Tezcatlipoca and Quetzalcoatl. These two deities dissipated the waters which had deluged the earth and hoisted the fallen sky, suspending it above the earth. With the earth suitably intact, Tezcatlipoca created fire for illumination, while other gods formed some of the fundamental elements of heaven and earth: rain, the night, stars, the underworld.

Then it fell to Quetzalcoatl to create humanity. He undertook a difficult journey

TABLE 6–1   TENOCHTITLAN SEQUENCE OF THE FIVE AGES, OR "SUNS"

Name of sun	Presiding deity	Human population	Fate of humanity	Type of destruction
1. *naui ocelotl* ("Four Jaguar")	Tezcatlipoca	Giants subsisting on acorns	Eaten by jaguars	Jaguars
2. *naui ehecatl* ("Four Wind")	Quetzalcoatl	Humans subsisting on piñon nuts (*acocentli*)	Transformed into monkeys	Hurricanes
3. *naui quiahuitl* ("Four Rain")	Tlaloc	Humans subsisting on an aquatic seed (*acecentli*)	Transformed into dogs, turkeys, butterflies	Fiery rain
4. *naui atl* ("Four Water")	Chalchiuhtlicue	Humans subsisting on wild seeds (probably *teocentli*, wild ancestor of maize)	Transformed into fish	Great flood
5. *naui ollin* ("Four Movement")	Tonatiuh	Humans subsisting on maize	To be devoured by *tzitzimime* (celestial monsters)	Earthquakes

to the underworld to collect bones and ashes of humans from the fourth disastrous age. He successfully acquired these lifeless remnants from the "Lord of the Underworld," Mictlantecutli. Quetzalcoatl and other deities, through autosacrifice, then splashed blood on the pulverized bones and ashes. From this mixture emerged a male child and then a female child. These two were the forebears of all historic and present humanity.

Heaven and earth were in proper order, fire provided light, and humanity was satisfactorily formed. But people could not survive without nourishment. Again the task fell to Quetzalcoatl. This adventurous god managed to secure a few grains of maize; disguised as a black ant, he was led to their source by a red ant. More grains were required if this food were to sustain all human beings, and after some godly competition, maize and other staple foods were guaranteed for mankind.

It was now time for the birth of the sun and moon; their creation by the gods is related in Chapter 5. From these events stemmed the quintessential duty of the Mexica and their neighbors: to provide the gods with nourishment through sacrifice. This cooperation between mankind and the gods was necessary if the present sun, or age, were to endure.

The Organization of the Universe   The perception by the Mexica of the celestial and terrestrial worlds—their components, organization, and meaning—closely reflected the people's notions of world genesis. And all these notions affected important aspects of everyday behavior.

The central Mexican organization of space may be divided into horizontal and vertical dimensions. These dimensions had their ultimate point of reference at the earth's navel. The earth itself was visualized as a disc located in the center of the universe and surrounded by a great circle of water. Horizontal spatial divisions, in the form of four world quarters facing the cardinal directions, radiated from the earth's navel. Vertical layers extended subterraneanly and into the heavens, again focusing on the center of the earth.

1. The Horizontal Dimension of Space   In the Aztec notions of horizontal space, the universe was divided into five directions—one associated with each cardinal direction, and one at the center. At the center was the Lord of Duality, the creator deity who lent support and omnipotent order to the universe. At each cardinal direction, a different god held up the lowest level of the heavens from the earth. The directions south, east, north, and west were viewed not as distinct points, but as quadrants radiating from the Lake Texcoco area. The entire realm of horizontal space was, therefore, divided into quarters. Each of these quadrants had distinctive qualities. Each was associated with a deity who helped support the heavens; each symbolized qualities of good, bad, or indifferent; each encompassed a 13-year section of the 52-year calendar round, representing a segment of time; and each had an associated color, tree, and bird or animal. These quadrants and some of their more important associations are summarized in Table 6–2.[2]

In this scheme, time and space were inextricably woven, and each segment of time-space had a special mood. The south, for example, was associated with the

----

[2] A table similar to the one presented here is in Nicholson (1971:405). In the documents, there are considerable variations in precise colors, trees, and birds.

TABLE 6–2   THE DIRECTIONAL QUADRANTS AND THEIR QUALITIES

Direction	Meaning	Quality	Probable associated deity	Year sign	Color
South (*huitztlampa*)	Region of Thorns	Neutral, uncertain	Mictlantecutli	Rabbit (*tochtli*)	White or blue
East (*tlapcopa*)	Place of Dawn	Fortunate, fertile	Tlahuizcalpantecutli (god of the planet Venus)	Reed (*acatl*)	Yellow or red
North (*mictlampa*)	Region of the Underworld	Dry, barren	A fire deity	Flint Knife (*tecpatl*)	Red or black
West (*cihuatlampa* or *imiquian* Tonatiuh)	Region of Women[3] or Place of the Sun's Death	Rainy, fruitless	Ehecatl-Quetzalcoatl	House (*calli*)	Blue-green or white

Compiled from Durán 1971:392–393; Sahagún 1950–1969, book 7:21–22, book 10:166; León-Portilla 1963:46–47; Nicholson 1971:403–405.

13 years under the sign of the Rabbit. These years were uncertain: "It was considered neither bad nor good, for in some years things went well and in others badly. These years were depicted in the form of a rabbit because he leaps to and fro and never stays in one place" (Durán 1971:393). Although Rabbit years were variable, the people recalled that the devastating famine in the mid-fifteenth century culminated in the year One Rabbit, and tended to fear the onset of this sign. But more frequent bad years apparently were remembered for the years associated with the north and west; when these signs came, moods of anxiety and uncertainty prevailed. The 13 years associated with the east were considered to have been uniformly favorable, happy, and productive; the moods of the population must have been correspondingly more cheerful. History itself seems to have a great deal to do with the attributes assigned to these time-space dimensions.

Certain concrete behavior patterns were also affected by this scheme. Method of burial was one:

. . . when an evil man died he was wrapped in old, thick cloth made of maguey fiber and was buried with his face toward the North. This was done because the people said he had gone to hell because of his wicked life; and, because of the terrible cold there, they wrapped him in those thick blankets to give him warmth. With him was buried food for him to eat, since the place was sterile (*ibid.*:392).

Religious ceremonies also frequently recognized the quadrants, as did architecture and city planning, and rites such as the dedication of a new house or the naming of an infant.

2. The Vertical Dimension of Space   On the vertical dimension, space was tiered. These tiers extended in 13 layers above the earth, and in 9 below. Each layered

[3] Called "Region of Women" because women who had died in childbirth accompanied the sun on its western descent.

arrangement began with the surface of the earth (level 1). Climbing upward, the heavens were chiefly the realms of the moon (level 2); the stars (level 3); the sun (level 4); the planet Venus or birds (level 5); comets and fire serpents (level 6); the color black, or winds (level 7); the color blue, or dust (level 8); storms (level 9); "White God" (level 10); "Yellow God" (level 11); "Red God" (level 12); finally reaching Omeyocan, the "Place of Duality," where reigned the primordial creators, the Lord and Lady of Duality (Nicholson 1971: table 2, León-Portilla 1963:49–52). The lowest heavenly layers provided the paths through which passed the most important observable celestial bodies. The more distant tiers were conceived as more abstract regions—as realms of winds, storms, and colors; as homes of untouchable gods.

The 9 layers of the underworld again began with the earth's surface (level 1). The remaining 8 layers were viewed as unpleasant and hazardous places. To the unrenowned soul, each of these layers served as a painful challenge on the soul's long journey to the ninth layer, Mictlan, or "Place of the Dead." There the soul rested for eternity (see Chapter 4).

THE DEITIES AND THEIR DOMAINS

In the Aztec supernatural world, the majority of the deities were anthropomorphic, or imbued with human characteristics. This applied to their physical appearance, aspects of their apparel, and especially their personalities. To oversimplify, Quetzalcoatl was typically depicted as benevolent, kind, and generous; Tezcatlipoca as capricious, youthful, and powerful.

Most of these deities were celestial dwellers. And a few resided in special heavenly districts: the Duality gods ruled the thirteenth heaven, where they continued their creative role by sending to earth the souls of unborn infants; and Tlaloc dwelled in Tlalocan, a verdant paradise said to be located somewhere in the east.

Most deities also served as patrons to specific groups of people. Fundamentally, each community and *calpulli* had its own patron god. These territorial units often coincided with occupational or ethnic categories, so that the patron of the community or calpulli was also the ethnic or occupational group patron. In many cases, however, such neat correspondences did not occur; then occupational or ethnic groups would have separate patrons. The midwives and curers, for example, although living in many diverse calpulli, celebrated as a unit the major ritual for their patroness Toci. The Mexica, spread over many calpulli and in fact in several cities, all worshiped Huitzilopochtli as their special protector. And the full-time professional merchants looked to Yacatecutli, the "Long-nosed God." Patron deities figured in any movements of the groups that worshiped them. When settled, the group's first substantial act would be to erect a temple to its patron. If a community were conquered, defeat was symbolized by the burning of the vanquished's patron god's temple; the god's image and sacred paraphernalia, if found, were then carried off by the victors.

By the time of the Spanish arrival, the Mexica had assembled an enormous and complex pantheon. Aside from their patron god, they also had a traditional collection of other Chichimec deities. Upon their arrival in the Valley of Mexico (and probably before), they assimilated a plethora of other deities long resident in the Valley of Mexico and beyond. The Mexica religion was not a proselytizing one, but an assimilative one. As the Aztec state accepted, absorbed, or conquered other peoples, it also adopted their gods.[4]

To lend some order to this diverse pantheon, a scheme devised by Nicholson (1971:410–430) is extremely helpful. Nicholson has discerned three paramount religious themes, each of which encompassed a number of deity complexes. These themes are celestial 'creativity—divine paternalism, rain—moisture—agricultural fertility, and war—sacrifice—sanguinary nourishment of the sun and the earth.

Celestial Creativity—Divine Paternalism The most abstract deity theme centered on original creative forces. As such, it included the Lord and Lady of Duality, sometimes represented as a single deity with combined male and female aspects. More direct ritual attention, however, was paid to another important creator, Tezcatlipoca. He was closely associated with the Duality gods, and shared many of their features. In particular, he possessed omnipotent power. He had many aspects, and it seems that some other independent deities, over time, had merged with this all-powerful god. As the "Smoking Mirror," he "could see all that took place in the world with that reflection" (Durán 1971:99). He was especially associated with the night, the jaguar, sorcery, and warfare. The range of his concerns was extremely broad, and the people and priests prayed to him to abate plagues, to prevent poverty (indeed, to bestow riches), to assist them in wars, and to assure them able rulers. He was obviously the source of all natural forces, human strength and frailty, wealth, happiness and grief. He was foreboding in appearance, typically depicted with two smoking mirrors—one at his head, the other covering one of his feet (see Figure 6–1). This second mirror replaced the foot Tezcatlipoca had lost to the earth monster.[5] His body was black, but his face was characteristically yellow with black horizontal bands. Since he was a young warrior, he carried military trappings: a shield, *atlatl* (dart thrower), and darts.

Also associated with creation was the ancient fire god, Xiuhtecutli (also called Huehueteotl, the "Old God"). Fire in both concrete and abstract forms was extremely important in central Mexico. From each small house to each awesome temple, secular and religious life centered on the fires. And fire itself seemed to symbolize enduring life, as in the new fire ceremony enacted every 52 years.

Rain—Moisture—Agricultural Fertility While the creativity—divine paternalism theme contained the most omniscient deities, the theme of rain, moisture, and agricultural fertility was clearly dominant in terms of priestly commitment, ritual activity, and diversity of deities. It focused on the most decisive life-sustaining forces and phenomena: rain, the earth, maize, maguey, and fertility in general.

[4] The flexibility of the pantheon is illustrated by the addition of the god Tloque Nahuaque, "Lord of the Immediate Vicinity," by the Texcocan ruler Nezahualcoyotl. This omnipotent invisible deity was worshipped by Nezahualcoyotl, but attracted few other followers.

[5] Tezcatlipoca as the jaguar was seen as the "Big Dipper" constellation in the night sky. The devouring of Tezcatlipoca's foot by the earth monster coincided with the periodic and regular dipping of one of the stars in that constellation below the horizon.

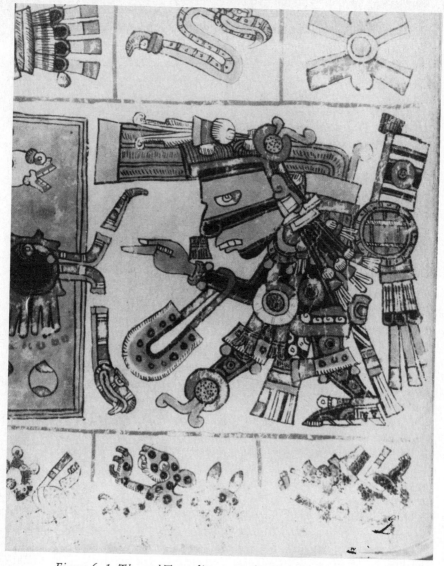

Figure 6–1: The god Tezcatlipoca (Codex Borgia 1963:page 21).

Here the supreme deity was Tlaloc, an ancient god of rain appearing in numerous aspects throughout Mesoamerica. His role in successful agriculture was crucial:

> To him was attributed the rain; for he made it, he caused it to come down, he scattered the rain like seed, and also the hail. He caused to sprout, to blossom, to leaf out, to bloom, to ripen, the trees, the plants, our food. And also by him were made floods of water and thunder-bolts (Sahagún 1950–1969, book 1:2).

Tlaloc was always portrayed with a distinctive facial mask; face front, this mask "gives him the appearance of wearing eyeglasses and a moustache" (Caso 1958:42).

His body and face were usually black, his mask and clothing were blue, and his headdress was topped with white heron feathers and green quetzal plumes. The black symbolized storm clouds, the blue represented water, and the white feathers symbolized white clouds. On his head and back he wore paper banners spattered with rubber. Stylized drops of water, his life-giving gift to humanity, are sometimes depicted with him (see Figure 6–2).

Tlaloc had a number of small celestial assistants, the Tlaloque, each of whom was associated with a mountaintop, where it was believed that storms were born. As with a great many of the more important deities, Tlaloc had a female consort, or counterpart. As Tlaloc's wife, mother, or sister, Chalchiuhtlicue ("Jade-Her-Skirt") reigned over water in general. Other lesser goddesses prevailing over salt and *oxitl*[6] seem simply to have been specialized aspects of this goddess.

Rain was necessary, but not sufficient to ensure human survival. People and cultivated plants must grow, be healthy, and reproduce. Fertility, therefore, was an essential task of a far-ranging group of deities. At the forefront were the female deities associated with the earth mother. Variously called "Mother of the Gods" (Teteoinnan), "Our Grandmother" (Toci), and "Heart of the Earth" (Tlalli iyollo), she was worshiped especially by the physicians and midwives, those dedicated to physical health and well-being. Many goddesses were closely linked to her, each with her own special realm and duties. Among the goddesses included in this earth mother concept were Coatlicue, the mother of Huitzilopochtli, and Tonantzin ("Our Revered Mother"), who later became associated with the Virgin Mary. In the abstract, all these goddesses symbolized the notion of fertility; in the concrete, they variously watched over pleasure and feasting, sexual desire and sin, pregnancy and childbirth.

Closely associated with these goddesses was the god Xipe Totec ("Our Lord the Flayed One"). He was a fertility god whose extraordinary rituals signaled the arrival of spring. It was for Xipe Totec that the gladiatorial sacrifice (see Chapter 5) was performed. As in ceremonies for the goddess Toci, the skin of the

Figure 6–2: The god Tlaloc (Codex Magliabecchiano, in the series CODICES SELECTI, vol. XXIII, Akademische Druck- u. Verlagsanstalt, Graz 1970, folio 34).

---

[6] Oxitl was a pine ointment used to relieve the sufferers of head scabies, head abscesses, and jigger fleas (Sahagún 1950–1969, book 10:140,152).

sacrificial victim was flayed and worn by a priest. This was a hallmark of the rites dedicated to Xipe Totec, and the god himself was characteristically portrayed as covered with a flayed skin.

Also included in this theme of rain—moisture—agricultural fertility are the gods who presided over maize and other cultivated plants. These were primarily youthful deities, headed by the goddess Chicomecoatl ("Seven Serpent"; see Chapter 2, Note 1) and the god Centeotl ("Maize God"). They were overseers not only of maize and other plants but also of many of the arts.

Maguey was the one other cultivated plant that warranted its own complex of deities. Mayahuel was the maguey goddess (see Chapter 2); her offspring were the "Four Hundred Rabbits," innumerable gods devoted to pulque, drunkenness, and pleasure.

War—Sacrifice—Sanguinary Nourishment of the Sun and the Earth   Under the theme of war and sacrifice may be grouped the deities who especially required the nourishment of human blood. By extension, these gods were variously imbued with qualities of warfare, human sacrifice, and death. A central deity in this theme, and in central Mexico generally, was Tonatiuh, the sun god. All warriors were dedicated to the sun's service: they supplied the sun with the blood of their captives; and if they themselves died serving the sun, they accompanied Tonatiuh on his daily journey from dawn to noon.

Huitzilopochtli, patron of the Mexica, also fits into this theme. His cult followers emphasized warfare and military dominance for the Mexica over neighboring peoples. Through his priests, he had led the Mexica on their long migration to the Valley of Mexico, always encouraging and promising them a future greatness. Like Tonatiuh, Huitzilopochtli required a regular supply of human blood, and many large-scale sacrifices were carried out at his lofty temple. As already noted, he was closely associated with the sun, and may also have been considered a solar deity. He was the Blue Tezcatlipoca, painted with blue stripes, wearing a precious quetzal feather headdress, and brandishing his trappings of war: a shield and the serpent which mythologically had been used to destroy his sister, Coyolxauhqui. Some depictions of Huitzilopochtli portray him with a hummingbird headdress, befitting his name "Hummingbird on the Left."

Other major deities who shared many of the qualities of Tonatiuh and Huitzilopochtli were Mixcoatl-Camaxtli, Tlahuizcalpantecutli, and Mictlantecutli. The first two were more closely associated with the stars and the planet Venus than with the sun, but they both had highly militaristic personalities. Mixcoatl-Camaxtli ruled the Milky Way. Under the name Camaxtli, he was also the supreme god of hunting, and patron of the Mexica's most ardent enemies, the Tlaxcallans. Tlahuizcalpantecutli was one of the gods of the planet Venus, Quetzalcoatl being the other. But while Quetzalcoatl was preeminently a beneficent god, Tlahuizcalpantecutli was warlike and malevolent (Nicholson 1971:427). Although they shared the same celestial body, these gods exhibited two very opposed personalities. Mictlantecutli ("Lord of Mictlan"), a god also associated with war and sacrifice, served as lord of the underworld, land of death and darkness (see Chapter 4). As with so many central Mexican deities, he supervised his realm with the aid of a female consort, the goddess Mictlancihuatl ("Lady of Mictlan").

Although Nicholson's thematic classification accommodates the roles of most of the deities of the central Mexican pantheon, like most systems of classification, it cannot neatly organize and account for all applicable data. Nicholson recognizes that some of the gods simply do not fit neatly into the scheme. The most important of these is Quetzalcoatl, the "Plumed Serpent." This ancient Mesoamerican deity is associated with the celestial creativity theme in his role as one of the fundamental creators and the provider of sustenance for mankind; he is linked with the rain—moisture—agricultural fertility theme in his role as Ehecatl, the wind: "he was the wind, the guide and roadsweeper of the rain gods, of the masters of the water, of those who brought rain" (Sahagún 1950–1969, book 1:3). Although not a militant or sanguinary deity, Quetzalcoatl as the planet Venus overlaps with the god Tlahuizcalpantecutli of the war—sacrifice—sanguinary nourishment theme. In this last aspect, the god Quetzalcoatl is confounded with a mortal, the Toltec ruler-priest, Topiltzin Quetzalcoatl. In the most famous Aztec legend, Topiltzin Quetzalcoatl was disgraced and sent from Tula by his enemy and stiffest competition, Tezcatlipoca. With both Quetzalcoatl and Tezcatlipoca, what is being related is undoubtedly a tale of the high priests of these gods. Nonetheless, Topiltzin Quetzalcoatl, as that god's most exalted mortal representative, traveled from Tula to the Gulf Coast. There, according to one version, he was cremated and ascended into the heavens as Venus, the Morning Star.

Quetzalcoatl was represented in a variety of ways in books and in sculpture. When painted, his face and body were black; and he characteristically wore a red mask, often in the shape of a bird's beak. Since he was featured as a high priest, he typically carried the hallmark of priestly paraphernalia: a copal (incense) bag. He always wore a conical headdress and his frontal garment was always designed as a sea shell. He sometimes wore a beard, which anthropomorphically identified him as an old man, or an ancient god (see Figure 6–3).

Figure 6–3: The god Quetzalcoatl (Codex Magliabecchiano, in the series CODICES SELECTI, vol. XXIII, Akademische Druck- u. Verlagsanstalt, Graz 1970, folio 61).

Quetzalcoatl, at one and the same time culture hero and beneficent god, was hailed in central Mexico as the ultimate provider of human sustenance, the calendar, and the fine arts. He was overseer of the schools where priests and other professionals were trained, the *calmecac*. He embodied all that the Mexica characterized as "civilization."

THE PRIESTLY HIERARCHY

Priestly Ranks   Each of the many deities was housed in its own special temples, surrounded by its characteristic paraphernalia, honored by its own rituals, and served by its own cadre of full-time priests. In addition to the priests, some deities were attended by priestesses, individuals who had made special vows to temporarily serve that deity, or other lay persons who felt a special affinity for that god. The *tlatoani* and *cihuacoatl*, as the supreme political officers, also served some important religious functions. Religion and politics were so intertwined that it is often difficult to separate the two, and perhaps the Mexica did not make such distinctions.

Training for the priesthood took place in the calmecac, under the tutelage of the priests. There were several calmecac, each associated with a different temple, and each probably emphasizing somewhat different ritual activities and duties. But, overall, boys were dedicated to the priesthood by their parents, and entered their priestly training under the title *tlamacazton* (little priests, or "little givers of things"). Under this title they performed mainly menial chores, until elevated to the next rank, that of *tlamacazqui* (young priest, or "giver of things"). The most qualified youths could later be promoted to the rank of *tlenamacac* ("fire giver"), the revered priests who, for the most part, wielded the obsidian knife at the moment of sacrifice. Movement from rank to rank apparently occurred at five-year intervals, and only the most devout were promoted. At the apex of the religious hierarchy were two priests equal in rank: *quetzalcoatl totec tlamacazqui* and *quetzalcoatl tlaloc tlamacazqui*. These priests managed the religious affairs at the great dual temple in Tenochtitlan: The former attended to Huitzilopochtli, the latter to Tlaloc. These priests were expected to exhibit special personal qualities, consistent with the Mexica image of Quetzalcoatl as "high priest" and symbol of civilization. Each was to be

> . . . of saintly life, of righteous life; of pure heart, good, and humane; who was resigned; who was firm and tranquil; a peace-maker, constant, resolute, brave; caressing, welcoming, and friendly to others; who was compassionate of others and wept for them; who had awe in his heart (*ibid.*, book 3:67).

These two high priests supposedly could be of either noble or commoner background. They were elected to their positions by secular authorities: the ruler and his most important chiefs and nobles.

The priesthood was in no way exclusively a male domain. As with boys, an infant girl might be dedicated to the priesthood by her parents. They indicated their intentions of offering their daughter to the service of the gods by taking the infant to a temple and offering the priest an incense ladle and copal incense. Apparently, this commitment was to be repeated every 20 days by gifts left at the temple. This symbolized an agreement that the girl would, when older, enter the priesthood as a *cihuatlamacazqui* (woman priest, or "female giver of things"). In spite of these arrangements, the girl supposedly entered the priesthood voluntarily (*ibid.,* book 2:215). Relatively few of these young priestesses, by comparison with the priests, made a lifelong career of the priesthood. While still young, they could leave the service of the deities and marry, as long as they received the blessings of their parents and the calpulli leaders.

But some women did dedicate their lives to the deities. Certainly, older priestesses in the temples supervised the younger priestesses, and priestesses serving a variety of deities played important roles in some of the monthly religious ceremonies. For instance, during the month of Ochpaniztli, the priestesses of Chicomecoatl celebrated side by side with that deity's priests:

> [The priestesses] bore upon their backs the ears of dried maize, seven ears each, striped, painted well with liquid rubber, well girt in paper and wrapped in costly capes. And the priestesses who carried them upon their backs had their faces painted and (their arms and legs) pasted with feathers. And also they proceeded singing as they went . . . (*ibid.*:116).

All in all, the number of persons fulfilling full-time priestly roles must have been enormous. Juan de Torquemada, admittedly sometimes given to exaggeration, noted that the dual temple of Tenochtitlan was served by 5000 persons (Caso 1958: 188–189). Although this was the largest temple in the Valley of Mexico, each of the other temples also had its own full-time religious staff, and temples were almost innumerable. With the addition of great numbers of lay persons from all walks of life involved in periodic religious care and events, the human involvement in religion in central Mexico must have been dramatic.

Religious Duties and Activities The priests, both in their day-to-day activities and in their periodic extravaganzas, operated in two distinct realms. On the one hand, they were deeply committed to the deities. They spent a considerable amount of time in the service of "their" deities: sweeping the temples; caring for the idol and its accoutrements; manufacturing and caring for the deity's sacred paraphernalia; managing the temples and supervising any necessary additions or repairs; keeping the temple fires lit; and offering the endless penances, prayers, and incense during the day and especially at night. The penances most commonly consisted of drawing blood from various fleshy parts of the body; indeed, for the priests, a "permanent red smear of blood on each temple was an important badge of their profession" (Nicholson 1971:437). Their bodies were usually dyed black, and they characteristically wore their hair long and bound. As will be seen, the priest was also responsible for managing and participating in any special events celebrated in honor of "his" deity. Of course, no one priest could perform all these roles, and the priestly organization was quite specialized. A given priest was attached to only one deity; and among those who served that deity, some were managers and some assistants, some only cared for the sacred paraphernalia so important to the deity, and some (the most junior members) performed menial chores. While active in the temple, the priest was expected to be a model of "the exemplary life," and also to remain chaste. There are, however, some indications that priests (or perhaps only some priests) could marry (Códice Xolotl 1951:75).

While the priests directed most of their attention to the deities they revered, they also were involved in the affairs of the society as a whole. They carried weighty responsibilities as the educators of noble boys in the calmecac, molding the minds of future leaders. Transmitting knowledge to the next generation, the priests also were the principal guardians of this knowledge, at times adding to it. They read and interpreted the sacred books, making predictions about the future and attaching meaning to omens. In short, they often made decisions and offered advice on affairs of great political import (see Chapter 8). And, as with most central Mexicans, the priests frequently engaged in warfare, often distinguishing themselves and receiving prized rewards. Even more impressive, the priests served as the critical link between deity and mortal, interpreting the will of the deities and the role of humanity in the overall scheme of the universe.

The range of duties assigned to priestesses seems to have been narrower than for priests. Priestesses engaged in similar day-to-day temple activities, especially sweeping and the offering of incense. They also helped orchestrate and participated in some of the major religious ceremonies. But a large amount of their time must have been spent in weaving and embroidering the fine cloths used to decorate the idol and the temple.

Religious duties were also an integral part of the activities of the highest Mexica political officials, the ruling tlatoani and his second-in-command, the cihuacoatl. The stated duties of the tlatoani included assuring religious observances as well as the administration of the state, of justice, of warfare and the general management of agricultural production (Pomar 1941:33; Sahagún 1950–1969, book 6:67–74). In encouraging religious observances, the ruler occasionally took an active role. Particularly in ceremonies dedicated to the sun and to maize, the ruler distributed food and drink to the poor, and also took part in ritual dancing (Broda 1978:235–239). Religious and political events were frequently entwined: Ritual sacrifices were performed at a ruler's coronation; the ruler distributed military rewards at a religious ceremony; the high priests were elected by the ruler and his nobles; the ruler and his Council of Four were installed by a cadre of priests.

In addition to the many people permanently invested with religious functions, lay persons participated in religious activities on a temporary or periodic basis. "Rotational priests" apparently served in monthly shifts and aided the full-time priests in their duties (Nicholson 1971:436). Additional help was gained from individuals, male and female, who vowed to serve a temple for a limited time. This was done, from the individual's point of view, primarily to gain supernatural favor to ensure future happiness or to procure a cure for illness (Torquemada 1969, vol. 2:189; Sahagún 1950–1969, book 3:6–9; Kubler and Gibson 1951: 29–30). The Tovar Calendar provides elaborate detail on penitents devoted to the god Huitzilopochtli:

> . . . especially they selected twenty men and twenty women who awaited the arrival of this god. All this time they were serving in the temple, the men by themselves, and the women by themselves, with much seclusion and chastity. The

men served by sweeping and guarding the temple, and the women by cooking for the idol different foods which they placed and offered before the idol and since they were there for so long the priests collected it for their ordinary sustenance (1951:29).

It was critical that these youths remain chaste; at the end of their yearlong penitence, their chastity would be tested. On the day they were to leave the temple, the priests uncovered mirrors called "the eyes of god." If the eyes were clear, all knew that the youths had completed their vows with distinction, and they were rewarded. But if the eyes were dusty or full of hairs, this was undisputable proof that the penitents had behaved improperly, and they were summarily hanged. There were rewards in undertaking these vows, but there were also risks.

Other lay persons were involved in religious activities on a regular, periodic basis. In particular, the members of certain calpulli or communities participated in special festivities honoring their patron deity. Similarly, members of specialized occupational groups revered their deities on the occasions of their festivities. For example, the florists participated in rituals to Coatlicue in the third month of the solar calendar, harlots and young warriors sang and danced in the festivities of the eighth and fifteenth months, curers and midwives were active in the ceremonies of the eleventh month, and hunters were the focus of activity in some rituals of the fourteenth month. As will be discussed, virtually every specialized occupation and residential group had festivities that called on its members to actively participate by singing, dancing, feasting, fasting, bloodletting, or making other forms of offerings.

Some ceremonies focused on even larger groupings of people. Children were ceremonially active, singing, dancing, and bloodletting during the third, fourth, and fifth solar calendar months. Women danced and sang during the religious events of the seventh month. Nobles feasted commoners in the eighth month, and all warriors were required to fast and fashion arrows in the fourteenth month. Virtually everyone in central Mexico had, at one time or another, an opportunity and an obligation to participate in the great and lesser religious rituals; everyone contributed in some manner to maintain the necessary relations with the deities. This, of course, included also the many warriors who periodically offered captured enemies for sacrifice, the captured warriors or purchased sacrificial slaves themselves, and especially those who impersonated the deities and were essentially deified through sacrifice.

RITES AND CEREMONIES

The Mexica celebrated their religion with both public and private ceremonies. In the public sphere were the grand ceremonial extravaganzas associated with each of the 18 months of the solar year, some major ceremonies observed less frequently, and "movable" rituals linked to the *tonalpohualli*, or 260-day ritual calendar (see Chapter 7).

Each individual ceremony had its own goal, participants, activities, and paraphernalia. Nonetheless, all major public ceremonies were characterized by some common elements. A "typical ceremonial occasion" began with several days of fasting, at least by the priests, and often by other penitents. The denial of food during fasting was ritually defined. Normally only one meal each day, without chile and salt, was allowed. Sexual abstinence and non-bathing were also expected. At the end of the fasting period, and usually the night before the major public event, a vigil was often held by the most important participants. The extravaganza itself consisted of singing with musical accompaniment, dancing, and colorful processions. Offerings were a part of virtually every ceremony, and ranged from incense and gifts (often food) to animals (usually quail) and human beings for sacrifice. Lavish feasting often marked the final phases of the ceremony (Nicholson 1971: 431–433).

Most of the Mexica's ritual time and energy were devoted to the 18 monthly ceremonies performed during each month in the 365-day solar year, or *xiuitl*. A brief sketch of the major features of each monthly ceremony is provided in Table 6–3.

Of these 18 monthly ceremonies, 11 were directly aimed at propitiating the rain and fertility deities. These ceremonies coincided with the most critical periods in the agricultural cycle; 9 of the 13 ceremonies celebrated from mid-February through October were devoted to this theme (see Chapter 7). The Mexica called upon the aid of these deities during the planting, growing, and harvesting seasons. Of the ceremonies not dedicated to rain and fertility, the Mexica dedicated 4 to their patron god Huitzilopochtli (who invariably shared center stage with Tezcatlipoca). Other groups and communities undoubtedly stressed their own patron deities in a similar fashion. And while this ceremonial round approximates the cycle of events in the Lake Texcoco urban setting, ritual activities and deities venerated in rural and outlying areas surely diverged from this pattern: Each group emphasized different gods and each culture placed different interpretations on how to propitiate those gods.

In addition to these monthly ceremonies, other major religious events were held on a regular but less frequent schedule. For example, every four years, additional ceremonies were included in the eighteenth month: impersonators of the fire god Xiuhtecutli were sacrificed, children were recognized by having their ears pierced and being assigned "godparents," and the nobles danced and displayed their most exquisite clothing and decorations. Every eight years the ceremony of Atamalcualiztli ("The Eating of Water Tamales") was observed. Feasting and dancing was preceded by seven days of strict fasting: everyone was permitted to eat only tamales soaked in water, with no chile, salt, saltpeter, or lime. And this sparse bland meal was to be eaten only at midday. The dancing was full of pageantry. Some dancers appeared in the guises of hummingbirds, butterflies, owls, or beetles; others impersonated "sleep," the poor, or a leper. One ethnic group, the Mazateca, honored Tlaloc by dancing for two days with snakes and reportedly swallowing them. The solemn event culminated with a feast of fruit tamales, and supplications by the elderly that they might live another eight years. The entire ceremony was considered extremely important for this reason:

Thus was respite given the maize every eight years. For it was said that we brought much torment to it—that we ate (it), we put *chili* on it, we mixed salt with it, we mixed saltpeter with it; it was mixed with lime. As we troubled (our food) to death, thus we revived it. Thus, it was said, the maize was given (new) youth when this was done (Sahagún 1950–1969, book 2:164).

Another periodic religious event was the solemn ritual of the new fire, held every 52 years to ensure the continuation of the universe. Its essential elements have been described at the beginning of this chapter.

Other ceremonial occasions were linked with the tonalpohualli, or 260-day ritual calendar. Since their dates were not "fixed" with respect to the solar (365-day) calendar, they were labeled "movable feasts" by the sixteenth-century Spanish friars, who saw parallels with the "movable" Christian ceremonies. Sahagún (*ibid.*: 35–41) discusses 16 of these feasts.[7] Much as mortals were inextricably linked with the day-sign of their birth, so also each deity had a special day-sign. Each movable feast commemorated the god or gods associated with the day-sign. Typically, the deity's image was ritually adorned; and offerings of incense, quail, food, and other goods were laid before the idol. Fasting, dancing, singing, and feasting were components of several movable feasts. Unique ritual activities were scheduled for some of these days. The merchants displayed their wealth on Four Wind; pulque was consumed in copious quantities on Two Rabbit; and the ruler bestowed gifts on warriors, singers, and other "royal employees" on One Flower. Human sacrifice occasionally was practiced, as in the feast of Four Movement, dedicated to the sun. Also on this day, all persons were obliged to draw blood from their ears in penance. At two other ceremonies, on One Rain and Four Wind, prisoners condemned to death were executed.

Most of these ceremonies had their own special groups of penitents and participants. The painters and seamstresses especially celebrated Seven Flower, the day-sign of their patron deities Chicomexochitl and Xochiquetzal. Maguey planters and dealers, revering the gods of pulque, were particularly active in the rituals of Two Rabbit. And in the ritual events of One Flower, One Reed, and One Death, nobles played important roles when they variously danced, sang, displayed their fine feathers, made offerings, and feasted. On the whole, though, these movable ceremonies were less extravagant than the monthly ceremonies.

Many aspects of Mexica life were geared to other non-calendric ritual activities. Some of these, such as the dedication of a temple, the triumphal return of a victorious army, or the coronation of a new ruler, were held on a grand public scale. But most of the non-calendric ritual that touched the life of the everyday Mexica did so on a much more personal plane. Events marking stages in the life cycle (e.g., birth and naming, marriage, confession of sins, death) all had religious components (see Chapter 4). Other rituals were performed by merchants when they returned from long journeys, by farmers when planting began in the fields (see Chapter 2), and by virtually everyone on a daily basis around the fire and altars of each household. These more private, personal rituals enlisted the aid not only of deities and priests but also of magic and astrologers.

---

[7] Since each deity probably had its own special day-sign, Sahagún provides only a small sample.

TABLE 6–3 MONTHLY CEREMONIES OF THE SOLAR YEAR

Month	Literal meaning	Dates[8]	Most important deities worshipped	Primary religious themes	Sample of ritual activities
1. Atl caualo	Ceasing of Water	Feb. 13–Mar. 4	Tlaloque, Chalchiuhtlicue	Rain—moisture—agricultural fertility	Papers hung on poles, fasting for rain, tamales offered, dancing, children sacrificed
2. Tlacaxipehualiztli	Flaying of Men	Mar. 5–Mar. 24	Xipe Totec	Rain—moisture—agricultural fertility	Dancing, vigils, feasting. Human sacrifices (including gladiatorial sacrifice with flaying, and child sacrifices), rewards presented to outstanding warriors
3. Toçoztontli	Little Vigil	Mar. 25–Apr. 13	Tlaloque, Centeotl, Chalchiuhtlicue, Chicomecoatl	Rain—moisture—agricultural fertility	Planting rituals (in fields); flowers, snakes, and tamales offered; children's rituals and sacrifices
4. Uey toçoztli	Great Vigil	Apr. 14–May 3	Centeotl, Chicomecoatl, Tlaloque, Quetzalcoatl	Rain—moisture—agricultural fertility	Fasting, offerings, mock battles between youths and maidens; seed maize blessed; children's rituals and sacrifices; deity impersonator sacrificed
5. Toxcatl	Our Drought	May 4–May 23	Tezcatlipoca, Huitzilopochtli	Celestial creativity—divine paternalism; war—sacrifice	Sacrifice of deity impersonators; dancing; feasting; incense, food and quail offered; children's rituals
6. Etzalcualiztli	Eating of Etzalli[9]	May 24–June 12	Tlaloc, Chalchiuhtlicue, Quetzalcoatl	Rain—moisture—agricultural fertility	Fasting for rain; etzalli offering and eating; offerings made to agricultural tools; deity impersonators sacrificed
7. Tecuilhuitontli	Little Feast Day of the Lords	June 13–July 2	Xochipilli, Huixtochihuatl	Rain—moisture—agricultural fertility	Singing, dancing, human sacrifices, nobles feast commoners
8. Uey tecuilhuitl	Great Feast Day of the Lords	July 3–July 22	Xilonen, Cihuacoatl	Rain—moisture—agricultural fertility	Nobles feast commoners, singing and dancing of warriors and prostitutes, deity impersonators sacrificed

9. Tlaxochimaco	Offering of Flowers	July 23–Aug. 11	Huitzilopochtli, Tezcatlipoca, all gods in general	War—sacrifice; celestial creativity—divine paternalism	Flowers offered and idols decorated, singing, dancing, human sacrifices, honoring of dead
10. Xocotl uetzi	Fall of Xocotl	Aug. 12–Aug. 31	Xiuhtecutli, Xocotl, Yacatecutli (patron of the merchants)	Celestial creativity—divine paternalism	Fire sacrifice; impersonator of Yacatecutli sacrificed; ceremony of Xocotl pole: boys strive to climb pole and retrieve image; honoring of dead
11. Ochpaniztli	Sweeping of the Road	Sept. 1–Sept. 20	Teteoinnan-Toci, Centeotl, Chicomecoatl	Rain—moisture—agricultural fertility	Harvest events: fasting, singing, dancing, offerings, feasting; deity impersonators sacrificed; mock battles; overall cleaning and repairing of houses, temples, and public structures; rewards presented to outstanding warriors
12. Teotl eco	The God Arrives	Sept. 21–Oct. 10	Tezcatlipoca, Huitzilopochtli, Xiuhtecutli, Yacatecutli, all gods in general	Celestial creativity—divine paternalism; war—sacrifice	Celebration of the return of the gods (including singing, dancing, offerings, feasting); fire sacrifices
13. Tepeilhuitl	Mountain Feast Day	Oct. 11–Oct. 30	Tlaloque, Xochiquetzal, pulque gods	Rain—moisture—agricultural fertility	Rain and pulque deities venerated with offerings and human sacrifices; rituals on hilltops for Tlaloque
14. Quecholli	Precious Feather	Oct. 31–Nov. 19	Mixcoatl-Camaxtli	War—sacrifice	Fashioning of hunting gear; hunting of animals; rewards and feasting for successful hunters; deity impersonators sacrificed
15. Panquetzaliztli	Raising of Banners	Nov. 20–Dec. 9	Huitzilopochtli, Tezcatlipoca	War—sacrifice; celestial creativity—divine paternalism	Large-scale fasting, dancing of warriors and prostitutes, processions, large-scale human sacrifices, feasting
16. Atemoztli	The Falling of Water	Dec. 10–Dec. 29	Tlaloque	Rain—moisture—agricultural fertility	Fasting, fashioning of Tlaloque images, offerings to Tlaloque, children sacrificed

TABLE 6–3   MONTHLY CEREMONIES OF THE SOLAR YEAR (*continued*)

Month	Literal meaning	Dates[8]	Most important deities worshipped	Primary religious themes	Sample of ritual activities
17. Tititl	Stretching	Dec. 30–Jan. 18	Cihuacoatl, all gods in general	Rain—moisture—agricultural fertility	Procession, deity impersonator sacrificed, women ritually harassed
18. Izcalli	Growth, Rebirth	Jan. 19–Feb. 7	Xiuhtecutli	Celestial creativity—divine paternalism	Feasting, fashioning of deity images, offerings, children raised by neck to ensure their growth, new fire ignited
Nemontemi	Barren or Useless Days	Feb. 8–Feb. 12	—	—	Evil days, fasting, penance, most usual behavior curbed (quarreling held to be particularly bad at this time)

Compiled from Sahagún 1950–1969, book 2; Durán 1971; Nicholson 1971: table 4.[10]

[8] Dates are from Caso 1971:341.
[9] Etzalli was a porridge consisting of maize and beans.
[10] The most detailed information is in Sahagún; a similar, more comprehensive chart appears in Nicholson 1971.

DIVINATION, MAGIC, AND OMENS: THE ROLE OF FATE

The formal, public religious system aimed primarily to propitiate grand and somewhat remote deities through prayer, supplications, and sacrifices. The Mexica believed that these deities directed people's lives and circumstances; the gods sent rain and drought, military success and defeat. In short, they ultimately determined the fate of the Mexica as a people. While this supernaturally determined fate extended to each individual, at the personal level one could do a great deal to both predict and influence one's destiny. Here, the realm of divination, magic, and sorcery operated alongside the formal religious system, with the two often overlapping. Some major deities, for example, were associated with magic and sorcery: Quetzalcoatl was a patron of magicians (shamans), Toci was patroness of curers and diviners, and one of Tezcatlipoca's guises was that of a sorcerer. Many of the activities undertaken by professional diviners and shamans coincided with the domains of major deities. For example, while Tlaloc and his many supernatural assistants (Tlaloque) were responsible for rain and storms of all kinds, certain specialized shamans (*teciuhtlazque*, "hail throwers," and *quiyauhtlazque*, "rain throwers") dedicated themselves to circumventing the devastating hailstorms and magically summoning the rains controlled by these deities. Some of these specialists may also have been practicing priests. But the shamanistic roles were quite different from the priestly roles. Instead of supplicating deities for the benefit of large groups, shamans attempted directly to manipulate the supernatural world for individuals, directing supernatural forces and magical paraphernalia to both beneficial and malevolent ends. In the beneficial arena were the diviners and such shamans as the "hail throwers"; in the evil arena were the sorcerers.

Divination and Beneficial Magic   At the core of the Mexica system of divination was the belief in a predetermined fate for each individual. These fates were laid out in the tonalpohualli, or ritual "count of days" already mentioned in many other contexts and described in detail in Chapter 7. A person's tonalpohualli birthdate was crucial in determining his or her destiny. One might be rich or poor, industrious or lazy, lucky or unlucky in life's fortunes. A *tonalpouhqui*, or reader of the day-signs, was always hired to interpret an infant's future; the tonalpouhqui exercised some control over the child's anticipated fate, in that he recommended the most auspicious day for the child's naming ceremony, thus diagnosing the most favorable destiny for the child (see Chapter 4). As diviners, the *tonalpouhque* also selected the most auspicious days for other events: the coronation of a ruler, a marriage, the planting of crops, or the beginning of a long journey or expedition. They were important to rulers and farmers alike, and few individuals dared embark on important affairs without consulting a tonalpouhqui.

In addition to generalized prediction, divination was used in many areas of problem solving and curing. To obtain a variety of divine information some shamans apparently would seek altered states of consciousness through the use of hallucinogens such as sacred mushrooms and peyote. In quite a different shamanistic practice, a thief might be revealed "by the *coatliquiyolitiani* ('who enlivens a snake'), who released a snake from a vessel, the latter crawling onto the guilty party" (Nicholson 1971:441). Determination of the causes and courses of illnesses also came under the careful scrutiny of the diviners. The *tlaolchayauhqui* ("one who scatters maize kernels") cast grains of maize and beans on a cotton cloak; the distribution of the kernels, read by the diviner, indicated the cause of the patient's illness. The *mecatlapouhqui* ("cord counter"), by knotting a cord and quickly yanking it, divined the course of a patient's illness; if the knot untied, the patient would recover, but if the knot held fast, the patient was destined to die. Other means of ascertaining the probability of a patient's recovery were also apparently used. In particular, if a child had suffered soul loss, the severity of the problem could be determined by the child's image reflected in water or in a special mirror; if the image were vague, the soul loss was severe; but if the image were clear, recovery was imminent.

Since some illnesses were believed to have been caused by supernatural means, it was often necessary that a shaman be employed for the cure.[11] For instance, a person might be diagnosed as suffering from soul loss, and a shaman would have to be consulted to cure the patient by magically retrieving the lost soul.[12] And for those made sick by the intrusion of some supernatural substance, a variety of magical practitioners could be engaged to remove the offending object (often worms, stone blades, or pebbles).

Sorcery   The practices of divination and beneficial magic were socially approved and deemed essential to counter the perils of everyday life. But the complex and varied behaviors associated with sorcery were considered dangerous and malevolent, and sorcerers were despised and feared. Any person, man or woman, noble or commoner, was particularly inclined toward a career of sorcery if born on the evil days of One Rain or One Wind. A person born on One Rain tended to become a *tlacatecolotl* ("human owl"), who

> . . . assumes the guise of an animal. (He is) a hater, a destroyer of people; an implanter of sickness, who bleeds himself over others, who kills them by potions—who makes them drink potions; who burns wooden figures of others. . . . (He) causes one to be possessed . . . destroys them by deception, depresses their hearts (Sahagún 1950–1969, book 10:31–32).

Although the procedures used to effect these malevolent acts are vague, the human owl typically transformed himself into an animal form: an owl, a turkey, a dog, a weasel, or other creature. Two illnesses already mentioned as requiring the services of magicians for curing (soul loss and intrusion) were believed to stem from the evil actions of these types of sorcerers. Sorcerers made their living, in fact, by hiring out to persons in need of their services. Any person desiring to destroy a hated enemy might hire a sorcerer to do this unpleasant work. Being generally feared and despised, a known sorcerer was rarely welcome in genial company, and usually lived alone and in unhappy circumstances.

Commoners born on the day One Wind were inclined toward other evil behaviors, which were quite specific:

---

[11] In addition to these cures, the Mexica had at their disposal an impressive apothecary of medicinal cures (see Chapter 7).

[12] Belief in soul loss as a cause of illness is still found in parts of Mexico today.

. . . he danced with the arm taken from a woman dead in first childbed; he was a destroyer of men; he burned images for one. Likewise, if it were a woman, she could enchant by taking apart or disarticulating the bones of the foot . . . (*ibid.*, book 4:101).

Often working in groups, the "dancers with the dead woman's forearm" typically cast their spells on the residents of homes they wished to rob. By ceremonially striking parts of the house with the woman's arm, they managed to stupefy the residents, and proceeded to help themselves calmly to all the household provisions. Like other sorcerers, these evildoers reportedly lived a life of suffering and unhappiness.

Omens Viewing their lives as ruled by fate, the Mexica believed that a great many omens might reveal to them their individual destinies. For travelers, the cry of the white hooded hawk might bring either good or evil tidings. If good, then "perhaps they would come upon something pleasing; perchance in something they would be favored; they would attain something beneficial" (*ibid.*, book 5:153). But if the hawk screamed long and loud, "they felt that perhaps something woeful would now betide them; they would come upon something perilous. Either some one of them would die; or sickness would come or somewhere they would be ambushed" (*ibid.*).

Some other omens drew on the natural world of birds and animals. For instance, a weasel crossing one's path meant serious trouble; one might not reach one's destination, or others might spread falsehoods about one. A rabbit entering a house meant that the house would be destroyed or the householder run away, much like a rabbit. And a skunk entering a house forecasted death for the resident (*ibid.*: 165–171). Additional omens were more supernatural in form. For example, a "night axe" and a "bundle of ashes," ominous specters, were taken to be guises of the capricious Tezcatlipoca; when encountered, these apparitions evoked great fright (*ibid.*: 157, 177).

The fear of evil omens and their portended consequences was extremely intense. Beginning 10 years before the Spanish conquest, curious omens appeared which foretold the impending disaster of the Aztec people. Eight of these were believed to have appeared in succession: (1) For a full year a huge flame appeared each night; (2) parts of the temple of Huitzilopochtli inexplicably burst into flames; (3) lightning struck a temple dedicated to Xiuhtecutli, the fire god; (4) a flaming comet raced through the afternoon sky; (5) with no wind, the waters of Lake Texcoco suddenly surged and boiled; (6) a wailing woman often appeared at night crying "O my beloved sons, now we are about to go!"; (7) a strange crane with a crest like a mirror was caught, and when Moctezuma looked into the mirror he saw warriors decked in battle gear and riding on deer; (8) two-headed people appeared, but when taken to Moctezuma, they vanished (*ibid.*, book 12:1–3). Such unexplained, awesome events would have struck intense fear into the hearts of a people as ruled by fate as the Mexica.[13]

---

[13] Some scholars hypothesize that the story of these omens was devised after the Spanish conquest.

Since Mexica life was so strongly dominated by religious practice and a belief in fate, it is no surprise that the people's intellectual and artistic achievements strongly manifested these themes. These achievements in the areas of calendrics, medicine, writing, architecture, sculpture, luxury craftsmanship, literature, and music are the subject of Chapter 7.

7/Intellectual and artistic achievements

It is said that he was a great astrologer; that he was much concerned with understanding the movement of the celestial bodies. Inclined to the study of these things, he would seek in his kingdoms for those who knew of these things, and he would bring them to his court. He would communicate to them all that he knew. And at night he would study the stars, and he would go on the roof of his palace, and from there he would watch the stars, and he would discuss problems with them (Torquemada 1969, vol. 1:188; translation in León-Portilla 1963:142).

This man seeking scientific knowledge was Nezahualpilli, ruler of Texcoco from 1472 to 1515. Both he and his father, the Texcocan ruler Nezahualcoyotl, exemplified the sophisticated intellectual life of fifteenth- and sixteenth-century central Mexico. They searched for scientific explanations of natural phenomena, patronized the arts, and made personal contributions to science, philosophy, engineering, and the literary arts. In so doing, they and others like them were expanding an intellectual heritage that had been undergoing centuries of development in Mesoamerica.

The people at the forefront of these traditions were known as *tlamatinime*, or "wise men." Serving as composers and creators, teachers, and advisors, they embodied knowledge and wisdom: "the philosophers and sages among them were in charge of recording all the sciences they knew and understood, and of teaching from memory all the songs that preserved their sciences and histories" (Alva Ixtlilxochitl 1965, vol. 2:18; translation by FFB). The achievements of the long forgotten sages, and those of the better known Aztec intellectuals, resulted in a system of knowledge that guided much of Aztec life. This knowledge combined features of empirical scientific discovery and culturally directed symbolism. For example, much of the complex system of calendrics was based on long-term astronomical observations, but the calendars were applied directly to divinatory and ritual ends. Medicine, on the one hand pragmatic with an abundance of ingenious herbal remedies, also relied on magic and divination for cures. Writing, architecture, sculpture, and the luxury crafts of metal casting, featherworking and stoneworking all relied on sophisticated technologies to produce exquisite works of art, works which served to record the affairs of an empire and to symbolize religious sentiments or social differences. In a more symbolic arena were literature and music. These forms of expression were most visible in religious contexts, where they clarified views of humanity's place in the Aztec universe, or served as essential elements in the conduct of most ritual events.

CALENDRICS AND THE RECKONING OF TIME

In their everyday life, the Aztecs were deeply concerned with the passage of time. To them, time was cyclical, with each unit persistently repeating itself. The universe had undergone four such cycles, each "sun" being born, destroyed, and born anew. But these recurring cycles were not viewed as endless. For the inevitable destruction of the fifth and present sun would put an end to all human beings.

Hand in hand with the notion of cyclical and repetitive time went a strong belief in fate. One's fate was believed to be determined by conditions and events pinpointed in time. It was therefore necessary that the Aztecs have accurate and meaningful calendars in order to divine the future, schedule activities, and keep track of the passage of time itself. All of these needs required two separate but interrelated calendars.

The Solar Calendar The solar year, or *xiuitl,* consisted of exactly 365 days grouped into 18 months of 20 days each. Although 20 days falls short of a full lunar cycle, these periods were nonetheless called *meztli,* meaning "moon." The year was rounded out at the end with five days (*nemontemi*) that were always viewed as unlucky and ill fated.

This calendar was used to decide the precise times for planting, harvesting, and other seasonal events. Marketing cycles were also geared to this calendar. Markets were held in many communities at five-day intervals, five days being equivalent to one Aztec "week." More rarely, major markets were held in their full splendor every 20 days.

Perhaps most noticeable, each month had its own special set of ceremonial activities, and these were among the most important ceremonies held during the year. These religious extravaganzas, in their month-by-month schedule, are described in Chapter 6 (see Table 6–3). The new fire ceremony was a major solemn ritual celebrated at the end of every 52 years, to predict and perhaps forestall the possible destruction of the universe (see Chapter 6). At the successful ending of each 52-year cycle, the people breathed a sigh of relief as a new cycle began its course.

The solar calendar was obviously based on astronomical observations, although there is no indication of how the Aztecs dealt with the reality that the solar year is 365.2422 days in length. If they did not account for this extra one-fourth of a day, as we do with our "leap year," the calendar would have gained on the seasons at the rate of 13 days every 52 years. Michel Graulich (1981) has recently presented a controversial interpretation of the solar calendar which suggests that, because of this problem, in 1519 the calendar was "off" 209 days in relation to the seasons. This would make the month of Atl caualo, for example, begin on September 10 instead of February 13 (see Table 6–3). However, this would have created a "mismatch" between the monthly ceremonies pertaining to agriculture and the practical demands of the agricultural cycle (see Chapter 6). Such a discrepancy by a people whose lives were so keyed to agriculture seems unlikely. It is more probable that the Aztecs adjusted for this leap-year dilemma in another, yet undiscovered, fashion.

The Ritual Calendar Less directly associated with astronomical phenomena was the ritual calendar, or *tonalpohualli*, of 260 days. This "count of days" was formed by joining 20 day names with the numbers 1–13; each day was associated with each number to produce 260 unique day-and-number combinations. The day names, their meanings, glyphic representations, and the fashion in which they were combined with the numbers 1–13 are displayed in Table 7–1. As can be readily seen by reading Table 7–1 from top to bottom, the first 13 day names were associated with the numbers 1–13. A new number sequence then began, linking the second series of numbers 1–7 with the remainder of the 20 day names. When the 20 names had run their course, then they began anew, joining the march of numbers. In this way the day name *cipactli* ("alligator") was first linked with the number 1, then 8, then 2, 9, and so on. In this fashion the name cipactli, and every other day name in the sequence, was tied to every number from 1–13 at the end of a 260-day period. At that time, a new sequence, beginning with *ce cipactli*, "One Alligator," was initiated.

The entire sequence of numbered day names (day-signs) provided the basis for the tonalpohualli. For ritual purposes these were divided into 20 discrete groups. Each group was led by the day name associated with the number one. The first group would therefore begin with One Alligator and include the days up to and including Thirteen Reed; the next group begin with One Jaguar and end with Thirteen Death; the next, One Deer to Thirteen Rain, and so on. Each of these sequences had a patron deity or deities who presided over the 13-day period. These were both major and minor deities of the pantheon, the major ones including Quetzalcoatl, Tlaloc, Tonatiuh, and Xipe Totec.

Each of the 20 day names also had its own patron deity, who lent special attributes to these days. For example, the patron of the days named *ehecatl* ("Wind") was Quetzalcoatl, who presided over the wind in one of his guises; the patron of the *tochtli* (rabbit) days was Mayahuel, goddess of the maguey whose intoxicating nectar foreshadowed a gloomy drunken fate for those born on the Rabbit days.

The *tonalamatl*, or sacred "book of days," contained the ritual calendar, or "count of days." The tonalamatl also portrayed 13 Lords of the Day, 13 "birds," and 9 Lords of the Night associated with this "count" (see Figure 7–1). The 13 Lords of the Day were major deities such as Tezcatlipoca, Tlaloc, and Quetzalcoatl. Each was associated with a particular bird (from hummingbirds and parrots to turkeys and quails) or a butterfly in these sacred almanacs. In addition, attached to the days themselves were the 9 Lords of the Night,[1] who were also major central Mexican deities such as Xiuhtecutli, Centeotl, and Mictlantecutli. The meanings carried by these many lords and birds are unclear. It is possible that the 13 Lords

---

[1] Each day had only one Lord of the Night, and these 9 Lords were repeated over and over again, allying themselves with each day in succession.

TABLE 7–1   THE TONALPOHUALLI, OR RITUAL CALENDAR ("COUNT OF DAYS")

Day Name	Meaning	Glyph	Associated Numbers				
cipactli	alligator		1	8	2	9	etc.
ehecatl	wind		2	9	3	10	
calli	house		3	10	4	11	
cuetzpallin	lizard		4	11	5	12	
coatl	snake		5	12	6	13	
miquiztli	death		6	13	7	1	
mazatl	deer		7	1	8	2	
tochtli	rabbit		8	2	9	3	
atl	water		9	3	10	4	
itzcuintli	dog		10	4	11	5	
ozomatli	monkey		11	5	12	6	
malinalli	grass		12	6	13	7	
acatl	reed		13	7	1	8	
ocelotl	jaguar		1	8	2	9	
cuauhtli	eagle		2	9	3	10	
cozcacuauhtli	vulture		3	10	4	11	
ollin	movement		4	11	5	12	
tecpatl	flint knife		5	12	6	13	
quiahuitl	rain		6	13	7	1	
xochitl	flower		7	1	8	2	

of the Day represented the 13 heavens and the 9 Lords of the Night were connected to the 9 layers of the underworld. It has also been suggested that the 13 Lords of the Day reigned over the 13 daytime hours while the 9 Lords of the Night presided over each of the 9 nightly divisions. Clear-cut evidence to support either of these possibilities, however, has not yet been unearthed.

The use of the tonalpohualli has been described throughout this book. In general terms, the ritual calendar was used to divine the fate of individuals, to foresee the

Figure 7–1: A page of the ritual tonalamatl, or "book of days" (Codex Borbonicus, in the series CODICES SELECTI, vol. XLIV, Akademische Druck- u. Verlagsanstalt, Graz 1974, page 13).

fortunes of empire, and to determine propitious days for the celebration of major events. Not only were the days themselves considered "good," "bad," or "indifferent," so were each of the 13 numbers, each of the patron day gods, each of the patrons of 13-day periods, and each of the 9 Lords of the Night. To understand the significance of these combined influences on a single concrete day required a great deal of specialized knowledge; and the *tonalpouhque*, or readers of the sacred almanacs, were respected specialists.

The Calendar Round and Astronomical Calculations   The 52-year period, or "calendar round," was the result of combining the 365-day solar calendar with the 260-day ritual calendar. In this system, there resulted 18,980 uniquely identified days. For example, Hernán Cortés entered the city of Tenochtitlan on November 8, 1519: the ninth day of the month of Quecholli in the solar calendar, that same day being Eight Wind in the ritual calendar. Tenochtitlan fell to the Spaniards on August 13, 1521: the second day of the month of Xocotl uetzi, One Snake in the tonalpohualli (Caso 1971:344, 342). These combined dates of Nine Quecholli/ Eight Wind and Two Xocotl uetzi/One Snake would not appear again in the calendrical system for another 52 solar years.

Each solar year was named after the day-number combination that fell at the end of the year. In this system only four of the day names were designated as year names or "year bearers": tochtli (rabbit), acatl (reed), tecpatl (flint knife), and calli (house).[2] Each of these four was joined with each of the numbers 1–13, to result in 52 distinct name-number combinations. For example, although the Spaniards designated the year of their arrival in Mexico as 1519, the Aztecs knew that year as *ce acatl*, or "One Reed"; the year of the Spanish conquest of Tenochtitlan, 1521, was known to the Aztecs as the year *yey calli*, or "Three House." This scheme of naming years, in brief, worked as follows:

1	Rabbit	9	Rabbit
2	Reed	10	Reed
3	Flint Knife	11	Flint Knife
4	House	12	House
5	Rabbit	13	Rabbit
6	Reed	1	Reed
7	Flint Knife	2	Flint Knife
8	House	3	House
			etc.

When a 52-year cycle was completed and One Rabbit again appeared, the entire calendar round would begin anew. The calendric system provided no concrete reference to any previous cycle, and in the early histories it is often difficult to know with assurance precisely in which 52-year cycle specific events took place.

The Aztecs made sophisticated astronomical calculations in addition to the solar year of 365 days. They calculated the revolutions of Venus (584 days) and of Mars (780 days). Like their earlier southern neighbors, the Maya, they undoubtedly had calculated the lunar cycle as 29–30 days, although this period does not appear in their calendars.[3]

MEXICA MEDICINE

The establishment of an accurate calendar system required rigorous systematic investigations of the heavens. Likewise, the Aztecs were scientifically involved in the discovery and use of medical cures for a variety of illnesses and injuries. The procedures used by a *ticitl*, or physician, were empirical and practical:

> The good physician (is) a diagnostician, experienced—a knower of herbs, of stones, of trees, of roots. He has (results of) examinations, experience, prudence. (He is) moderate in his acts. He provides health, restores people, provides them

[2] These days were spaced at intervals of 365 days; 365 days from the day One Rabbit was the day Two Reed, 365 days from Two Reed was Three Flint Knife, and so on.

[3] See Aveni 1980 for a detailed treatment of Mesoamerican archaeoastronomy.

splints, sets bones for them, purges them, gives emetics, gives them potions; he lances, he makes incisions in them, stitches them, revives them, envelopes them in ashes (Sahagún 1950–1969, book 10:30).

The Aztecs recognized a variety of ailments as being medically curable. These included injuries, minor infections, other small irritations, and a few graver ailments. For injuries such as broken bones, dislocations, sprains, burns, lacerations, and head wounds, an assortment of cures was used. Broken bones, for example, were first set and then splinted with poultices of specific ground roots or herbs. Apparently, there was no firm rule for these treatments, for individuals might use the ground roots or herbs in a number of ways: spread them on the injury, bathe in them, or drink them with pulque. A number of specific remedies existed for head wounds. These injuries may have been quite common, many of them suffered in warfare. In one remedy, the wound was first washed. Hot maguey sap was then applied directly to the wound, followed by a mixture of maguey sap, lampblack, and salt. The wound was then bound (Sahagún 1950–1969, book 10:161–162). In a very different procedure, a ground herb (*iztac palancapatli*) was applied to the wound. As the wound healed, a powdered pine resin and feathers were applied (*ibid.*, book 11:152). If one bit one's tongue, chile cooked with salt was applied to the injury, followed by the more soothing bee honey or maguey sap.

The Aztecs used herbal remedies for at least 40 specific ailments other than injuries. In all, at least 132 herbs were considered to have curative properties (*ibid.*: books 10 and 11). These ailments included pimples, nosebleed, headache, inflamed eyes, gout, diarrhea, fatigue, festered skin, coughs, chest pains, nausea, epilepsy, and a variety of infections and fevers. Some ailments were served by a great diversity of herbal cures; 45 different herbs were said to cure fevers, 18 herbs could be applied to festered skin, and 10 different herbs could be prescribed for the patient who suffered a relapse. By the same token, some herbs were almost panaceas, having multiple uses. For example, the herb *tlatlanquaye* was used to relieve bleeding, vomiting, side and chest pains, sluggishness, and weakness (*ibid.*, book 11:174–175). The herb *picietl* was prescribed for fatigue, gout, or a swollen stomach (*ibid.*:146). Many herbs, however, were used only for a single illness. The complete cure for most ailments involved more than one herbal or other remedy. Specific herbs, roots, or other plants (such as cacao) were frequently mixed into a single curative potion or poultice. A sweatbath was often recommended as an adjunct to the cure, and was particularly important in problems of childbirth, skin festering, and traumas. Above all, the sweatbath was considered to be relaxing and soothing and helpful in recoveries in general.

Medicinal remedies were often combined with other procedures to effect a cure. The use of divination and magic in both the diagnosis and curing of illness has been discussed in Chapter 6. In addition, some ailments entailed strict taboos: A patient with a head wound was to abstain from eating meat or fish, and one with a fever was not to eat hot tortillas or chiles (*ibid.*:152, 156, 161). There was also a preventative element in Aztec medicine; some herbal remedies were recommended for perfectly healthy individuals to prevent the onset of illnesses. For example, the herb *acocoxiuitl* was available to those who were not at all sick; it was said to aid the digestion and restrain the onset of fever. Likewise, a nursing mother was not to eat avocados, since the infant might develop diarrhea from them (*ibid.*:162). And lisping and stammering problems could be prevented by weaning children when they were very young (*ibid.*, book 10:148).

HIEROGLYPHIC WRITING

The ritual calendar, or tonalpohualli, was set down in the tonalamatl, or "book of days." This book was only one of several types of manuscripts, or codices, composed by the Aztec scribes. Their libraries housed other religious, ritual, and astrological records; tribute accounts; histories and the genealogies of rulers; maps of large and small scale; and legal records. Most of these books were written on *amatl*, paper made from the inner bark of the *amaquauitl*.[4] The bark was soaked in water, beaten to separate and smooth the fibers, and treated with various materials to make a firm, even writing surface. Typically, these long "sheets" of paper were not bound, but folded accordion style; this is certainly the case for the surviving pre-Hispanic ritual codices. Other codices, particularly maps and tribute records, were most likely to be composed on single unbound, unfolded sheets. In either style, the scribe usually wrote his hieroglyphic message on both sides of the bark paper. This message was written in a kaleidoscope of bright colors outlined in black, the most common being red, yellow, green, and blue; in fact, writing itself was known as *in tlilli in tlapalli*, "the red, the black."

The Aztec writing system was based on a great number of glyphs which served as mnemonic devices. Being non-alphabetic, the glyphs provided only guides or clues to the entire message. Learning to read, therefore, involved much more than merely learning the glyphic symbols: It was essential to have learned, or memorized, the messages themselves. In other words, the reader (and the writer) required a great deal of knowledge not directly expressed in the glyphs.

The glyphs were formulated in at least three different ways. By far the most common method was pictographic: a picture of the item was drawn (e.g., snake, flower, water, house). Although painted with a certain artistic license, these stylized pictographs were readily intelligible and carried simple, direct meaning. The second means of composing glyphs was ideographic. Slightly more abstract than pictographs, ideographs are aspects or qualities of an object that are selected to represent the entire object (e.g., a stylized speech scroll to represent speech, or a noble's headband to indicate a high-ranking noble, or *tecutli*). Other common ideographs were footprints for travel; speech scroll with flowers for song or poetry; a shield and arrows for warfare; a burning temple for conquest; and "year-bundle," or bundle of reeds, to symbolize the "binding of the years" at the completion of the 52-year cycle. The third means of glyphic formation was phonetic. Phoneticism took the form of rebus writing, in which one word, easily represented pictorially, is used for another word or set of words that has the same sound. For example, the glyph for the place name Coatlan contains two elements: *coatl* for "snake" or "serpent" and *tlan(tli)* for "teeth." While *-tlan* does indeed mean "teeth," it also means "place

---

[4] Amaquauitl refers to certain trees of the genus Ficus (F. benjamina, F. involuta).

of." In this case, the entire glyph means "Place of Snakes," and "place of" is symbolized glyphically by its homonym *tlantli*, or "teeth." Similarly, a banner (*pantli*) stood for the syllable *pan* ("on"), a ball of thread (*icpatl*) expressed *icpac* ("on top of"), a human posterior (*tzintli*) conveyed the meaning "little," and a road (*ohtli*) represented the sound of the vowel "o." These are but a few of the many examples of phoneticism in the codices. Most such examples are found in place and personal name glyphs, which most commonly were composed of two or more discrete glyphic elements (see Table 7–2).

In addition to the form of the glyphs, other written details conveyed information. For example, the size of human figures was important. The larger individuals represented more important or dominant persons, the smaller ones indicated subservient or less significant persons. Color also provided valuable information. Various types of feathers would have been indistinguishable from one another except for color; so would grass, reeds, and canes, which were all portrayed in different colors. Other details, such as the prominent wrinkles on an old man's face or the specific decoration of a deity, served to enhance the writing system and allow it to record and transmit a variety of information.

Since only the "high points" were actually written, both reader and writer had to rely on intellectual skills sharply honed in the *calmecac* in order to "fill in" the necessary unwritten information. It comes as no surprise that this skill, taught only in the calmecac, was reserved for the nobility. Precisely these people would occupy the administrative and religious positions which would require literacy. Nor is it surprising that the scribes, who carefully and laboriously composed the many colorful codices, were a highly specialized and highly regarded group in Aztec society.

SCULPTURE AND THE LUXURY CRAFTS

Much as the scribes specialized in painting manuscripts, other trained artists and artisans produced an amazing quantity and variety of sculpture; metalwork; featherwork; and mosaics of stone, shell, and other materials. Most of the artistic techniques and content were adopted from earlier Mexican cultures; the Aztecs admired the Toltecs for their exceptional achievements in the artistic realm. None-

TABLE 7–2   GLYPHS WITH PHONETIC DERIVATIONS

Tochpan: "on the rabbits" or "place of the rabbits"

    toch(tli): rabbit
    pan(tli): banner, on

Tulantzinco: "little place of reeds"

    tul(li): reed
    (t)lan: place of
    tzin(tli): human posterior, diminutive
    co: in(not shown glyphically)

Icpatepec: "on top of the hill"

    icpa-c: ball of thread, on top of
    tepe(tl): hill

theless, the Aztecs compared favorably with their antecedents in both the quantity and quality of artistic production.

Sculpture   The Aztec stoneworkers excelled in the art of sculpting, and the "good stoneworker" was able to earn regard as a fine craftsman: "He is of skilled hands, able hands, accomplished (after the manner of) Tula" (*ibid.*:27). Particularly in their colossal stone sculptures, the Aztecs far surpassed any of their predecessors in quantity, quality, and diversity of production. Their expertly carved works ranged from over two and a half meters high to miniature figures a mere two or three centimeters in height.

Using tools made of stone, they executed realistic sculptures in the round and meticulous relief carvings. Items depicted "in the round" included idols; animal figures; skulls; masks; people; and replicas of temples, drums, year-bundles commemorating the end of a 52-year cycle, and other cultural artifacts. The idols were the most colossal stone sculptures. Every deity was apparently represented in stone and placed in its appropriate temple. Some of these carved idols were decorated with elaborate care. Having seen the idol of Huitzilopochtli first hand, the conquistador Bernal Díaz del Castillo wrote many years after the conquest that

> . . . it had a very broad face and monstrous and terrible eyes, and the whole of his body was covered with precious stones, and gold and pearls, and with seed pearls stuck on with a paste . . . and the body was girdled by great snakes made of gold and precious stones, and in one hand he held a bow and in the other some arrows. . . . Huichilobos [Huitzilopochtli] had round his neck some Indians' faces and other things like hearts of Indians, the former made of gold and the latter of silver, with many precious blue stones (1956:219).

Almost without exception, these idols were depicted in very formal, rigid stances; and they undoubtedly made a powerful impression on the faithful. One such idol, that of the goddess Coatlicue, stood over 2½ meters high and weighed over 16 metric tons.

Animals were among the most popular subjects for Aztec sculpture, and were extremely realistic. A favorite theme was the serpent, sometimes portrayed as a realistic snake, sometimes carved in a feathered style to represent the god Quetzalcoatl, the "Plumed Serpent." But the Aztecs also carved other animal figures in great abundance: dogs, jaguars, frogs, turtles, monkeys, rabbits, eagles, grasshoppers, and even tiny fleas. More rarely, plants such as squashes were deemed appropriate subjects for sculpture. Most of these animal and plant figures probably served as ritual paraphernalia in and around the temples. Serpent heads were typically situated at the bases of temples. Indeed, recent excavations in downtown Mexico City have exposed serpent heads projecting from the base of the Mexica's great temple (*Templo Mayor*), flanking the two stairways leading to the abodes of Huitzilopochtli and Tlaloc (H. B. Nicholson, personal communication).

Carvings of skulls and masks also served as important religious accoutrements. Skulls, emphasizing the Aztec preoccupation with death, were carved frequently. Although found most often as relief carvings, many skulls were realistically carved in the round from precious and semi-precious stones such as rock crystal. Masks were a key element in Aztec ceremonialism. Their importance lay in the belief that certain mortals, especially priests and those about to be sacrificed, became deified. The masks symbolized this transformation from mortal to supernatural status.

Human figures also were carved in stone, the most prevalent portrayals being of commoners and warriors. Carved in minute detail, these realistic images often served as standard bearers at the bases and entrances of Aztec temples.

The Aztecs were also fond of carving replicas of a variety of objects. These most often symbolized religious and military themes and included depictions of year-bundles, drums, a temple, staffs, and shields. If these items were functional, they most likely served as cult objects accompanying the deity images in the temples.

The same religious and military themes predominated in Aztec relief sculpture. Some deities were represented in relief, as were a multitude of warriors in elaborate military costume. Calendric dates were also often carved in relief, and probably designated historic as well as religious points in time. Unlike the monolithic sculptures in the round, the relief carvings, like the pictorial codices and other paintings now lost, could portray a collection of individuals, gods, and objects in a sequence of events; they could convey religious beliefs, military feats, or historical events; they could record complex mythologies or tales.

The vast bulk of Aztec carving, whether in the round or relief, expressed religious themes or served religious functions. The symbolism used by the sculptors was highly standardized, and the products of their efforts are readily identifiable as "Aztec." For the more massive sculptures, they may have worked in teams; once, 14 sculptors were commissioned by the ruler Moctezuma Xocoyotzin to carve a monumental statue in his likeness; at another time, numerous sculptors worked together on an enormous stone to be placed atop the temple of Huitzilopochtli (Tezozomoc 1975:668–669, 662). Such team effort suggests that the training received by skilled sculptors was regulated and consistent. Perhaps the sculptors, like the makers of luxury goods, were organized into formal guilds in the major cities. In post-conquest times and probably before, they were concentrated in the cities of Tenochtitlan and Texcoco, although they often traveled to other parts of the empire in their search for work (Motolinía 1950:214).

The Luxury Crafts: Gold, Feathers, and Mosaics   Standard techniques and styles were also a hallmark of the work of the luxury artisans. As discussed in Chapter 2, these skilled artisans were organized into formal urban guilds which controlled both membership and the transmission of specialized knowledge used in the craft.

The metalworkers manufactured ornate objects of gold, silver, and copper. None of these metals was found locally in the Valley of Mexico; each was obtained from the more distant reaches of Mesoamerica by means of tribute, market exchange, or foreign trade. All were mined in the mountains, and gold was also panned in mountain streams and coastal rivers. Although the Triple Alliance capitals were major centers for the manufacture of metal objects, other important centers of metalwork did flourish. From some areas, such as the Oaxaca region to the south, the Aztecs received in tribute not only raw gold but also finished gold and copper objects. The Aztecs certainly had no monopoly on the production of ornate metal objects.

In fashioning their precious objects of gold the Aztecs used several techniques, among them the complicated "lost-wax" technique. To make a hollow object the craftsman began with a core of ground charcoal and clay. When this core dried, it was sculpted in the shape of an animal, bird, fish, human being, or other form. Then melted beeswax was rolled out very smoothly, thinly, and evenly (like a "cobweb"), and placed carefully over the carved core. This was then covered with a paste of ground charcoal, and the entire form was encased in a clay-charcoal mixture. After drying for two days, this form was heated to melt the beeswax, which flowed out through openings left in the form. Molten gold, heated in a charcoal fire, was poured into the space left vacant by the melted wax. The result was an exact gold duplicate of the wax form (Sahagún 1950–1969, book 9:73–78). Masks, figures, and pieces of jewelry were made in this fashion, all richly polished and burnished. The entire process was undertaken with meticulous care, and each piece was a unique work of art, since the molds had to be broken to free each golden masterpiece.

The techniques of the featherworkers were no less elaborate. They worked with both local and exotic feathers; great quantities of precious feathers from distant regions reached the Triple Alliance capitals as tribute, through foreign trade, and by way of marketplace exchanges. These feathers were fashioned, with the aid of glue or maguey cord, into exquisite headdresses, standards, shields, fans, armbands, godly cloaks, and royal dress.

If an item were to be fashioned by glueing, the craftsmen began with a paper pattern; the intricate designs were drawn by scribes, who may have been employed by the featherworkers for this purpose. Then the craftsmen prepared a thin, shiny piece of cotton. They pressed and thinned out the cotton on a flat maguey leaf, glued and reglued the surface of the cotton until it was glossy, and then carefully peeled the cotton from the maguey leaf. This delicate but stiff length of cotton was then placed over the paper pattern, and the design was traced on the cotton. When the design was complete, a paper backing was attached to the cotton to reinforce it. This cotton-paper form was cut along the lines of the design to form a stencil; the pattern was then transferred to another glue-hardened piece of cotton with a maguey leaf backing. The featherworker now began to attach feathers to the design, beginning with inexpensive local feathers, since they would not show when the work was completed. In the manner of an artist, the feather-worker typically dyed these feathers to imitate the more expensive feathers that would cover them; he worked as carefully with these inexpensive feathers as with the ones that would actually show. This first layer of feathers was then covered with the exotic feathers: quetzal, parrot, spoonbill, hummingbird, and others. Together these feathers formed a mosaic in an exquisite kaleidoscope of colors. Shields, some fans, and other rigid objects were fashioned and decorated in this manner.

Objects that capitalized on the loose, flowing quality of the feathers, such as headdresses and shirts, were fashioned by tying and sewing. The feathers were individually attached with maguey thread to a rigid backing or, in the case of clothing, to cotton cloth. Quetzal feathers, being especially long and graceful, were prized for headdresses and other items that emphasized a flowing appearance (see Figure 3–1).

In all of these procedures, there was a definite division of labor. The men prepared the patterns, stencils, and other backing material and chose and applied the feathers; the women dyed and sorted the feathers; and the youngsters undergoing their apprenticeship prepared the glues (*ibid.*:93–97).

Most featherwork involved arranging not only feathers but also gold and other ornaments to make the finished item truly exquisite. Whether the feathers were used by themselves or in combination with other precious materials, the result was typically a mosaic pattern.

Mosaics were also produced by the lapidaries, who combined numerous stones and shells into intricate patterns. They typically worked on a wooden surface, painstakingly arranging the colorful stones and shells. More rarely they developed the mosaic on pottery, bone, shell, gold, or stone. Although they produced ornaments and figures from stones such as jade, rock crystal, and amethyst, their favorite mosaic stone was turquoise. With turquoise, malachite, and other stones and shells they created vivid mosaics. Masks, shields, staffs, vessels, ear plugs, nose plugs, and bracelets were elaborately decorated with mosaic designs. Some of these objects adorned and accompanied the deities; others were reserved for members of the aristocracy. The mosaics and polished stone jewelry manufactured by the lapidaries, along with precious objects of gold and feathers, set the nobility apart from the rest of the population and emphasized their special social and material prerogatives.

LITERATURE AND MUSIC

Members of the Aztec elite were prolific creators and reciters of oral literature—epic and lyric poetry, hymns, plays, orations, chronicles, and histories. Many of the major epic poems, hymns, orations, and histories became standardized and were handed down from generation to generation. The Aztecs were heirs to a long tradition of oral literature. Other forms of this art, particularly lyric poetry, were created in profusion by the Aztec elite, including the renowned rulers of Texcoco, Nezahualcoyotl and his son Nezahualpilli, as well as rulers and nobles from many other Valley of Mexico cities.

Fine oratory of all kinds was esteemed by the Aztecs, and only those who were most highly skilled in oral expression performed at the major political and religious events. The "good narrator" was a producer of "pleasing words, joyful words, he has flowers on his lips. His speech overflows with advice, flowers come from his mouth. His speech, pleasing and joyful as flowers; from him come noble language and careful sentences" (León-Portilla 1969:27).[5] To attain these skills, training in the calmecac was necessary. There the noble children learned literary forms and rules; memorized the standardized sagas, songs, and histories; and learned to key their memory to the "written reminders" in the pictorial codices. But many of the religious songs and dances were also taught in the *cuicacalli*, or "house of song," attended by youths and maidens. Since many public religious ceremonies required the participation of people from all walks of life, it was necessary that these persons receive the requisite training in song and dance. And there

---

[5] "Flowers," usually in a combined "flower-and-song" metaphor, refers to poetry and art.

were apparently also professional singers, whose valued qualities were similar to those of a fine orator: a clear expressive voice, sharp memory, and creative ability (Sahagún 1950–1969, book 10:29). Such singers were apparently employed by the Aztec rulers to create songs extolling their feats and those of their ancestors: "In their kingdoms songs had been composed describing their feats, victories, conquests, genealogies, and their extraordinary wealth" (Durán 1971:299). Other singers were attached to the various temples and composed hymns to and about the gods (*ibid.*). In charge of this group was a *tlapizcatzin*, or "caretaker":

> The Caretaker took charge of the songs of the devils, of indeed all the sacred songs, that none might do ill (with them). Greatly was he concerned that they teach the sacred songs, and he cried (the summons) that the singers be gathered, or the chiefs, that they might be taught the songs (Sahagún 1950–1969, book 2:195).

Thus, a variety of persons were involved in the presentation of poetry, dialogues, and chants. The professionals were composers as well as reciters and singers; the lay population learned new works and the more ancient creations by rote in order to participate in ceremonial events.

Poetry   Aztec poetry was of two types: epic and lyric. The epic poetry encompassed the great myths: they told of the creation of the Four Suns, the birth of the present sun, and the origin of human beings; they recounted beliefs about major deities such as Huitzilopochtli, Quetzalcoatl, and the agricultural deities; and they expressed conceptions of the afterlife. Through the skillful use of repetition and minute detail, the epics presented vivid and exciting sagas, especially of creation and destruction. (The content of many of these myths has been presented in earlier chapters.)

Lyric poetry, much of which has survived to the present day, expressed the personal musings of the intellectual elite. They pored over great philosophical questions: the nature of the supernatural world, the meaning of human existence, and the secret of death. A poem composed by Cuauhtencoztli expresses some of these philosophical thoughts:

> I, Cuauhtencoztli, here I am suffering.
> What is, perchance, true?
> Will my song still be real tomorrow?
> Are men perhaps real?
> What is it that will survive?
> Here we live, here we stay,
> But we are destitute, oh my friends! (León-Portilla 1969:82).

Aztec lyric poetry also expressed more mundane themes: the glory of war, the grandeur of the Aztecs, the joy of love and friendship, and the meaning of poetry itself. Although much of this poetry expressed doubts and pessimism, some was hopeful in tone:

> Now, oh friends,
> listen to the words of a dream:
> each spring brings us life,
> the golden corn refreshes us,
> the pink corn makes us a necklace.
> At least this we know:
> the hearts of our friends are true! (*ibid.*:83).

Like the great epics, lyric poems relied heavily on the use of repetition and meta-phors. In the optimistic poem, for example, lines 3–5 convey the same meaning in a different and colorful way.

Lyric poetry provided a means by which the thoughtful intellectuals could express their reflections on the human condition and human relations. The Aztec culture itself, through a religious doctrine emphasizing fate, provided answers to many questions posed by the poets. Yet these philosophers apparently were not totally satisfied with the generally accepted cultural explanations; and they expressed intense doubts, fears, and hope in their poetry.

Songs and Hymns The Dominican friar Diego Durán described the types of song and dance common in Aztec culture:

> . . . some were sung slowly and seriously; these were sung and danced by the lords on solemn and important occasions and were intoned, some with modera-tion and calm, (while) others (were) less sober and more lively. These were dances and songs of pleasure known as "dances of youth," during which they sang songs of love and flirtation. . . . There was also another dance so roguish that it can almost be compared to our own Spanish dance the saraband, with all its wriggling and grimacing and immodest mimicry . . . I have seen this per-formed in some villages, and it is permitted by our friars as a recreation, but I do not consider this wise because it is highly improper (1971:295).

Aside from these lively songs and dances, Durán also described the religious hymns or chants sung in honor of the deities. Each deity apparently had its own reper-toire of songs, and long rehearsals preceded the public ceremonies. These sacred songs formed part of more extensive ceremonies in which they served to pay honor to the deities, and in which the priests asked for supernatural protection and good-will and reaffirmed their beliefs in the omniscience of the deities. One such song was dedicated to the goddess Cihuacoatl:

> The eagle, the eagle, Quilaztli,
> with serpent blood painted,
> with eagle plumes crowned,
> is protectress of the Chalmeca and (goddess) of Colhuacan.
> The maize is our hands and our feet in the field of the god,
> who resteth upon her rattle board.
> Maguey thorns, maguey thorns rest in my hand;
> Maguey thorns rest in my hand.
> In the field of the god she resteth upon her rattle board.
> The grass bunch resteth in my hand.
> In the field of the god she resteth upon her rattle board.
> Aumei quauhtli, our mother, goddess of the Chalmeca,
> deliver me with the dread dart of thorns.
> It is my son Mixcoatl (Sahagún 1950–1969, book 2:211).[6]

Song and poetry often overlapped, since poems were frequently set to music and accompanied by flutes and drums. Also, with song and poetry, the Aztecs occasion-ally created dramatic presentations. Combining songs, recitations, and dances, the participants would often disguise themselves to assume special identities. Deities, jaguars, eagles, monkeys, dogs, hunters, and the neighboring Huaxtecs were common

[6] This is only the first part of the hymn to Cihuacoatl. The maguey thorns refer to auto-sacrifice.

disguises (Durán 1971:296). Some of these dramas were amusing, such as the one involving a juggler and a "simpleton . . . who pretended to understand all his master's words backward, turning around his words" (*ibid.*:297). Others were more serious, such as the dance-drama dedicated to the goddess Xochiquetzal. The area set aside for the event was decorated with sweet-smelling flowers and artificial trees. Boys disguised as birds and butterflies climbed the trees, enjoying the flowers on the way. Adults disguised as gods then arrived and danced about, shooting at the birds and butterflies with blowguns. Xochiquetzal then appeared and sat the gods beside her, offering them flowers and tobacco and treating them with respect and reverence (*ibid.*:296). In other religious dramas, such as the one dedicated to Tlaloc, priests and perhaps calmecac students would enact a dialogue between the deity, a priest, and the populace.

Prose: Chronicles and Narratives   In their literature, the Aztecs expressed an interest in the lives and feats of mortals as well as in the exploits and powers of the gods. In their chronicles, they preserved the histories of entire peoples and the adventures of individual heroes, often in intimate and vivid detail. The Mexica chronicles, for example, recorded the migration to the Valley of Mexico, the founding of Tenochtitlan, events under the domination of Azcapotzalco, the birth of the Triple Alliance, and the process of empire building: victories, defeats, the lives of rulers, memorable ceremonial occasions. These histories also frequently included dates and the names of specific people and places, providing a detailed historical tradition for succeeding generations. These histories were among the esoteric materials learned by young noblemen in the calmecac.

Another major form of Aztec prose was the *huehuetlatolli*. These "speeches of the elders" were presented to individuals and/or groups at critical points or periods in their life cycles: birth, adolescence, marriage, and death. Special life cycle events such as the coronation of a new ruler were also appropriate occasions for these lengthy narratives. In these discourses the Aztecs revealed and taught their most cherished values: Through them infants were introduced to a precarious and dangerous world, youths were taught proper etiquette and humility, and a new ruler was advised of the heavy burdens he must assume with his office (see Chapters 4 and 5).

Many of these intellectual and artistic achievements suffered a sad fate when the Spaniards arrived. The numerous books that glyphically preserved calendrical and literary knowledge were destroyed as "books of the devil," leaving only a few original manuscripts. Much of the sculpture, representing idolatry to the Spaniards, was also destroyed; and many of the exquisite gold and silver masterpieces were melted down. The loss of these intellectual accoutrements symbolized the even greater impact of the Spanish conquest on Aztec life in general. The conquest and its traumatic effects on the Aztec people are covered in Chapter 8.

8/The consequences of conquest

During the fifteenth and early sixteenth centuries the Aztecs had formed a powerful empire encompassing most of present-day central and southern Mexico and extending into Guatemala. They had developed an effective centralized political structure with an elaborate bureaucracy that administered the affairs of empire. A major goal of this empire building was the control of economic resources; through tribute of conquered provinces the Aztecs obtained vast quantities of utilitarian and exotic goods. But merchandise from throughout Mesoamerica flowed daily into the Valley of Mexico through other channels. Through foreign trade and other mercantile efforts, professional Aztec merchants dealt profitably in luxury wares; through the lively marketplaces, goods of all kinds changed hands and filtered from community to community, from region to region. Surpluses were produced in great quantities, supporting a wide range of non-food-producing specialists. Some of these, in the highest echelons of the society, served as full-time political or military officials. Others devoted their lives and energies to the priesthood, serving a religion that was complex in both belief and ritual. Some of these same high-ranking persons, as well as many of humbler social station, specialized in science and the fine arts. They embellished the Triple Alliance cities so finely that these centers were not only the seats of imperial power but also magnificent symbols of that power.

Throughout this time of empire building, across the Atlantic, Spain was enmeshed in events and processes which were to leave an indelible mark on the Aztecs and their way of life. In 1469, amidst tense political intrigue, Ferdinand of Aragon married Isabella of Castile. When the dust settled some 10 years later, Ferdinand and Isabella had succeeded in consolidating the strongest kingdoms in Spain, and in priming Spain for a glorious century of expansion and conquest. Since the eighth century, Moors had occupied parts of the Iberian Peninsula, and the war waged by the Spaniards against these invaders was fairly continuous for most of the next eight centuries. Not until 1492, in Granada, did the Moors meet their final defeat at the hands of the Spanish armies. At that time, Spain could boast of a great many highly trained military officers and soldiers. And as the Spanish kingdoms reconquered more and more of the Iberian Peninsula from their Moorish enemies, they established an efficient pattern of administering and settling territories, many of which were deeply immersed in Moorish language, culture, and religion. A logical extension of the reconquest was Spanish expansion into North Africa, where they established several important footholds in the early sixteenth century. In the 1490s, Spain also moved beyond its shores into the Atlantic. Against fierce resistance, Spanish forces subdued the Canary Islanders and began early experiments in colonial government, establishing patterns that would later be transferred to the New World. And in 1492, Columbus succeeded in reaching the Indies, claiming for Spain a new world of unimagined riches. Spanish expansion was not only military and political but mercantile as well. Concentrated in the city of Seville, experienced merchants carried on extensive trade in the Mediterranean region. They were accustomed to long-distance commerce, and well prepared to reap profits from the new Spanish possessions.

Despite this flurry of expansion, Spanish traditions remained essentially feudal and agrarian. Large estates owned by noblemen and their families were not only a reality but also an ideal to be cherished and preserved. The system was paternalistic and patriarchal. The feudal ideals extended in varying forms to other aspects of social and political life: Political offices of many kinds were viewed as lifetime prerogatives and normally carried a great deal of respect; government was characterized by a strong sense of legalism and record-keeping was prodigious. The people of Castile in particular were characterized as hardy and austere, able to withstand considerable hardships. Ideals of personal independence and individuality prevailed in fifteenth- and sixteenth-century Spain.

While the Catholic religion was important to the pious Spaniards, the Catholic Church was not a powerful institution in Spain. For example, bishops and heads of the orders of regular clergy (friars) essentially served at the pleasure of the Spanish government. The Inquisition was controlled by the state as much as by the church; even confiscations of property went directly into the state coffers (Merriman 1962:88). In general, relations were cordial between the Pope and the Spanish monarchs:

> The sovereigns would gladly promise unswerving loyalty to Rome, and enthusiastic devotion to the advancement of the interests of the church in all their dominions; but in return they demanded from the Pope wellnigh complete control of the clergy of Spain and all her dependencies (*ibid.*:152).

These religious obligations and rights formed the cornerstone for Spanish religious policy in the New World.

In this historical setting, the Spaniards arrived in the New World. They came armed with formidable experience in military, administrative, and mercantile matters. And they carried certain characteristic traditions and traits: feudalism, "idealization of nobility," hardiness, and individuality.

ARRIVAL OF THE SPANIARDS

The earliest Spanish colonial experience in the New World was in the Caribbean. In 1492 Columbus set foot on San Salvador (Watling's Island), and in the following year he returned to the Caribbean outfitted for settlement. In this second expedition, 17 ships carried 1500 men of diverse occupations (including craftsmen, soldiers, and general laborers) and large quantities of livestock, seeds, and tools. Although women did not accompany this expedition, its purpose was clear: to establish a permanent colony in the New World and solidify Spain's claim to the new-found territories. Settling on the island of Hispaniola, the adventurous party was almost immediately beset with problems: Their health deteriorated in the unfamiliar climate, morale was low, discipline was ineffective, and many colonists deserted. Relations with the "Indians," as the Europeans called all the native New World peoples, were consistently poor and often resulted in violent encounters.

Despite this floundering and inauspicious beginning, Spain began settling the islands of the Caribbean, drawing out what little gold they had to offer and establishing cattle ranching and sugar cultivation. At the same time, several expeditions were launched from the major islands to explore the region more fully. These years of colonization in the Caribbean provided the Spaniards with their undamental colonial institutions and policies: economic institutions, policies t)ward Indians, political structures, settlement patterns, and attempts at religious conversion.

From the beginning of the Caribbean settlements, the Spanish crown was determined to retain absolute economic and political control. Very early, the crown began withdrawing the rights and privileges it had originally granted Columbus in the New World. The crown established agencies and offices to govern the colonies, regulate trade, supervise immigration, and ensure taxation for the royal coffers. It also formulated Spanish policy toward the Indians: They were to be regarded and treated as Spanish subjects, not slaves. In this policy the crown was vehemently supported in the New World by many liberal friars.

But the goals and ideals of the crown were often thwarted by the personal goals of the Spanish settlers. Conflicts between the crown and the settlers often revolved around the institution of the *encomienda*. Encomiendas consisted of grants of Indian labor to privileged Spanish colonists. The institution was based on Spanish prototypes, and Columbus initiated the practice in the New World when he allotted a number of Indian communities to rebellious and dissatisfied Spaniards in the settlement party of his second voyage. Encomienda grants did not allocate land, only rights to the tribute and labor of specified Indian groups (Gibson 1964: 58–59). The institution was legally constrained by royal orders. Instead of seemingly unlimited rights and control over the Indian population in his domain, the Spanish *encomendero* had a specific set of legal obligations toward them. He must pay wages, offer protection, and provide for instruction in the Catholic faith. The rights of the Indians were formally set down in the Laws of Burgos in 1512, which specified

Limitation of the periods of the labor of the natives, regulations concerning their food and shelter, and a provision for the nomination of inspectors to see that the orders of the crown were actually carried out, . . . but as the inspectors were themselves encomenderos, they had every inducement to neglect the discharge of their functions. We have here again, in fact, the selfsame difficulty which crops up in every phase of the Spanish administration of the New World to the very end. The regulations made by the home government were usually excellent, but distance and defective means of communication rendered it well-nigh impossible to carry them out (Merriman 1962:234–235).

However, the crown could barely enforce its rules, and the personal goals of many encomenderos were stronger than their obedience to the Spanish law. Wages were often not paid to the Indians, work hours were gradually increased, and care and instruction were often disregarded. Despite attempts by the crown to restrict and control it, the encomienda became the single most important economic institution in the Spanish colonies.

Much of the Indian labor mobilized on the islands through the encomienda system was used for mining. The search for gold and other forms of mineral wealth was a major goal of many Spanish colonists. Success in mining meant that the colonists could live in the "Spanish style" in the colonies, since precious metals were easily exchanged for Spanish manufactured goods. Mining also provided the Spanish crown with unbelievable wealth. The crown, claiming ultimate rights to all mineral deposits, exacted a tax of one-fifth, known as the "royal fifth." But in the Caribbean the mineral deposits were exhausted after about 25 years. While some colonists switched to cattle ranching or sugar cultivation, those who sought mineral wealth were forced to look elsewhere.

The crown quickly established formal governmental institutions in its Caribbean possessions to attain some direct control. This always included a viceroy or royal governor; an *audiencia*, or high court of six or seven judges appointed for life; and royal treasury officials. While these royal officers conducted the high-level affairs of the colonies and protected the interests of the Spanish crown, local government was typically controlled by a *cabildo*, or town council. The members of this council were the most prominent and wealthy Spaniards of the town, and typically encomenderos. These men grew progressively more powerful and wealthy. For example, the cabildos reserved the right to distribute mining sites in the form of grants; the most lucrative grants they typically allocated to the already wealthy encomenderos.

The Spaniards strongly preferred living in urban settings. Urban residence was so important to the Spanish colonists that Santo Domingo, the main city of the island of Hispaniola, soon gave its name to the entire island.[1] This general pattern of settlement—with Spaniards and Spanish culture concentrated in urban settings and Indians and Indian culture dominating the countryside—was firmly established in the Caribbean and later transferred to conquered Mexico.

Hand in hand with Spanish political and economic control of the West Indies went a strong desire to convert the indigenous population to Christianity. Beginning with Columbus's second journey, friars accompanied virtually every voyage bringing colonists to the Caribbean. Their explicit duties revolved around conversion, but many also became staunch and outspoken supporters of Indian rights. This stance, of course, often brought these churchmen into direct conflict with the many encomenderos who mistreated the Indians granted to them. Aside from the friars attached to the regular orders (e.g., Dominicans, Franciscans), bishops and

[1] Later the name of Santo Domingo was transformed into the Dominican Republic.

priests began to arrive in the second decade of the sixteenth century. The priests were often attached to encomenderos, receiving care and a share of the encomendero's tribute. In this arrangement, the priest was basically dominated by the encomendero. This was consistent with the Spanish policy and practice in which secular bodies exercised dominance over the church.

In the Caribbean Islands the gold played out early and the Indian population was decimated by epidemic diseases and the trauma of conquest. Soon many Spaniards became dissatisfied and restless in their quests for wealth and souls. Early explorations in the region, many of them touching on the mainland, whetted the appetites of these Spaniards. By 1502, the entire eastern coast of the mainland from Honduras to Brazil had been explored by Spanish navigators, and settlements were established in Honduras as early as 1509. Spaniards traveling to these areas brought back to the islands rumors of gold and talk of large Indian populations. The coast of Mexico, however, remained undiscovered until 1517, when Hernandez de Córdoba was driven off course and landed on the coast of Yucatan. Córdoba explored much of the Yucatan coastline and engaged in frequent skirmishes with the Indians. He and his men were particularly surprised to find large communities with substantial stone buildings, and were delighted to see the inhabitants dressed in fine clothing and wearing polished gold and silver adornments. An expedition by Juan de Grijalva in the following year confirmed Córdoba's reports of wealth and a large unfriendly Indian population.

In addition to the information these expeditions obtained, they also seasoned many men who would participate in the conquest of Mexico. From the Grijalva expedition alone, at least 38 men returned to Mexico in 1519 with Hernán Cortés,[2] having already gained valuable experience on their earlier voyage. In addition, Cortés also inherited a Yucatecan Indian brought back by Córdoba. The Indian learned some Spanish in Cuba and served Cortés as an interpreter in the very early part of his expedition. Cortés would further ease his communication problems by discovering Jerónimo de Aguilar, a Spaniard shipwrecked on the Yucatecan coast several years earlier and fluent in the Yucatecan Mayan language.

For the Spanish empire in the New World, the Caribbean served as a transitional area. Not only did the Spaniards experiment with and establish colonial practices and policies, but they also began to acquire knowledge of the New World and to adopt selected parts of the culture and language. In fact, many words derived from the island languages were carried by the Spaniards to Mexico and applied to indigenous people and things there: *cacique* is an Arawak word for "chief," and Moctezuma and other great rulers were given this title by the Spaniards; *maguey*, a word also from a Caribbean language, was carried to Mexico by the colonists and replaced the Aztec term *metl*; and the Spaniards adopted from the Caribbean peoples the *canoa* ("canoe") as both a term and a tool. In the Caribbean, the Spaniards developed institutions, policies, goals, and expectations which were to serve as the keystone for their colonial experience in Mexico.

---

[2] Wagner (1942:51–52); Prescott (1931:141) states that more than 100 of Grijalva's men joined Cortés.

THE CONQUEST

The Cortés expedition was organized on the initiative of Diego Velásquez, governor of Cuba. Cortés agreed to pay two-thirds of the expedition expenses and make all the necessary arrangements—acquisition of the ships, recruitment of the men, and outfitting of the expedition in general. In return, he expected to receive a handsome profit; and the prospect of a great mainland encomienda undoubtedly loomed in his mind. Like many other men of his time, Cortés was extremely well equipped to handle the task of exploration. He came from a respectable family, was a wealthy encomendero in Cuba, an astute businessman, and a cabildo member. Somewhat unusual among his peers, he had studied law at the University of Salamanca in Spain.[3] Usually portrayed as a handsome, flashy, swashbuckling adventurer, he exhibited strong leadership qualities, a decisive temperament, and a tenacious will. He also was bored with his sedentary life in Cuba, and more than willing to accept the challenge and the position of captain. He had very little trouble finding men to follow him; the mineral resources of the islands were exhausted by 1519, and men seeking fame and fortune were looking to the mainland.

Like the Córdoba and Grijalva missions, the Cortés expedition was designed only for exploration and trading. Another purpose of the Cortés voyage was to find Grijalva; although some of his expedition had returned with tempting tales of fabulous wealth, Grijalva had not yet shown up in Cuba. But while Cortés was preparing his expedition, Velásquez became suspicious of his captain. He feared that Cortés was becoming too powerful, and that once away from Cuba Cortés would act independently and not respect his ties to his governor. To make matters worse, Grijalva returned and Velásquez apparently tried to prevent Cortés from embarking. Despite the protests of his governor, the determined Cortés and his loyal adventurers set sail. They indeed left Cuba on a sour note. In all, 11 ships were laden with approximately 600 men, of whom 50–100 were sailors. The men were from many walks of life. Some were encomenderos in Cuba, many of these superior to Cortés in social status. Others felt themselves important enough to have encomiendas, but did not. These men were extraordinarily loyal to Cortés, for they had everything to gain and nothing to lose. Still others were a varied lot of adventurers of much lower social station, including mechanics, miners, musicians, and sailors. Many of these sailors were foreigners: Genoese, Portuguese, Greeks, and even a Frenchman (Wagner 1944:38). A few of the men were armed with crossbows, and even fewer carried muskets. Both light and heavy cannon supplemented these arms. Sixteen horses were also carried on the ships.

So in February 1519 Cortés departed from Cuba, and in approximately a week anchored off the island of Cozumel. Here, just off the coast of Yucatan, the Spaniard Jerónimo de Aguilar joined him. Having survived nearly eight years stranded on the peninsula, Aguilar had become conversant in the Yucatecan Mayan language. He proved invaluable to Cortés as an interpreter and an advisor on Indian customs.

---

[3] In contrast, Francisco Pizarro, credited with the conquest of the Inca, never learned to sign his name.

Sailing along the coast of Yucatan to Tabasco, Cortés met a large force of Indians; the encounter was a violent one, resulting in perhaps 300 Indian deaths and some 70 wounded Spaniards. The Indians were defeated, and later brought gifts of gold, turquoise, food, and women to Cortés. Among these women was Marina, fluent in both the Mayan and Nahuatl tongues. Later, when her talents were recognized, she and Aguilar together served Cortés in translations; Marina would translate from Nahuatl to Mayan, Aguilar from Mayan to Spanish.

With an uneasy peace established in Tabasco, Cortés sailed along the Mexican coast to Veracruz. There he met, for the first time, envoys sent from the great Moctezuma.

For his part, Moctezuma Xocoyotzin was growing increasingly uneasy over the arrival of these strangers from the east. For 10 years prior to the Spanish arrival, he had been plagued by a series of troublesome omens (see Chapter 6). Although the unusual signs were difficult to interpret, Moctezuma feared that they foretold doom for himself and his empire. Then his own messengers reported that strangers—perhaps men, perhaps gods—had appeared off the Mexican coast.[4] Moctezuma's apprehension grew. Approximately one year later the Spaniards reappeared, this time under the command of Hernán Cortés. Moctezuma sent five high-ranking emissaries, along with great quantities of rich gifts and godly attire, to greet the strangers. These messengers were welcomed aboard the Spanish craft, where they proceeded to dress Cortés in the elaborate attire of the god Quetzalcoatl. Apparently Cortés retained his composure. He did, however, provide the emissaries with a display of Spanish military might: After firing one of his large cannons, he challenged them to combat. Shocked by the cannon blast and terrified by all they had seen, the Aztecs refused the challenge and rushed back to Tenochtitlan.

This initial encounter marked the beginning of the series of events and circumstances that was to end in the eventual defeat of the Aztecs. Moctezuma was apparently unable to decide whether the invaders were gods or mortals. His first delegation treated Cortés as a god, but his second envoy included sorcerers, who tried magically to dispose of the strangers. The Spaniards spent about five months on the Veracruz coast. During this time Moctezuma learned a great deal about the strangers, their horses, and their arms; but he continued to vacillate about their natural or supernatural identity. His emissaries informed him that the mysterious Cortés sought Moctezuma specifically; this frightened the *tlatoani* so much that he tried to hide, but he could find no suitable place. When he realized that the Spaniards had begun to march inland, he resolved to await their arrival, periodically sending envoys to try to discourage the resolute Spaniards.

Meanwhile, Moctezuma's adversary was not idle. Cortés had many nagging problems, and he attacked them one by one. Diego Velásquez was antagonistic toward him, and Cortés knew that he would receive no support or rewards from the Cuban governor. He therefore ignored Velásquez's orders and proceeded to establish a settlement on the mainland, and to move inland with the intent of conquest. Having undertaken a course of action certain to alienate his immediate

---

[4] They must have meant the Grijalva expedition of 1518 (Anderson and Dibble 1978:11–12).

superior, Cortés began to woo King Charles V of Spain by sending him precious gifts received from Moctezuma's emissaries. Some men in Cortés's party were supporters of Velásquez and objected to these actions, so Cortés destroyed his vessels to prevent this faction's return to Cuba. He had a talent for diplomacy, and through flattery and cajolery managed to unify his little band.

Cortés had not developed friendly relations with the Indians, although he did discover one reassuring fact: Some Indian communities in Mexico were not altogether loyal to Moctezuma. Cortés viewed such groups as potential allies. In his first major incursion inland, to Cempoalla, he encouraged the inhabitants to seize a group of Aztec tribute collectors, a terrible affront to the Aztec ruler. Although Cortés later arranged for the release of the tax collectors, the destiny of the Cempoallan people and their "fat chief" was sealed; they had defied the authority of Moctezuma, who had only recently conquered them, and their only recourse was to ally themselves with the European invaders.

Cortés did not endear himself to his new allies. His religious zeal compelled him to have idols hurled from temples and destroyed, much to the shock and dismay of the local inhabitants. He then transformed the Cempoallan temple into a church.

In late summer 1519, Cortés, 300–350 of his men,[5] 15 horses, and some warriors from Cempoalla began moving inland toward Tenochtitlan. After about two weeks of travel through difficult terrain and inclement weather, they reached the borders of the province of Tlaxcalla. At that time Tlaxcalla was an independent state surrounded by conquered Aztec provinces. In one province bordering Tlaxcalla, the Spaniards learned a great deal about Moctezuma and his great empire: the vast Aztec armies, Moctezuma's voluminous stores of precious metals, and the grand and impregnable city of Tenochtitlan. Far from dampening the ambitions of the adventurers, such talk inspired them to forge ahead more eagerly, for "Such is the nature of us Spaniards that the more [the local ruler] told us about the fortresses and bridges, the more we longed to try our fortune, although to judge from Olintecle's description the capture of Mexico would be an impossible enterprise" (Díaz del Castillo 1963:136–137). And talk of Moctezuma's extraordinary wealth only made the Spaniards more resolute in their desire to discover and control the source of these riches. The Spaniards were also advised by these Aztec subjects not to enter the lands of the Tlaxcallans, since the latter were bitter enemies of Moctezuma. Cortés had already decided to contact and solicit the support of the Tlaxcallans because they would be of inestimable value to him in a confrontation with the powerful Moctezuma.

Cortés did not win the support of the Tlaxcallans easily. The two forces engaged in small skirmishes and two major battles. Cortés's few hundred men held their own against several thousand fierce Tlaxcallans.[6] These encounters left many Tlaxcallans dead and wounded, 2 horses dead, and relatively few Spaniards wounded. The

---

[5] Cortés had left 150 of his men at La Villa Rica de la Vera Cruz, the Spanish settlement on the mainland. Others had died of sickness and wounds suffered in earlier battles.

[6] Cortés reported confronting forces of 100,000 and 139,000 Tlaxcallans (1928:43, 44). These figures are greatly exaggerated, although he may have faced an army as large as 32,000 men (Wagner 1944:150).

Tlaxcallan rulers, seeing that they were unable to defeat the invaders, finally sued for peace. A mutually advantageous alliance was arranged: Both Cortés and the Tlaxcallans were eager to subdue the mighty Aztecs, and their combined forces might achieve that conquest.

The Spaniards spent 20 days in the city of Tlaxcalla. The rulers presented Cortés with modest gifts; maguey fiber cloth, inexpensive stones, and a small quantity of gold. They also offered some of their daughters to serve as wives for Cortés and his captains. With his religion always in mind, Cortés attempted to convert the rulers, who refused to forsake their traditional beliefs. He also insisted that the maidens be baptized before he distributed them among his captains. From the Tlaxcallan rulers Cortés learned impressive details about the Aztecs, their capital city, and their tlatoani. During this time, ambassadors from Moctezuma arrived in Tlaxcalla to woo Cortés. Moctezuma feared Cortés's alliance with his old enemies the Tlaxcallans, and his ambassadors tried to dissuade Cortés from that alliance. The Spanish captain was in an enviable political position between ancient enemies, each of whom wished his support and insisted on the evil intents of the other.

The Mexica ambassadors stayed with Cortés in Tlaxcalla, and served as his guides to Tenochtitlan. Against the advice of his Tlaxcallan allies, he traveled through neighboring Aztec-dominated Cholula, where he heard rumors of an ambush by Aztec warriors. Perhaps to prevent the ambush, to reward the Tlaxcallans with some booty, or merely to dishearten the Aztecs, Cortés ordered a massacre of the Cholulans, killing some 4000–5000 and imprisoning many others (Wagner 1944: 174–175). The city was looted; the Tlaxcallans were given cotton clothing and salt, which they lacked in their province, while the Spaniards kept the gold.

Cortés spent another 20 days or so in Cholula, leaving for Tenochtitlan on November 1. Along with about 350 Spaniards and several thousand Tlaxcallan allies, he arrived at his destination on November 8, 1519. Much of his time was spent parleying with Moctezuma's numerous messengers. Emissaries brought the Spaniard expensive gifts and amiable words to dissuade him from advancing, soothsayers and sorcerers tried to bewitch him and his company, and commoners were sent to block the road and make him detour. But Cortés was not to be dissuaded, bewitched, or deceived. He proceeded straight to the causeways that linked Tenochtitlan with the mainland, gathering lakeshore allies along the way. Meanwhile, in Tenochtitlan, Moctezuma and the Mexica had resigned themselves to their fate: " 'So be it,' the common folk said. 'Let us be accursed. What more can be done? We are bound to die, we are already bound to perish. Yes, we can only await death' " (Anderson and Dibble 1978:27).

Finally, Moctezuma sent his nephew, Cacama, ruler of Texcoco, to meet the advancing Spaniards and guide them to the Mexica capital. They moved along the broad causeways, painfully aware of their own vulnerability. As they approached the city, Moctezuma arrived to greet Cortés. Their meeting was a dramatic historical moment:

> When Cortés saw, heard, and was told that the great Montezuma was approaching, he dismounted from his horse, and when he came near to Montezuma each bowed deeply to the other. Montezuma welcomed our Captain, and Cortés, speaking through Doña Marina, answered by wishing him very good health.

Cortés, I think, offered Montezuma his right hand, but Montezuma refused it and extended his own. Then Cortés brought out a necklace which he had been holding. . . . This he hung round the great Montezuma's neck, and as he did so attempted to embrace him. But the great princes who stood round Montezuma grasped Cortés' arm to prevent him, for they considered this an indignity (Díaz del Castillo 1963:217–218).

The visitors were housed in luxurious quarters, the palace of Moctezuma's father, Axayacatl. There they discovered some of Moctezuma's opulent treasure, which many eagerly seized. They were provided with the finest food and provisions. And Moctezuma took Cortés on a tour of the city. From the summit of the great temple, Cortés and his men gaped at the size of the city, its orderly marketplace, and its long causeways. They nervously pondered their strategic predicament: so few men essentially trapped within the city. But these fears did not deter Cortés from expressing his religious zeal once more. He ordered idols

. . . to be dragged from their places and flung down the stairs, which done I had the temples which they occupy cleansed for they were full of the blood of human victims who had been sacrificed, and placed in them the image of Our Lady and other saints all of which made no small impression upon Muteczuma and the inhabitants (Cortés 1928:90–91).

Under the circumstances, his actions were extraordinary: He personally smacked the idol of Huitzilopochtli between the eyes with a long rod! This won Cortés no support from the powerful Aztec priesthood, who were appalled at his behavior.

To strengthen his shaky position, Cortés seized Moctezuma and held him prisoner in Axayacatl's palace. The Mexica ruler did not resist, but simply accepted his fate. He declared his obedience and subservience to Charles V of Spain, and ordered that his noble subjects do the same. But instead of rallying to Moctezuma's side, the Mexica elite deserted him:

When Moctezuma was kept a captive by the Spaniards, these noblemen went into hiding not only to get away from the Spaniards but to express their disgust and anger with Moctezuma (Anderson and Dibble 1978:34).

Moctezuma had lost his Mexica following, and the city was plunged into political chaos. His nephew Cacama, ruler of Texcoco, plotted to unseat his uncle; but Moctezuma betrayed him and he also became a prisoner of Cortés.

While in Tenochtitlan, Cortés received word that 18 ships with 900 men had arrived at Veracruz. The expedition was under the command of Pánfilo de Narvaez, and had been sent by Cortés's archrival Velásquez to apprehend him. The Spaniards, as well as the Aztecs, were split by internal rivalries. Cortés left 80 men in Tenochtitlan under Pedro de Alvarado, and took the remainder to meet the threatening Spanish forces. His task was simple: he easily captured Narvaez, whose men immediately surrendered. These forces then joined with Cortés: he now had over a thousand men and nearly 100 horses. He returned confidently to Tenochtitlan, only to find that the city had been in an uproar.

In his absence, a feast in honor of Huitzilopochtli had been celebrated. While the participants sang and danced, the impetuous Alvarado surrounded the courtyard and his men began massacring the celebrants. The Aztecs retaliated, and all-out war resulted. The Spaniards retreated to Axayacatl's palace and placed Moctezuma in irons. Cortés returned to find the city quiet, but his men and their Tlaxcallan allies were trapped and completely cut off from supplies; starvation was a real possibility. Both sides now began fighting in earnest; in the melee Moctezuma was killed.[7] By this time, the Mexica had selected a new tlatoani, Cuitlahuac. In contrast to his brother Moctezuma, he had from the beginning advised the Mexica to resist the intruders. Although he was a valiant warrior, his reign lasted less than six months. He was an early victim of smallpox, the deadly disease that would ravage sixteenth-century Mesoamerica.

For several days the Spaniards and Tlaxcallans were locked in a fierce struggle with the Aztecs. As the invaders' forces rapidly diminished and their supplies dwindled, it became clear that their only real hope lay in evacuation.

The Spaniards undertook their escape on a drizzly July night in 1520. They moved out of the city along the causeway to Tlacopan, meeting harsh and sustained resistance from Aztec warriors; the Aztecs pursued them along the causeway on foot, and attacked from the lake in canoes. The damage done to Cortés's forces was so severe that the night was labeled *noche triste*, or "sorrowful night."[8] Authorities do not agree on the number of men involved, but perhaps as many as 600–700 Spaniards and 2000–3000 Tlaxcallans were lost, along with all the Aztec hostages (including Cacama, the Texcocan ruler). Indeed, when the bedraggled force finally reached Tlacopan, they counted only 425 Spaniards and 23 horses.[9] All surviving Spaniards and horses were wounded (Wagner 1944:300). The greatest casualties were among the Tlaxcallans and the forces of Narvaez. These groups formed the rear guard, and Narvaez's men were reputedly so weighted down with gold that they had little chance of escape.

From Tlacopan an exhausted group of Spaniards and Tlaxcallans began a slow march to Tlaxcalla. The Mexica and their allies harassed this force every step of the way. After more than 10 days of painful travel, the small company reached friendly territory, but were greeted by the Tlaxcallans with mixed emotions. Some were angry that the Spaniards had caused so many Tlaxcallan deaths; others were pleased to see any of the company return. The latter attitude prevailed, and Cortés and his men nursed their wounds in a generally amiable atmosphere.

The Spaniards spent some five and a half months in and around Tlaxcalla. They recuperated, raided nearby Aztec-dominated cities, and sent for reinforcements. In late December Cortés set out for Tenochtitlan; he intended to isolate and besiege the city, then attack when it was debilitated. But Tenochtitlan was already weakened:

[7] Mystery shrouds Moctezuma's death. Native sources claim that he was killed by the Spaniards; Spanish chronicles claim he was stoned by his own people while pleading with them for peace (Anderson and Dibble 1978:51).

[8] Many of the Spaniards lost on the Noche Triste were laden with melted-down gold and other valuables from Moctezuma's treasure. In early 1981, a slightly curved gold bar, 26.5 × 5 × 1 centimeters, was uncovered along the old Tlacopan causeway. It has been suggested that this bar, of a size and shape to fit neatly under Spanish armor, accompanied an unlucky conquistador that night.

[9] The distance from Axayacatl's palace to Tlacopan was four and a half miles; the Spaniards traveled most of this distance between midnight and dawn. The "count" was probably very chaotic, in tune with the events of the night. Later, when the exhausted party reached Tlaxcalla, 440 Spaniards were tallied (Wagner 1944:300).

Many were dying of smallpox, including Cuitlahuac, who was succeeded by his cousin Cuauhtemoc. Cuauhtemoc began preparations for the expected Spanish onslaught: he sent emissaries to conquered provinces in search of aid and reinforcements, brought extra supplies into the city, and trained warriors. However, many of the subject cities abandoned the Mexica, preferring an alliance with Cortés. Among the most powerful of these was the Triple Alliance city of Texcoco, whose allegiance to Cortés was soon copied by many of the lakeshore cities. Tenochtitlan was virtually severed from the mainland, although some mainland cities remained loyal. Cortés spent until mid-April 1521 subduing opposition around the Valley of Mexico, wooing more allies, and preparing for the siege and final attack.

The formal attack began on April 28, 1521. Cortés now had over 900 Spaniards; untold thousands of Indian allies; 86 horses; 15 cannon; and 13 brigantines, which he had ordered constructed in Tlaxcalla and Texcoco. Cortés's land forces approached the city along the three causeways, while the brigantines (manned by 300 of his men) blockaded the city, attacking and stopping all canoe traffic on the lake. The street fighting, which lasted several days, was fierce but inconclusive. The Spaniards would take a position, only to lose it; the Mexica would push the invaders back, only to be attacked more ferociously. The brigantines were temporarily immobilized by large stakes placed in the lake by the Mexica. In the course of the fighting, about 50 Spaniards were captured alive; their comrades watched stupefied as these men were marched up the temple steps, forced to dance with fans before the image of Huitzilopochtli, and finally sacrificed. While the Mexica celebrated their temporary victory, their enemies regrouped. Many of the Spaniards had been killed, most were wounded, and all were exhausted. Large numbers of the Spaniards' Indian allies had deserted. Under the circumstances, Cortés decided to minimize the fighting and concentrate on his blockade to prevent supplies from reaching Tenochtitlan. This strategy, beginning on May 30, took a heavy toll on the already beleaguered city:

> There was hunger. Many died of famine. There was no more good, pure water to drink—only nitrous water. Many died of it—contracted dysentery which killed them. The people ate anything—lizards, barn swallows, corn leaves, salt-grass; they gnawed . . . leather and buckskin, cooked or toasted; or sedum and adobe bricks. Never had such suffering been seen; it was terrifying how many of us died when we were shut in as we were (Anderson and Dibble 1978:79).

In mid-July the Spaniards renewed their assault on the city, finally overwhelming the last remnants of resistance in Tlatelolco, and capturing the retreating Cuauhtemoc on August 13.

The siege had lasted 75 days, and each day had seen at least some fighting (Cortés 1928:228). The devastation wrought by the Spaniards and their Indian allies was cataclysmic: Entire quarters of the city were demolished, many Aztec survivors were slaughtered, and the city was sacked mercilessly. Out of perhaps 300,000 original Aztec defenders, only about 60,000 survived (Wagner 1944:355).

It has often been asked how such a small group of Spaniards could be militarily successful against such overwhelming odds. To add to the conquistadores' difficulties, they were fighting in a strange land, on terrain familiar to their adversaries. Cortés and his men occasionally became distressed and despondent. While engaged in the war with Tlaxcalla, "there was not one amongst us who was not heartily afraid at finding himself so far in the interior of the country among so many and such warlike people and so destitute of help from any part" (Cortés 1928:47).

Spanish success was based on several factors: technology, military goals and tactics, and the loose structure of the Aztec empire. The Aztec armory consisted mainly of lances, bows and arrows, and clubs insert with sharp obsidian blades. Wooden shields and thick cotton armor offered some protection in battle. While the Spaniards very early adopted the native cotton armor, they had steel swords and shields, muskets and cannon. Of these arms, the most effective were the swords; competent swordsmen could swiftly and easily smash wooden shields and inflict serious wounds in hand-to-hand combat (see Figure 8–1). The muskets and cannon provided some "shock value," but could not have inflicted much serious damage, since they were awkward to use and reload. The horses and large dogs brought by Cortés also terrified and astounded the Indians, but only until the Tlaxcallans killed two horses and realized the animals were mortal. The horses remained tactically useful to the Spaniards by providing great mobility on the field of battle. Coupled with these differences in military equipment, the goals and tactics of the two adversaries tipped the balance in favor of the Spaniards. The Indian warriors engaged in their traditional style of warfare, taking great chances in hand-to-hand combat in order to capture the enemy for sacrifice. The Spaniards traditionally fought to vanquish, not capture, the enemy. The advantage of an enormous number of Indian warriors was muted by the indigenous practice of advancing in a closed body, with only a small part of the force actually confronting the adversary at any one time. Under these conditions, it is not startling to read that a typical Indian-Spanish battle could result in several hundred Indians dead and some Spaniards only wounded. After leaving the coast, the Spaniards always fought in the company of Indian allies. They defeated the Tlaxcallans with the aid of warriors from Cempoalla; arrived at Tenochtitlan with a formidable body of Tlaxcallan and

Figure 8–1: Spaniards and Indians engage in battle (Lienzo de Tlaxcala 1892: lámina 77).

Cempoallan warriors; and made the final assault on the Mexica capital aided by Tlaxcallans, Texcocans, Xochimilcas, and warriors from a multitude of other nearby cities. The Tlaxcallans had a history of formal hostilities with the Aztecs; the others were apparently capable and willing to rebel against Mexica domination. The belief that Cortés may have been the god Quetzalcoatl may have caused some initial hesitation on the part of the indigenous rulers, but they must not have held this belief for long. It is unlikely that Moctezuma would have sent sorcerers to work malevolent magic against a god, and equally improbable that the Tlaxcallans and others would have taken up arms against any deity, much less one so highly favored and benevolent.

With the scales tipped in their favor, the Spaniards had conquered a great city, and were destined to transform an entire civilization. These painful changes would penetrate deeply into the everyday lives of the Indian population of the sixteenth century.

INDIGENOUS ADAPTATIONS TO SPANISH RULE

The full impact of the Spanish conquest fell differently on each indigenous community in central Mexico. However, the major effects of the conquest treated in this chapter were distributed generally throughout central Mexico. This "generalizing approach," by its very nature, tends to mask variation. Yet each indigenous individual and community assumed a slightly different strategy in adapting to the new colonial order. The generalizations also obscure the fact that, on the whole, the indigenous groups retained their ethnic identities and dealt with each other and the Spanish administration as Xochimilcas, Chalcas, Tlaxcaltecas, and so on, not as "Indians." While the term "Indian" is used here, the Spanish documents usually contain the term *naturales* ("natives") to express the same concept, and the Nahuatl documents use *nican tlaca*, or "here people."

Demography and Settlement Patterns   One of the most immediate effects of European entry into the New World was a devastating decline in the native population. In central Mexico, the indigenous population plunged from an estimated 12–15 million[10] to just over 1 million at the beginning of the seventeenth century. This decline was due to warfare, the ravaging effects of European epidemic diseases, famine, dislocation of many people from their traditional lands, and overwork on Spanish estates and mines.

After the fall of Tenochtitlan, 10 years passed before most of Mesoamerica came effectively under Spanish control. While some groups were readily subdued, others persistently resisted Spanish domination. All of the military confrontations, beginning in 1519, exacted a heavy toll from the indigenous forces. The total of these battlefield casualties is almost impossible to estimate, although it was surely in the tens of thousands, and mostly men in their prime.

---

[10] "Central Mexico" roughly corresponds to the area of the Aztec empire, plus the Tlaxcallan and Tarascan states. Estimates for the indigenous population in 1519 range as high as 25,200,000 (Cook and Borah 1963).

Warfare continued only for a limited time; except for an occasional local rebellion, it ceased to reduce the Indian population by the middle of the sixteenth century. More insidious and devastating was the onslaught of epidemic diseases introduced by the Spaniards. Smallpox, measles, and typhus were particularly destructive to the Indians, who lacked immunities to these diseases. Tenochtitlan suffered its first epidemic in 1520 while Cortés prepared for his final military onslaught on the stricken city. Severe epidemics in 1545–1548 and 1576–1581 resulted in a vast depopulation of the central Mexican Indian population. The loss, in total numbers, was greatest in the central Mexican highlands, where the population was concentrated in towns and cities. But the greatest impact was felt in the tropical lowlands, where the diseases spread unabated and wiped out entire communities. Famine often accompanied the loss in population, as fields lay idle and crops untended.

Famine also ensued from dislocations of the Indian population. Some of these dislocations resulted from a drastic decline in local populations; Indians voluntarily abandoned severely depopulated settlements and joined larger, more stable communities, or wandered off to live as vagabonds. A great deal of agricultural land was abandoned in the process, and this remained unused or was easily acquired by Spaniards eager for extensive land holdings. Some Spaniards also bought or traded for traditional lands, which the Indians were often hungry and desperate enough to sell. Throughout the 1550s, the Indian council of Tlaxcalla wrestled with the problems of Spanish encroachment on Indian lands, decreeing that Spaniards could not live in Tlaxcalla and preventing nobles from selling their landed estates to Spaniards. Nonetheless, some Spaniards apparently did reside in Tlaxcalla and farm Tlaxcallan lands (Anderson, Berdan, and Lockhart, n.d.). Indian peoples from all parts of central Mexico were displaced from their traditional lands; in 1547 the Tlaxcallan council grappled with the problem of controlling and assessing taxes on its many newcomers—Indians from Texcoco, Mexico City (Tenochtitlan), and other cities (Anderson, Berdan, and Lockhart 1976:121).

The movements, groupings, and regroupings of indigenous peoples were attempts, often involuntary, to adjust to the massive population decline and the impingement of Spaniards on traditional lands. This process of adjustment was accelerated in the late sixteenth and early seventeenth centuries by the Spanish policy of *congregación*. Under this policy, Indians in outlying areas were resettled in larger, more stable communities. Spanish secular officials favored the policy, which greatly simplified their tasks of census taking, tribute assessment, and general administration. The Catholic clergy welcomed the policy: More Indian souls became readily available for conversion to Christianity. And Spaniards in general benefited from the policy: vast tracts of land were abandoned and open to Spanish ownership. But relatively few Spanish immigrants were farmers, and the removal of the Indians from these lands often resulted in famine, for the lands went unused and the Indians removed to larger settlements did not immediately adjust to their new conditions.

Also contributing to the native population decline, although in unknown proportions, was overwork and the trauma of surviving under alien conditions. The encomienda system placed whole Indian communities under the control of a single

Spanish overlord, and although Spanish royal policy demanded that the Indians be treated as wards of the crown, they were sometimes reduced to hopeless bondage; they were undernourished, maltreated, worked long hours, and died young. Many encomienda Indians were transferred from their communities to mines, where they were often driven to despair by the strenuous and debilitating conditions.

These many adverse conditions, especially disease, resulted in millions of Indian deaths. Some estimates place the population decline at more than half by 1570, and others suggest a loss of two-thirds by that time. A century after the Spanish conquest, the Indian population may have declined by as much as 90 percent (Gibson 1964:138). Some provinces and communities suffered tragically. In 1563 the Indians of Xochimilco estimated their provincial population at 6000–7000—down from perhaps 30,000 in 1519;[11] by the early seventeenth century some other communities had plummeted from "8000 to 300, from 6000 to 200, and from 4000 to 150" (ibid.). Around 1620, the Indian population began to increase, recovering from a century of trauma. Even with these demographic setbacks, Indians as a whole continued to outnumber any other group in the population throughout the colonial period.

From the earliest Spanish arrival, a new population began to emerge. Typically the offspring of a Spanish father and an Indian mother, this person of mixed blood and combined heritage was called a mestizo. As the centuries passed, mestizo married mestizo, Spaniard married mestizo, and Indian married mestizo; this complicated category came to include all persons of mixed Spanish-Indian background. While "pureblooded" Spaniards probably never constituted more than 5 percent of the total population in central Mexico, the mestizos steadily increased in numbers, until by the end of colonial rule in 1821, they comprised one-third of the total population (Gerhard 1972:25). In a sense, this process of "mestizoization" also contributed to the statistical decline in Indian population, although not to any decline in total population, since many Indian women were producing mestizo, rather than Indian, children.

In the New World, as in Spain, the Spaniards preferred to live in towns and cities; only rarely did they settle in the countryside. In some cases, the Spaniards founded entirely new cities such as Puebla and Veracruz; these cities became administrative, economic, and religious centers for Spanish endeavors.[12] In many other cases, Spaniards came to reside in traditionally Indian towns and cities: the razed Tenochtitlan was rebuilt as Mexico City, and numerous other indigenous towns had relatively small but powerful Spanish minorities by the mid-sixteenth century. Although Spaniards and Spanish interests were concentrated in the urban centers, the culture and activities they introduced had a profound and lasting impact on life in the countryside as well. Their arrival was felt in transformations of the traditional economy, society, polity, and religion.

Economy   The economy of Aztec Mexico was based primarily on agriculture. To this important production system the Spaniards added technologies, foodstuffs,

---

[11] William Sanders (1970:449–450), relying on documentary analysis, has suggested an approximate population of 15,000 for Xochimilco proper in 1519.

[12] Almost 35 Spanish towns had been established in New Spain by 1575 (West and Augelli 1966:270).

goals, and institutions novel to the Indian way of life. Machetes were widely adopted by Indians, and eased the task of clearing land for cultivation. The wheel, as a practical tool, was also introduced, and greatly facilitated transportation and commerce throughout Mesoamerica. The concept of the wheel was apparently well known in Mesoamerica long before the arrival of the Europeans; engaging little ritual objects depicting jaguars, monkeys, and dogs on wheels, dating several hundred years before Columbus, have been found in the state of Veracruz. But without robust draft animals, the wheel was of little use applied to carts or wagons. The Spaniards brought carts, wagons, draft animals, and even the pottery wheel. While some noble Indians acquired plows and the necessary oxen shortly after the conquest, most Indian cultivators continued to rely on the traditional technology until the eighteenth century. Until that time, the plow remained a tool primarily for Spanish agricultural enterprises.

Livestock, including cattle, horses, sheep, goats, chickens, pigs, donkeys, and mules, was a standard part of the Spanish production system. Of these animals, the chicken became the most widespread, raised by Spaniard and Indian alike, and a common item of encomienda tribute. The chicken was the new animal most readily adopted by the Indians; they were already experienced in raising its relative, the indigenous turkey, and found chickens easy to raise and reliable in production. Some Indian nobles and communities developed substantial sheep herds, but their lack of experience severely limited production; in the mid-sixteenth century the Indian council of Tlaxcalla agreed to place its substantial sheep herd in the care of a Spaniard for the explicit purpose of increasing production (Anderson, Berdan, and Lockhart, n.d.). On the whole, Indians had little interest in raising cattle (although they enjoyed eating beef). They were restricted in their use of horses, and limited in the sizes of other herds they could maintain. Livestock raising was predominately a Spanish activity throughout the sixteenth century, and Indians often complained about Spanish livestock overrunning and destroying their crops. The animals required pasturage and fodder; and Indian lands were often appropriated by Spaniards for grazing livestock. And some crops were geared toward feeding livestock, not people; in times of famine, people and animals often competed for a limited supply of maize and other foodstuffs.

In addition to livestock, certain crops also accompanied the Spaniards. Wheat, sugarcane, grapes, olives, and a variety of European fruits were more desirable to the Spanish palate than were the indigenous foods. By the same token, the Indians were reluctant to adopt these Spanish foods, and continued to prefer their own diet of maize, beans, squashes, and chiles. In the highlands, much of the fertile irrigated flatlands was devoted to the European crops; wheat especially was produced on a large scale under plow cultivation. In the tropical lowlands, vast tracts of land came under sugarcane cultivation. The introduction of both livestock and Spanish crops substantially reduced the area allotted to traditional Indian maize cultivation. This change was commensurate with the drastic decline in Indian population.

Privileged Spaniards not only acquired extensive tracts of land but also dominated Indian labor. Many Indian communities were granted as encomiendas to Spaniards who had distinguished themselves in the conquest and who had special political connections. Through this system, much Indian labor was diverted from traditional cultivation to satisfy the demands of the landed Spanish aristocracy. The inhabitants of communities held in encomienda were obligated to cultivate the encomendero's fields and provide him with tribute (typically Spanish pesos, chickens, indigenous-style cloaks and household service). In the mid-1500s the wealthier encomiendas received 4500–17,000 pesos annually in tribute from their subjects (Chevalier 1963:118–119).[13] These encomienda grants diverted considerable wealth from the crown to individuals; the crown eventually curtailed the institution, usually by refusing to renew the grant for the next generation.

Many Indians produced fine crafts and other manufactures in pre-Hispanic times, and much of this specialized activity continued throughout the colonial period. Communities noted for special crafts retained their distinction—Azcapotzalco for silverwork, Cuauhtitlan for pottery, Coyoacan for masonry, Xochimilco for carpentry and masonry, and Texcoco for a variety of crafts from fine stoneworking to lacquer work (Gibson 1964:350–351). Specialized production of Aztec status goods, however, was greatly reduced. In the new society, elegant feathered headdresses and gold lip plugs were no longer signs of elevated social status, even if the few surviving Indian nobles could have afforded them. Rather, the demand was for carpenters, masons, potters, canoe makers, and the like; and much of this production continued in indigenous hands. New specializations were perfected by some Indians. Tailoring became a particularly active occupation, geared toward local Spanish consumption:

> . . . they can make breeches, doublet, coat or waistcoat of whatever kind you ask for as well as in Castile, and all other garments, whose styles are innumerable—for they (i.e., the Spaniards) do nothing but change their clothes and seek for new fashions (Motolinía 1950:242).

Commerce thrived in New Spain. Although the *pochteca* guilds quickly dissolved after the Spanish conquest, both long-distance and local trade continued at a lively pace. The Spaniards interfered little with the local markets, or *tianguiz*, where Indians came as both producers and middlemen to buy and sell. Spaniards, mestizos, or acculturated Indians also probably frequented these marketplaces, since Spanish goods were often in evidence. The late sixteenth-century marketplace of Toluca offered candles, metal knives, and shirt collars (Lockhart 1976:115); and the mid-sixteenth century Coyoacan marketplace displayed candles, hides, and shirt collars, although indigenous goods dominated (Anderson, Berdan, and Lockhart 1976:138–149). Some Spaniards and mestizos became involved in commerce, especially on a larger scale. Many Texcocan mestizos, for example, became cacao entrepreneurs in the sixteenth century, transporting cacao over ancient trade routes from Guatemala to Mexico City (Leslie Lewis 1976:131). The more strictly Spanish commercial activity was somewhat complex, being carried on in the tianguiz and with overseas companies and individuals.

European demands for a few indigenously produced goods caused major transformations in the lives of some Indians. For example, in 1553 the Indian council

---

[13] Most tributaries paid one or one and a half pesos each, while widows usually were assessed half a peso.

of Tlaxcalla had a heated discussion on the evils of extensive cultivation of the cochineal cactus.[14] The council members cited many unsavory consequences of the activity, which was geared toward a Spanish overseas market: Commoners were neglecting their food crops, which made famine possible, and were wasting their money income on unnecessary luxuries; they were flaunting their cash and losing respect for the nobles; and they were working Sundays on cochineal production, instead of attending mass. Drunkenness, improper relations between the cochineal dealers and the women dye collectors, and exploitation by Spaniards were also noted as leading to a deterioration in the traditional Tlaxcallan life-style. Although probably somewhat overplayed, the concern of the council points out the fragile and dependent nature of the Indian economy in the colonial period (Anderson, Berdan, and Lockhart, n.d.).

Some material introductions by the Spaniards transformed the face of New Spain. New Spanish-style towns were planned on a grid pattern, buildings were constructed in Spanish architectural traditions, and tile roofs dotted the landscape. Catholic churches were frequently built on the sites of indigenous temples and were often constructed of stones from the razed temples. The extensive Spanish construction efforts accelerated a process of deforestation and erosion already under way in pre-Spanish times. Wood was a high-demand commodity, being used in colonial times for lumber, fuel, lime production, and enormous pilings for building supports in Mexico City. Very early in the colonial period the Spaniards had begun draining Lake Texcoco to provide more land for urban construction and crop production; however, the soft lakebed required firm foundations for the stone buildings, and some of the area remained too saline for agricultural purposes (Gibson 1964: 303–305).

The Spanish friars, often alarmed and indignant at the brevity of native clothing, insisted on some elements of Spanish attire for the Indians. This especially applied to males, with the indigenous loin cloth being replaced by the more modest Spanish trousers. On the whole, however, few elements of Spanish material culture found their way into Indian homes. Partly for economic reasons and partly from cultural preference, most of the indigenous people continued to sleep on mats, thatch their roofs, plant with digging sticks, and walk to their fields. By the same token, Spaniards rarely adopted ingredients of the Indian life-style. Most Spaniards who migrated to New Spain emphasized retaining, and if possible enhancing, an aristocratic Spanish life-style. For their homes and activities these Spaniards imported European tools, household goods, and personal adornments. To obtain these goods, the wealthier Spaniards developed mining enterprises or acquired large landed estates. Mineral wealth in particular provided Spaniards with a medium universally accepted in exchange for European manufactures. Less well-to-do Spaniards emulated their wealthier counterparts as best they could, often earning a livelihood in commerce, transport, or small-scale farming. All of this resulted in a dual economy: an indigenous subsistence economy geared toward Indian consumption, and a Spanish import-export economy supporting a more elevated Spanish standard of living.

---

[14] The intense red cochineal dye was made from tiny insects that lived on the nopal, or prickly pear, cactus. The dye was processed in Mexico and exported to European markets.

Social Stratification   Spaniards of both humble and aristocratic origins migrated to New Spain. Many of the conquistadores had been penniless adventurers, although some were from the Spanish noble class. Whatever their backgrounds, these men formed the upper echelon of New Spain society. For the most part, they were not settlers or colonists like those of Plymouth Plantation or Jamestown. They were neither equipped nor prepared to farm, but wished to live in the style of a new aristocracy, even though many were, by elite standards of the day, illiterate, unrefined, and coarse in their everyday speech and behavior.

On the heels of the conquerors came a more learned segment of Spanish society: educated clergymen, genteel professionals, and high-ranking administrators of honorable descent and impressive political connections. Some of these arrivals developed strong attachments to the land and people of New Spain, such as the Franciscan friar Toribio de Benavente. Fray Toribio lived and worked in New Spain and Guatemala from 1524 until his death in 1569, and was known as Motolinía, "the Poor One," because of his characteristic appearance in bare feet and tattered habit. He wrote of many Spaniards who wished only to return to the familiar comfort of Spain, but he was not one of these (Motolinía 1950:16). Less celebrated immigrants also adopted New Spain as their permanent home. In 1558, one struggling farmer in Puebla, Antonio Mateos, wrote his wife in Spain that he was anxious for her to join him:

> With the desire to prepare for your arrival, I went to the valley of Atlixco, where they grow two crops of wheat a year, one irrigated and the other watered by rainfall; I thought that we could be there the rest of our lives (Lockhart and Otte 1976:141).

Many other Spaniards would have much preferred living in Spain; but their wealth and social status were so remarkably improved by their activities in New Spain that they opted to stay.

Over the course of the colonial period, people who were born in Spain and immigrated to New Spain were called Peninsulares. The highest governmental and religious offices were reserved for these persons, a procedure often prompting jealousy and frustration in those of "pure" Spanish blood born in New Spain. The latter, called Criollos, were held by the Peninsulares to be "innately lazy, effete, irresponsible, and lacking in both vigor and intelligence" because of the perceived detrimental effects of the New World climate (Meyer and Sherman 1979:207). For their part, the Criollos considered the Peninsulares to be "arrogant, hypocritical, and rapacious" (*ibid.*). The Criollos usually held secondary, although lofty, positions in the political and social life of New Spain. They entered the administrative and religious organizations, but were usually denied the highest offices. Many Criollos gained substantial wealth in commercial, ranching, agricultural, and mining ventures. In the remoter areas of New Spain, which the Peninsulares disdained, Criollos served as the local aristocracy (*ibid.*:208).

Compared with Spanish men, relatively few Spanish women immigrated to New Spain. A great many male immigrants, therefore, acquired Indian wives and/or mistresses. The process of *mestizaje*, or the creation of a mestizo population, began even before the Spanish conquest was complete. Noble Indian women were occasionally given as gifts by local rulers to Cortés and his captains; the offspring of these unions created the first generation of mestizos. Most early mestizos were considered illegitimate under Spanish law. But as New Spain became established under colonial rule, more and more Peninsulares and Criollos were encouraged to find available Indian wives: The crown wished greater stability, the church sought a higher morality. Many later mestizos, therefore, were considered legal heirs. Their status in colonial society was extremely variable and often ambiguous. Most, ignored by their Spanish fathers, were raised by their Indian mothers; these mestizos were often culturally indistinguishable from Indians (Gibson 1964:144–147). A few others, from wealthy backgrounds, penetrated Spanish society and more closely mirrored Spanish culture. An extreme case was that of Don Martín Cortés, son of Hernán Cortés and Doña Marina; he went to Spain at an early age, became a knight, and served in the Spanish army. By all appearances, he was a Spaniard with full Spanish rights (Meyer and Sherman 1979:210).

Large numbers of African slaves were brought to the Caribbean Islands, and lesser numbers to the mainland of New Spain. While some resided in the Mexican highlands as personal slaves of the aristocracy and as laborers in mines, the majority toiled on the sugarcane plantations of the tropical lowlands and Caribbean Islands. A mulatto population emerged very early, following patterns similar to the creation of the mestizo. Unions usually involved Spanish men and black women, and the social status of the offspring depended largely on personal circumstances. A mulatto might be awarded a free status or relegated to slavery. If free, mulattoes might engage in commercial ventures (as did some mulatto women in Texcoco) or earn small wages by hiring out as skilled laborers (Leslie Lewis 1976:131; Lockhart 1976:112). The ambiguous status of mestizos and mulattoes in New Spain is highlighted by some documents which describe both as indigent and troublemakers (Gibson 1964:147), and mestizos specifically as "the lame, the destitute, the abandoned" (Lockhart 1976:112).

Indian society, highly stratified in pre-conquest times, became increasingly homogeneous under the force of Spanish rule. Initially, some local rulers were allowed to maintain certain titles, retain some traditional perquisites, and were even given new positions such as "governor." While individual Spaniards sometimes obstructed tlatoani rule by tampering with rules of succession and inheritance, the crown did grant special rights to Indian rulers and nobles. They were allowed to "carry swords or firearms, to wear Spanish clothing, to ride horses or mules with saddles and bridles, or in other ways to demonstrate their status within Indian society" (Gibson 1964:155). Many tlatoque and tetecutin were able to control considerable amounts of wealth, often through ventures combining Indian and Spanish modes of production (e.g., traditional maize cultivation on some fields, grazing sheep on others). It is small wonder that these caciques, as the Spaniards called the ruling nobility, became rapidly acculturated to the Spanish way of life: They had both legal and economic access to the trappings of Spanish culture. Proximity to the centers of Spanish activity, of course, was also a crucial variable in the rate of acculturation. Adoption of Spanish culture was relatively rapid where Catholic friars earnestly educated young Indians in Spanish and Latin, where Spanish goods were a part of the everyday scene, and where Spanish values were everywhere in evidence. Many Indians attached to urban Spanish households as servants became quickly acculturated. And the presence of Spaniards more powerful than the native caciques opened new avenues of social mobility for the humble *macehualli*. Enterprising Indian commoners often exploited the new order by gaining wealth in trade or other ventures, acquiring land, and simply assuming nobility status. Others, favored by Spanish clergymen or encomenderos, garnered favors and privileges theoretically reserved for the indigenous nobility (*ibid.*:156). Over time, the native nobility status became depressed and imaginative commoners could acquire both wealth and prestige, posing a very real threat to the hereditary Indian nobility. Spanish policy often aided this equalization process. For example, in 1565 the cacique of Tlacopan requested Indians as agricultural laborers. In pre-Spanish times, these Indians would have probably been *mayeques*, owing him their labor by way of customary tribute. But the Spanish colonial government ruled that these commoners, if they worked the cacique's fields, were to be given daily food and wages (*ibid.*:157). Such rulings quickly undermined the economic bases for cacique authority, seriously weakening these nobles' political role and social standing in the Indian communities. All in all, colonial rule tended to deemphasize heredity (ascription) as a criterion for Indian prestige and authority, and instead stressed initiative and personal capabilities (achievement). This is a common pattern in "conquest societies."

Highly disruptive of the native stratification system, Spanish rule also forced other changes in Indian social life. Many of the trappings and rules associated with indigenous social class were dissolved: Heredity as a basis for rule was weakened, warfare ceased to serve as an avenue for social mobility, and ornate costume no longer symbolized rank. The monogamous Spanish code forbade the practice of polygyny, long a perquisite of the Indian elite. Institutions associated with the Aztec state collapsed almost immediately upon conquest. In particular, formal education was transferred from the *calmecac, cuicacalli*, and *telpochcalli* (see Chapter 4) to the friars in religious schools. The *calpulli*, however, remained essentially intact. It was similar to the Spanish *barrio*, and the Spaniards continued to treat the calpulli as a tribute-paying and labor-drafting unit, although it ceased to act as a military unit, and the calpulli patron deity was replaced by a Catholic patron saint. On a more personal level, Indian marriages continued to be established without the blessing of a Christian ceremony, many couples preferring the less expensive family rituals, or no formality at all. But the Spanish custom of *compadrazgo*, or godparenthood, was readily borrowed by the Indians; it provided surrogate parents for children at a time when plagues and famine threatened the family structure.

Political Life   The fall of Tenochtitlan marked the dissolution of the Aztec state and empire. The highest levels of political administration were now occupied by Spanish officials, the king's representatives in New Spain. This included a viceroy; members of the royal audiencia, or high court; treasury officials; and a variety of lesser bureaucrats. With only weak communications between Spain and New Spain, the viceroy often made decisions without royal direction or approval, and occasionally did not execute orders when they did reach him. He was, indeed, a powerful colonial figure.

Early in the colonial period the Spanish administration typically awarded *cabecera* status to any community with a well-entrenched tlatoani rule. As a tlatoani's capital, a cabecera was the "head town" of a region, usually with a number of *sujetos* ("subjects"), or tribute-paying dependent settlements, under its jurisdiction. The cabecera-sujeto relationship served as the basic political structure in New Spain. It defined dominant-subordinate relations and fixed tribute obligations. Since the cabecera commanded the tribute of its sujetos, communities ardently sought this prestigious and lucrative designation, irrespective of their pre-Hispanic status. With the Aztec imperial bonds severed, many communities asserted themselves as prominent political centers, hoping either to maintain traditional rights or to gain unprecedented favors under the new colonial order. Unstable political links among communities had been characteristic of the pre-Hispanic period, as empires rose and fell and conquerors became the conquered. Under Spanish rule, the fortunes of specific communities continued to change.

The Triple Alliance capitals were defined as cabeceras, but lost enormous subject areas. In fact, these cities were reduced in importance, since they no longer served as powerful imperial centers. The tribute-paying dependencies of Tenochtitlan were restricted to a few communities in its immediate area; Texcoco and Tlacopan fared only slightly better. Tlacopan, in fact, was given in encomienda to one of Moctezuma's daughters. Some communities, formerly subjects of the Triple Alliance, came to enjoy cabecera status. Under Aztec rule they retained their tlatoque; under Spanish rule they were relieved of their obligations to the former imperial capitals, and exacted tribute from their own sujetos. And other traditional tribute-paying settlements petitioned for cabecera status, even though they lacked a full-fledged tlatoani tradition. The Spanish arrival provided these communities with the opportunity to throw off the yoke of former subjugation, and Indian community vied with Indian community for prominence and wealth. The Spanish courts overflowed with jurisdictional disputes as each community sought to preserve or elevate its position under Spanish rule. In the course of such litigation, the presence of a resident tlatoani as the main criterion for cabecera status began to falter, and new criteria emerged: size, location, antiquity, and the presence of markets or churches (Gibson 1964:54).

The status of the tlatoani was progressively weakened throughout the sixteenth century in yet another way. Initially, many of the traditional positions and perquisites of the native rulers were recognized by the Spanish administration. In the mid-sixteenth century the rights of Don Juan de Guzmán, hereditary ruler of Coyoacan, included an impressive assemblage of lands, laborers, household services, and market tax revenues (see Chapter 2). Some especially high-ranking native persons such as the legitimate heirs of Moctezuma were awarded handsome encomiendas. This compensated in some measure for the loss of vast portions of their traditional holdings and, of course, transformed these nobles into encomenderos. However, the tlatoque in general were losing their laborers and large tracts of their lands. Thus, they also began to lose their political footing. This process was prompted by the institution of an elected governor and cabildo, or municipal council, as a Spanish-style body politic. A typical cabildo had two *alcaldes* and three or four *regidores*.

Under Spanish dominion, the political affairs of each cabecera were directed by a governor and council. Often the governor was also the local tlatoani, who could carry the dual title of "cacique and gobernador" (*ibid.*:167). But it became increasingly common for the governor to be a different person from the tlatoani, thus undermining the tlatoani's rule. This procedure was favored and encouraged by the Spanish administration, which on the whole could not tolerate powerful native rulers (cf. Whitecotton 1977:188).

The governor and municipal council deliberated on a variety of community affairs such as tribute collection, labor drafts, public projects, management of municipal property, law and order, drunkenness, Spanish-Indian relations, and the furtherance of the Christian faith (*ibid.*:179; Anderson, Berdan, and Lockhart, n.d.). From the mid-sixteenth century on, these New Spain political bodies began to look more and more like their Spanish counterparts. The position of tlatoani was separated from the office of governor; the Spanish administration recognized the governor/cabildo as the significant town-governing body; and the community officials were rewarded through salaries, which often included Spanish money as well as household goods and services. All of these officials were elected, the councilmen annually, and the governors annually or every other year. Although these municipal offices were to be held only by Indians, by the seventeenth century several important cabeceras had mestizo or mulatto governors and councilmen. Considerable direct Spanish influence was also exerted on the Indian cabildos. The cabecera-level Spanish bureaucrat, the *corregidor,* attended council meetings, issued directives, and swayed opinions. The elections of all governors and councilmen were subject to approval or disapproval by the viceroy. And some Spaniards—whether representing private, secular, or religious interests—interfered directly with municipal elections and affairs (Gibson 1964:179). A rather extreme example was the priest of the community of Jalostotitlan. In 1611 an alcalde of this town complained to higher church authorities that the local priest had severely abused him, broken his staff of office, and blatantly maltreated other residents and officials of the community—all for no apparent reason (Anderson, Berdan, and Lockhart 1976:166–173).

The institution of the cabildo required some significant native adjustments. The idea of councils and elections was certainly not novel to the Indians, but they had always been coupled with the hereditary rule of a tlatoani. In pre-Hispanic times, elections were not held annually, but only upon the demise of a ruler; and councils were advisory bodies, not separate decision-making entities. In New Spain the emphasis in Indian political life shifted from traditional hereditary rule at imperial and city-state levels to the governance of individual communities by elected officials responsible to the colonial government.

Religion   Even before the military conquest of the Aztecs, Hernán Cortés had fiercely struck the idol of Huitzilopochtli in Tenochtitlan. Three years later the first 3 Franciscan friars set foot in New Spain, followed by a company of 12 Franciscans in 1524. Thus began the spiritual conquest of the Aztecs.

Christianity was a proselytizing religion, and Spain had been named by the Pope as the official arm of the Roman Catholic Church. But the brand of Christianity spread to New Spain was not that typically found in Spain. The Spanish religious elite sought to teach a more "pure" Christianity in the New World, discarding folk customs commonly associated with Spanish religious practices: "In Spain 'devils' dance in churches in some fiestas, devotees walk barefoot over live coals, maidens stick pins into images of the Virgin, a representation of a saint may be hung upside down in a well or stones may be thrown at his bare navel—all in the name of religion" (Foster 1960:165). Although some of these customs did find their way into parts of New Spain, they were not part of the official religion taught by the friars and secular clergy. The insistence on a "pure" Christianity was also manifested in the Inquisition. Although very active in Spain, the Inquisition was not introduced officially into New Spain until 1571, and relatively few persons were sentenced to the stake. These were mostly Spanish colonists, not Indians. Although indigenous religious practices continued for some time, and appeared deplorable and paganistic to the Spaniards, Indians were considered "unenlightened," and were rarely brought before the Inquisition.

First the Franciscan friars, and later the Dominicans and Augustinians, shouldered the responsibility of converting the native peoples to Christianity. Living pious lives and forsaking many everyday comforts, the friars were admired by the Indians who shared these ideals of hardship. The friars established primary schools, replacing the native formal educational system with missionary schools which emphasized religious and moral instruction. Distinctions between noble and commoner boys were generally maintained, with commoners receiving instruction only in the mornings, and nobles boarding at the monasteries. In addition to religion, the curriculum included reading, writing, ciphering, singing, and the playing of musical instruments (Ricard 1966:209–210).

In 1536 the first native college was established, the Colegio de Santa Cruz in Tlatelolco. Religion and Latin were emphasized, since the fundamental goal of the college was to train native priests. But although a highly literate, educated elite did emerge from its halls, no natives were allowed to be ordained as priests. Young girls attended schools run by nuns, where they were taught religious beliefs and practices, manners, and household skills and tasks. Girls left the schools at age twelve, when they typically married students trained in the missionary schools (*ibid.*:210–211). This formal education, for boys and girls, focused on the young. Some adults did receive training of a different sort from the friars. They were instructed in a variety of crafts and trades: painting, sculpting, carpentry, tailoring, and pottery. With these skills they produced Spanish-style objects for religious and secular purposes. The training of the young, like that of native adults, was modeled on Spanish customs and styles, and served as a direct means of acculturation to the Spanish way of life. The fact that only the young received intense religious instruction often created serious strains along generation lines within the Indian community: Children spied on their parents, parents were alienated from their children (Madsen 1967:374–375). The friars insisted that idolatry cease, and the zealous schoolchildren often served the friars by smashing idols and reporting continuing Aztec religious practices.

The friars quickly learned Nahuatl, the Aztec language, and most instruction was conducted in this language. However, the indigenous hieroglyphic writing system was considered inadequate by the friars, who introduced the Latin alphabet and script writing to their young scholars. Training in the native hieroglyphics had certainly ceased. The vast Aztec libraries had been destroyed in the violence of the conquest; and many volumes had been burned by zealous Spanish religious officials, who considered them "books of the devil." So Nahuatl was rendered in a new medium of writing, alphabetic. Not only did the written form change, but the language itself underwent important modifications. Most noticeably, Spanish words penetrated Nahuatl in profusion. Rarely, however, did a word enter the vocabulary unscathed: Nahuatl lacked sounds for "b" and "d", so a word such as *cabildo* ("council") sometimes became *capilto*; Spanish plurals were not always perceived, so *alcaldes* ("judges") often became *alcaldesme* with the Nahuatl plural *-me* tagged on to the Spanish plural *-s* (Anderson, Berdan, and Lockhart 1976: 30–31).

These linguistic changes took place not only in the schools but also in a variety of everyday contexts. The colonial experience often brought Aztec and Spanish languages and cultures into intimate contact; the process of acculturation that ensued typically involved some compromise. Nowhere was this more visible than in the religious belief systems.

The spiritual conquest of the Aztecs came immediately in the wake of the military conquest. Public worship of Aztec deities was forcibly suppressed, and the central Aztec themes of warfare and human sacrifice were destroyed. Huitzilopochtli and Tezcatlipoca, having promised victory to the Mexica, had failed and were discredited.[15] Human sacrifice, always believed necessary for the continuation of the universe, was abolished—yet the sun still rose and set. The Aztecs were faced with a sudden rupture in their belief system.

The alternative they faced was Christianity. Although the efforts of the missionaries were tireless, actual conversion of the Indians to Christianity was slow. Religions are tenacious, and the Aztecs were reluctant to reject many features of their religion.[16] Many of the people were bitter over the military conquest and were unwilling to adopt any trappings of the new imposed order; and a number of irreconcilable differences existed between the two religions.

Christianity was a monotheistic, proselytizing religion; Aztec religion was polytheistic and tended to absorb, rather than reject, foreign deities. Although the missionaries insisted on worship of the Christian god alone, a typical Aztec response was to simply absorb this god as one of many in their pantheon. There was also a native tendency to link Aztec deities with individual Catholic saints. The results of this syncretism can be seen in some Mexican villages today. In Tepoztlan, El Tepozteco is both god of the wind and son of the Virgin Mary (Oscar Lewis 1951:256), and in Tecospa,

> Catholic saints have lost their saintly character and become human-natured divinities who lie, lose their tempers, wreak revenge, and indulge in love affairs as the Aztec gods used to do. . . . With the consent of God and the help of Aztec rain dwarfs, San Francisco miraculously produces rain in Tecospa even when the saints of other villages have failed in this task (Madsen 1967:381).

---

[15] Another version states that these gods, through a priest, had threatened to abandon the Aztecs if they failed to dispel the foreigners (Madsen 1967:370–371).

[16] There was no disenchantment with, especially, the many fertility deities, and their cults continued in secret.

These notions were incompatible with European Christian beliefs, and by the mid-sixteenth century the clergy began prohibiting all aspects of the native religion. The task was enormous and not often successful, for the religions differed significantly. The Aztec gods required human assistance through sacrifice; the Christian god was omnipotent and required no such assistance. The Aztec gods were represented by idols; the Christian god was an abstraction. The Aztec values emphasized collective responsibilities in maintaining order in the universe; Christian values promoted the ideal of individual perfection. The course of individual Aztec lives depended on fate, those of individual Christians on free will. The type of afterlife awaiting an Aztec was determined by the circumstances of his or her death; the afterlife awaiting a Christian was a result of his or her conduct in life. And the afterlives available to the Aztecs did not include eternal torture, although the journey to Mictlan was never easy.

Alongside these contradictions were a number of remarkable similarities between the two religions. Both shared rites of baptism and confession, although in Aztec belief a person could confess only once. As a result, the colonial Indians tended to confess to a Catholic priest only when death seemed imminent. Nonetheless, the willingness of the Indians to submit to these Christian rites gave the outward appearance of acceptance of the newly introduced religion. The missionaries soon learned that this was simply not the case. A further point of similarity centered on the notion of virgin birth: Huitzilopochtli had been miraculously conceived by the Aztec mother goddess, much as Jesus Christ had been conceived by the Virgin Mary. With the meshing of these female religious figures, the two religions actually fused. In 1531 an Indian, Juan Diego, reported seeing a dark-skinned Virgin on a hill that was traditionally the abode of the Aztec goddess Tonantzin. Although the Virgin was Indian in appearance, she requested that a church be erected on that very spot; and she displayed love and mercy, attributes not associated with the Aztec goddess. The fusion of these two figures into the Virgin of Guadalupe set the tone for the style of Catholicism which would typify central Mexico in the centuries to follow.

But the path to a religious and cultural compromise was not accepted by the Indians willingly or passively. In 1524, some Aztec sages were confronted by 12 Christian friars, who challenged the precepts of the Indian religion. The reply of Aztec wise men expresses their submission to the new lords of the land and the tragic fate of their own gods, but also discloses their firm determination to hold on to their age-old beliefs and traditions, even in the face of possible reprisals:

> Perhaps we are to be taken to our ruin, to our destruction. But where are we to go now? We are ordinary people, we are subject to death and destruction, we are mortals; allow us then to die, let us perish now, since our gods are already dead. . . . You said that we know not the Lord of the Close Vicinity, to Whom the heavens and the earth belong. You said that our gods are not true gods. New words are these that you speak; because of them we are disturbed, because of them we are troubled. For our ancestors before us, who lived upon the earth, were unaccustomed to speak thus. From them we have inherited our pattern of life which in truth did they hold; in reverence they held, they honored, our gods. They taught us all their rules of worship, all their ways of honoring the gods. Thus before them, do we prostrate ourselves; in their names we bleed ourselves; our oaths we keep, incense we burn, and sacrifices we offer. It was the doctrine of

the elders that there is life because of the gods; with their sacrifice, they gave us life. . . . And now, are we to destroy the ancient order of life? . . . We know on Whom life is dependent; on Whom the perpetuation of the race depends; by Whom begetting is determined; by Whom growth is made possible; how it is that one must invoke, how it is that one must pray. Hear, oh Lords, do nothing to our people that will bring misfortune upon them, that will cause them to perish. . . . We cannot be tranquil, and yet we certainly do not believe; we do not accept your teachings as truth, even though this may offend you . . . (León-Portilla 1963:63–66).

The culture these sages fought so determinedly to perpetuate had truly ancient roots in Mesoamerica, much of it predating the ascendance of the Mexica. The Mexica had arrived in the Valley of Mexico in the thirteenth century and had quickly become subordinated to an existing powerful city-state. After a century of subjugation they had overthrown their overlords. During the next 90 years they and their allies reigned as the supreme lords of the land. But like so many other empires, they succumbed to yet more powerful forces and became a subordinated population again. Over the course of the following 450 years, Aztec culture blended with Spanish culture to produce the unique way of life that characterized much of Mexico into the twentieth century. In the remotest areas of central Mexico, some elements of the ancient Aztec culture still persist, relatively unchanged, to the present day.

Glossary

Acculturation: In the context of culture contact, the process whereby a subordinate culture is transformed to conform to the dominant culture.

Achieved status: Position attained through personal effort and accomplishment.

Acolhuaca: Ethnic group in eastern part of the Valley of Mexico; Acolhuacan capital of Texcoco was a strong partner of the Triple Alliance.

Affines: Relatives defined through marriage.

Amanteca: Professional featherworkers.

Anthropomorphic: Having human characteristics; especially pertaining to deities.

Ascribed status: Position assigned through birthright.

Aztec: General term for the dominant late post-classic peoples of central Mexico. The Mexica are also popularly known as Aztecs.

Barrio: Spanish term for a territorial division of a town or city.

Barter: Exchanges involving goods for goods.

Bilateral descent: Kinship traced through both male and female lines.

Cabecera: Head town of a region or province in the colonial period.

Cabildo: Colonial period town council.

Cacique: Local Indian ruler during the Spanish colonial period.

Calendar round: Fifty-two year cycle reached by combining the 365-day solar calendar with the 260-day ritual calendar.

Calmecac: School administered by priests and attended by noble boys.

Calpixqui (pl. *calpixque*):   Aztec tribute collector.

Calpulli: Territorial and land-holding unit of a town or city; a district or ward.

Chichimecs: Nomadic hunting and gathering tribes of the northern desert regions of Mexico.

Chinampas: Agricultural plots built in shallow lakebeds by alternating layers of vegetation and mud.

Cihuacoatl: An important office in the Tenochtitlan political structure, second only to the ruling tlatoani (literally "Woman serpent"). Also the name of an "earth mother" deity.

Consanguines: Relatives defined through descent, or "blood."

Criollos: Spaniards born in the New World.

Cuicacalli: School devoted to the teaching of song, dance, and the playing of musical instruments.

Encomienda: Grant of Indian labor to a privileged Spanish colonist.

Enculturation: The process of learning one's culture.

Endogamy: A rule requiring a person to marry within a particular social group of which he or she is a member.

Exogamy: A rule requiring a person to marry outside a particular social group of which he or she is a member.

Guild: Closed organization of professional craftsmen or merchants.

Huehuetlatolli: Speeches of the elders embodying moral teachings.

Huitzilopochtli: Patron god of the Mexica; a war god associated with the sun.

Joint family: Family composed of two or more married couples, often united through siblings.

Macehualli (pl. *macehualtin*):   "Free commoner."

Mayeque (sing. and pl.):   Rural tenant. Also called *Tlalmaitl*.

Mesoamerica: Culture area encompassing the area of high civilizations in pre-Hispanic Mexico and Guatemala.

Mestizo: A person of mixed Spanish-Indian heritage.

Mexica: The Chichimec group that founded Tenochtitlan and later became the dominant partner of the Triple Alliance. Also popularly known as Aztecs.

Nahuatl: Predominant language of central Mexico in late pre-Hispanic times.

Nuclear family: Family composed of parents and their children.

Patolli: A game resembling pachisi.

Peninsulares: Spaniards born in Spain.

Pilli (pl. *pipiltin*):   Member of the nobility class; literally "son of nobility."

Pochtecatl (pl. *pochteca*):   Professional merchant.

Polygyny: Marriage of one man to two or more women at the same time.

Polytheism: A religious belief system involving the worship of many deities.

Port of trade: Politically neutral trading center.

Quachtli: Large plain cotton cloaks, perhaps used as a form of money.

Quetzalcoatl: A beneficent creator god and patron of the arts.

Shaman: Part-time religious specialist deriving magical power from a supernatural source.

Sujeto: A subject community, in Spanish colonial times.

Teccalli: Household of a *tecutli*, or high-ranking noble.

Tecutli (pl. *tetecutin*):   High-ranking noble, or "chief."

Telpochcalli: *Calpulli* school for commoner boys.

Tepaneca: Ethnic group in western part of the Valley of Mexico; Tepanec capital of Tlacopan was the smallest partner of the Triple Alliance.

Tequiua: Seasoned warrior; title attained through the capture of four enemy warriors.

Tezcatlipoca: A capricious, omnipotent deity; patron of young warriors.

Tianquiztli: Marketplace.

Tlachtli: Ball game.

Tlacolol: Fallowing system of agriculture.

Tlacotli (pl. *tlacotin*):   Slave.

Tlaloc: God of rain.

Tlamatinime: "Wise men," or sages.

Tlatoani (pl. *tlatoque*):   Ruler of a region or community.

Tolteccatl (pl. *toltecca*):   Luxury artisan. Also person of Tula.

Tonalamatl: Astrological, divinatory guide for the ritual calendar.

Tonalpohualli: Ritual 260-day calendar (literally "Count of days").

Tonatiuh: The sun deity.

Tribute: Revenue collected by a militarily dominant state from its conquered regions.

Triple Alliance: The military alliance of Tenochtitlan, Texcoco, and Tlacopan.

Tula: Ancient capital of the Toltecs; idealized by the Aztecs as a center of fine craftsmanship.

Tzompantli: Skull rack.

Xiuitl: The 365-day solar year.

Yaoxochitl: "War of flowers"; ritualized warfare to obtain sacrificial victims and train warriors.

References and Additional Readings

AGI (Archivo General de Indias, Seville), Patronato 20, no. 5, ramo 22
Del orden que tenian los indios en el tiempo de Moctezuma en la sucesion del Valdios y Jurisdiccion de las tierras (originally written: ca. 1537).

AGN (Archivo General de la Nación, Mexico), Tierras 1735, exp. 2
Juan Hidalgo Cortes Moctezuma y Guzman, principal de esa villa, contra Maria, Petronila y Teresa Guzman, por posesion del cacicazgo que disfruto Juan de Guzman Ixtolinque (originally written: ca. 1560).

AGN (Archivo General de la Nación, Mexico), Tierras 2692, exp. 16
1578. Tecomastlahuaca. Diligencias de información sobre el patrimonio que pide Don Francisco de Arellano, cacique del pueblo de Tecomastlahuaca.

Alva Ixtlilxochitl, Fernando de
1965. *Obras Históricas*, 2 vols. Mexico: Editora Nacional (originally written in early seventeenth century).

Anawalt, Patricia
1980. Costume and control: Aztec sumptuary laws. *Archaeology*, vol. 33, no. 1, pp. 33–43.

Anderson, Arthur J. O., Frances Berdan, and James Lockhart
1976. *Beyond the Codices: The Nahua View of Colonial Mexico*. Berkeley: University of California Press.

Anderson, Arthur J. O., Frances Berdan, and James Lockhart
n.d. *The Actas of Tlaxcala: Guide, Calendar and Selection of Minutes of the Cabildo of Tlaxcala, 1547–1627*. Ms. in preparation.

Anderson, Arthur J. O., and Charles Dibble (transl. and eds.)
1978. *The War of Conquest: How It Was Waged Here in Mexico*. Salt Lake City: University of Utah Press.

Anonymous Conqueror
1971. Relación de algunas cosas de la Nueva Espana y de la Gran Ciudad de Temestitan Mexico; escrita por un compañero de Hernán Cortés. In *Colección de Documentos para la Historia de Mexico*, J. C. Icazbalceta, ed., vol. 1, pp. 368–398. Mexico: Editorial Porrua (originally written: sixteenth century).

Aveni, Anthony F.
1980. *Skywatchers of Ancient Mexico*. Austin: University of Texas Press.

Berdan, Frances F.
1974. Mesoamerican Money: Problems of Equivalency. Paper presented at the XLI International Congress of Americanists, Mexico City.

Berdan, Frances F.
1975. Trade, Tribute and Market in the Aztec Empire. Doctoral dissertation, University of Texas at Austin.

Berdan, Frances F.
1980. The Matrícula de Tributos—Provincial tribute. In *Matrícula de Tributos (Códice de Moctezuma)*, Frances F. Berdan and Jacqueline de Durand-Forest, commentators. Codices Selecti vol. LXVIII. Graz, Austria: Akademische Druck u. Verlagsanstalt, pp. 27–45.

Bray, Warwick
1968. *Everyday Life of the Aztecs*. New York: Putnam.
Bray, Warwick
1972. The city state in Central Mexico at the time of the Spanish conquest. *Journal of Latin American Studies*, vol. 4, no. 2, pp. 161–185.
Broda, Johanna
1978. Relaciones políticas ritualizadas: El ritual como expresión de una ideología. In *Economía Política e Ideología en el México Prehispánico*, Pedro Carrasco and Johanna Broda, eds., pp. 221–255. Mexico: Editorial Nueva Imagen.
Calnek, Edward
1972. Settlement pattern and chinampa agriculture at Tenochtitlan. *American Antiquity*, vol. 37, no. 1, pp. 104–115.
Calnek, Edward
1974. The Sahagún texts as a source of sociological information. In *Sixteenth Century Mexico: The work of Sahagún*, Munro S. Edmonson, ed., pp. 189–204. Albuquerque: University of New Mexico Press.
Calnek, Edward
1976. The internal structure of Tenochtitlan. In *The Valley of Mexico*, Eric R. Wolf, ed., pp. 287–302. Albuquerque: University of New Mexico Press.
Carrasco, Pedro
1964. Family structure of sixteenth-century Tepoztlan. In *Process and Pattern in Culture*, Robert Manners, ed., pp. 185–210. Chicago: Aldine.
Carrasco, Pedro
1971. Social organization of ancient Mexico. In *Handbook of Middle American Indians*, vol. 10, pp. 349–375. Austin: University of Texas Press.
Carrasco, Pedro
1974. Sucesión y alianzas matrimoniales en la dinastía Teotihuacana. *Estudios de Cultura Nahuatl*, vol. 11, pp. 235–241.
Carrasco, Pedro
1976. Estratificación social indígena en Morelos durante el siglo XVI. In *Estratificación Social en la Mesoamérica Prehispánica*, Pedro Carrasco and Johanna Broda, eds., pp. 102–117. Mexico: Centro de Investigaciones Superiores del Instituto Nacional de Antropología e Historia.
Caso, Alfonso
1958. *The Aztecs: People of the Sun*. Norman: The University of Oklahoma Press.
Caso, Alfonso
1971. Calendrical systems of central Mexico. In *Handbook of Middle American Indians*, vol. 10, pp. 333–348. Austin: University of Texas Press.
Chevalier, Francois
1963. *Land and Society in Colonial Mexico: The Great Hacienda*. Berkeley: University of California Press.
Codex Borbonicus
1974. Codex Borbonicus. In *Codices Selecti*, vol. 44. Graz: Akademische Druck u. Verlagsanstalt (originally composed: early sixteenth century).
Codex Borgia
1963. Codex Borgia. In *Comentarios al Códice Borgia*. Eduard Seler, ed., 2 vols. and facsimile reproduction of the codex. Mexico: Fondo de Cultura Económica (originally composed: pre-Hispanic).

Codex Boturini
   1964. Codex Boturini o Tira de la Peregrinación. In *Antigüedades de Mexico*, vol. 2, pp. 7–29. Mexico: Secretaría de Hacienda y Crédito Público (originally composed: sixteenth century).
Codex Magliabecchiano
   1970. *Codex Magliabecchiano*, commentary by Ferdinand Anders. Graz: Akademische Druck u. Verlagsanstalt (originally composed: mid-sixteenth century).
Codex Mendoza
   1938. *Codex Mendoza*, James Cooper Clark, ed., 3 vols. London: Waterlow & Sons (originally composed: 1540s).
Codex Telleriano-Remensis
   1964. Codex Telleriano-Remensis. In *Antigüedades de Mexico*, vol. 1, pp. 151–337. Mexico: Secretaría de Hacienda y Crédito Público (originally composed: ca. 1562–1563).
Códice Xolotl
   1951. *Códice Xolotl*, Charles E. Dibble, ed. and commentator. Mexico: Publicaciones del Instituto de Historia, 1st series, no. 22 (originally composed: sixteenth century).
Coe, Michael D.
   1964. The chinampas of Mexico. *Scientific American*, vol. 211, no. 1, pp. 90–98.
Cook, Sherburne F., and Woodrow Borah
   1963. The aboriginal population of Central Mexico on the eve of the Spanish conquest. *Ibero-Americana*, vol. 45. Berkeley: University of California Press.
Cortés, Hernán
   1928. *Five Letters of Cortés to the Emperor*, J. Bayard Morris, transl. New York: W. W. Norton (originally written: 1519–1526).
Craine, Eugene R., and Reginald C. Reindorp (transl. and eds.)
   1970. *The Chronicles of Michoacan*. Norman: The University of Oklahoma Press (originally written: 1539–1541).
Davies, Nigel
   1973. *The Aztecs: A History*. New York: Putnam.
de Fuentes, Patricia (ed. and transl.)
   1963. *The Conquistadors*. New York: Orion.
Díaz del Castillo, Bernal
   1956. *The Discovery and Conquest of Mexico*, A. P. Maudslay, transl. New York: Noonday (originally written: 1560s).
Díaz del Castillo, Bernal
   1963. *The Conquest of New Spain*. Baltimore: Penguin (originally written: 1560s).
Durán, Diego
   1964. *The Aztecs: The History of the Indies of New Spain*, Doris Heyden and Fernando Horcasitas, transl. New York: Orion (originally written: 1581).
Durán, Diego
   1967. *Historia de las Indias de Nueva España e Islas de la Tierra Firme*, 2 vols. Mexico: Editorial Porrua (originally written: 1581).
Durán, Diego
   1971. *Book of the Gods and Rites* and *The Ancient Calendar*. Fernando Horcasitas and Doris Heyden, transl. Norman: University of Oklahoma Press (originally written: 1570 and 1579).

Elliott, J. H.
  1964. *Imperial Spain: 1469–1716.* New York: St. Martin's Press.
Foster, George M.
  1960. *Culture and Conquest: America's Spanish heritage.* Chicago: Quadrangle.
Gerhard, Peter
  1972. *A Guide to the Historical Geography of New Spain.* New York: Cambridge University Press.
Gibson, Charles
  1964. *The Aztecs under Spanish Rule.* Stanford, Calif.: Stanford University Press.
Gibson, Charles
  1971. Structure of the Aztec empire. In *Handbook of Middle American Indians,* vol. 10, pp. 376–394. Austin: University of Texas Press.
Graulich, Michel
  1981. The metaphor of the day in ancient Mexican myth and ritual (with comments and reply). *Current Anthropology,* vol. 22, no. 1, pp. 45–60.
Harner, Michael
  1977. The ecological basis for Aztec sacrifice. *American Ethnologist,* vol. 4, no. 1, pp. 117–135.
Harvey, Herbert R.
  1979. Aspects of Land Tenure in Ancient Mexico. Paper presented at the XLIII International Congress of Americanists, Vancouver.
Hicks, Frederic
  1976. Mayeque y calpuleque en el sistema de clases del México antiguo. In *Estratificación Social en la Mesoamérica Prehispánica,* Pedro Carrasco and Johanna Broda, eds., pp. 67–77. Mexico: Centro de Investigaciones Superiores del Instituto Nacional de Antropología e Historia.
Historia de los Mexicanos por sus Pinturas
  1941. Historia de los Mexicanos por sus pinturas. In *Nueva Colección de Documentos para la Historia de Mexico,* 2nd ed., J. García Icazbalceta, ed., vol. 3, pp. 207–240. Mexico: Editorial Salvador Chávez Hayhoe (originally written: ca. 1535).
Historia General de las Cosas de Nueva España por Fr. Bernardino de Sahagún
  1926. *Edición completa en facsimile colorido del Códice Florentino,* vol. 5. Mexico: Talleres Gráficos del Museo Nacional de Arqueología, Historia y Etnografía (originally written by 1569).
Hunt, Eva
  1972. Irrigation and the socio-political organization of Cuicatec cacicazgos. In *The Prehistory of the Tehuacan Valley,* vol. 4, pp. 162–259. Austin: University of Texas Press.
Katz, Friedrich
  1972. *The Ancient American Civilizations.* New York: Praeger.
Keen, Benjamin (ed.)
  1955. *Readings in Latin-American Civilization: 1492 to the Present.* Boston: Houghton Mifflin.
Kirchhoff, Paul, Lina Odena Guëmes, and Luis Reyes García (eds.)
  1976. *Historia Tolteca-Chichimeca.* Mexico: CIS-INAH and INAH-SEP (originally composed: mid-sixteenth century).
Kubler, George, and Charles Gibson
  1951. The Tovar calendar. *Memoirs of the Connecticut Academy of Arts and Sciences* (New Haven, Conn.), vol. 11 (originally written: ca. 1585).

Las Casas, Bartolomé de
  1967. *Apologética Historia Sumaria*. Mexico: Universidad Nacional Autónoma de Mexico (originally written: 1555–1559).
León-Portilla, Miguel
  1963. *Aztec Thought and Culture*. Norman: University of Oklahoma Press.
León-Portilla, Miguel
  1969. *Pre-Columbian Literatures of Mexico*. Norman: University of Oklahoma Press.
Lewis, Leslie
  1976. In Mexico City's shadow: Some aspects of economic activity and social processes in Texcoco, 1570–1620. In James Lockhart and Ida Altman, eds., *Provinces of Early Mexico*, pp. 125–136. Los Angeles: UCLA Latin American Center Publications.
Lewis, Oscar
  1951. *Life in a Mexican Village*. Urbana: University of Illinois Press.
Lienzo de Tlaxcala
  1892. Lienzo de Tlaxcala. In *Antigüedades Mexicanas*, Alfredo Chavero, ed., Publicadas por la Junta Colombina de Mexico. Mexico: Secretaría de Fomento (originally composed: ca. 1550).
Lockhart, James
  1976. Capital and province, Spaniard and Indian: The example of late sixteenth-century Toluca. In James Lockhart and Ida Altman, eds., *Provinces of Early Mexico*, pp. 99–123. Los Angeles: UCLA Latin American Center Publications.
Lockhart, James, and Enrique Otte (eds.)
  1976. *Letters and People of the Spanish Indies: The Sixteenth Century*. New York: Cambridge University Press.
Madsen, William
  1967. Religious syncretism. In *Handbook of Middle American Indians*, vol. 6, pp. 369–391. Austin: University of Texas Press.
Matrícula de Tributos
  Manuscript in the Museo Nacional de Antropología, Mexico City (originally composed: early sixteenth century).
Merriman, Roger Bigelow
  1962. *The Rise of the Spanish Empire in the Old World and in the New. Volume II: The Catholic Kings*. New York: Cooper Square Publishers.
Meyer, Michael, and William L. Sherman
  1979. *The Course of Mexican History*. New York: Oxford University Press.
Motolinía, Toribio (de Benavente)
  1950. History of the Indians of New Spain. In *Documents and Narratives Concerning the Discovery and Conquest of Latin America*. Elizabeth A. Foster, transl. and ed. new series, no. 4, Berkeley, Calif.: The Cortés Society (originally written: ca. 1536–1543).
Motolinía, Toribio (de Benavente)
  1971. *Memoriales, o Libro de las Cosas de la Nueva España y de los Naturales de Ella*. Mexico: Universidad Nacional Autónoma de México, Instituto de Investigaciones Históricas (originally written: ca. 1536–1543).
Nicholson, H. B.
  1971. Religion in pre-Hispanic central Mexico. In *Handbook of Middle American Indians*, vol. 10, pp. 395–446. Austin: University of Texas Press.

Noguera, Eduardo
   1971. Minor arts in the central valleys. In *Handbook of Middle American Indians*, vol. 10, pp. 258–269. Austin: University of Texas Press.
Ortiz de Montellano, Bernard R.
   1978. Aztec cannibalism: An ecological necessity? *Science*, vol. 200, pp. 611–617.
Oviedo y Valdés, Gonzalo Fernández de
   1851–1855. *Historia General y Natural de las Indias, Islas y Tierra Firme del Mar Océano*, José Amador de los Ríos, ed., 4 vols. Madrid: Impr. de la Real Academia de la Historia (originally written by mid-sixteenth century).
Parsons, Jeffrey R.
   1976. The role of chinampa agriculture in the food supply of Aztec Tenochtitlan. In *Cultural Change and Continuity*, Charles E. Cleland, ed., pp. 233–257. New York: Academic Press.
Pomar, J. B.
   1941. Relación de Tezcoco. In *Nueva Colección de Documentos para la Historia de Mexico*, 2nd ed., J. García Icazbalceta, ed., vol. 3, pp. 1–64. Mexico: Editorial Salvador Chávez Hayhoe (originally written: 1582).
Prescott, William H.
   1931. *History of the Conquest of Mexico and History of the Conquest of Peru.* New York: Modern Library.
Reyes, Luis
   1975. Calpulli y Barrios en Tenochtitlan. Paper presented at the symposium Organización Social del Mexico Antiguo sponsored by the Centro de Investigaciones Superiores del Instituto Nacional de Antropología e Historia, Mexico.
Ricard, Robert
   1966. *The Spiritual Conquest of Mexico.* Berkeley: University of California Press.
Sahagún, Bernardino de
   1950–1969. *Florentine Codex: General History of the Things of New Spain.* Arthur J. O. Anderson and Charles E. Dibble, transl. Salt Lake City, Utah and Santa Fe, New Mexico: University of Utah and School of American Research, Santa Fe (originally written by 1569).
Sanders, William T.
   1970. The population of the Teotihuacan Valley, the Basin of Mexico and the central Mexican symbiotic region in the sixteenth century. In Sanders *et al.* (eds.), The Natural Environment, Contemporary Occupation and Sixteenth Century Population of the Valley. *The Teotihuacan Valley Project Final Report*, vol. 1:385–457. Occasional Papers in Anthropology, Department of Anthropology, no. 3. University Park, Pa.: The Pennsylvania State University.
Sanders, William T.
   1971. Settlement patterns in central Mexico. In *Handbook of Middle American Indians*, vol. 10, pp. 3–44. Austin: University of Texas Press.
Sanders, William T., Jeffrey R. Parsons, and Robert S. Santley
   1979. *The Basin of Mexico: Ecological Processes in the Evolution of a Civilization.* New York: Academic Press.
Simpson, Lesley Byrd
   1966. *The Encomienda in New Spain.* Berkeley: University of California Press.

Soustelle, Jacques
1961. *Daily Life of the Aztecs on the Eve of the Spanish Conquest*. Stanford, Calif.: Stanford University Press.

Spores, Ronald
1967. *The Mixtec Kings and Their People*. Norman: University of Oklahoma Press.

Tapia, Andrés de
1971. Relación hecha por el Sr. Andrés de Tapia, sobre la conquista de Mexico. In *Colección de Documentos para la Historia de Mexico*, J. Icazbalceta, ed., vol. 2, pp. 554–594. Mexico: Editorial Porrúa (originally written: sixteenth century).

Tezozomoc, Fernando Alvarado
1949. *Crónica Mexicayotl*. Mexico: Universidad Nacional Autónoma de Mexico (originally written: 1609).

Tezozomoc, Fernando Alvarado
1975. *Crónica Mexicana*, 2nd ed. Mexico: Editorial Porrúa (originally written: 1598).

Torquemada, Juan de
1969. *Los Veinte i un Libros Rituales i Monarchia Indiana*, 3 vols. Mexico: Editorial Porrúa (originally published: 1615).

Tozzer, Alfred M. (transl. and ed.)
1941. Landa's Relación de las Cosas de Yucatan. *Papers of the Peabody Museum of American Archaeology and Ethnology* (Cambridge, Mass.), vol. 18.

Vaillant, George C.
1966. *Aztecs of Mexico*. New York: Doubleday.

Wagner, Henry R.
1942. *The Discovery of New Spain in 1518, by Juan de Grijalva*. Henry R. Wagner, transl. with an introduction. Berkeley, Calif.: The Cortés Society.

Wagner, Henry R.
1944. *The Rise of Fernando Cortés*. Berkeley, Calif.: The Cortés Society.

West, Robert C., and John P. Augelli
1966. *Middle America: Its Lands and Peoples*. Englewood Cliffs, N.J.: Prentice-Hall.

Whitecotton, Joseph W.
1977. *The Zapotecs: Princes, Priests and Peasants*. Norman: University of Oklahoma Press.

Wolf, Eric
1959. *Sons of the Shaking Earth*. Chicago: University of Chicago Press.

Zorita, Alonso de
1963. *Life and Labor in Ancient Mexico*. Benjamin Keen, transl. New Brunswick, N.J.: Rutgers University Press (originally written: 1570s or 1580s).